Smalltalk

Alec Sharp

McGraw-Hill
New York   San Francisco   Washington, D.C.   Auckland   Bogotá
Caracas   Lisbon   London   Madrid   Mexico City   Milan
Montreal   New Delhi   San Juan   Singapore
Sydney   Tokyo   Toronto

Library of Congress Cataloging-in-Publication Data

Sharp, Alec.
    Smalltalk by example : the developer's guide / Alec Sharp.
      p. cm.
    Includes index.
    ISBN 0-07-913036-4 (pbk.)
    1. Smalltalk (Computer program language) 2. VisualWorks.
  QA76.73.S59S55 1997
  005.13'3—dc21   96-47061
                                            CIP

McGraw-Hill

A Division of The McGraw-Hill Companies

2 3 4 5 6 7 8 9 DOC/DOC 9 0 2 1 0 9

PN 0-057779-X
Part of
ISBN 0-07-913036-4

The sponsoring editor of this book was John Wyzalek. The editing supervisor was Scott Amerman, and the production supervisor was Pamela Pelton. This book was set in New Century Schoolbook. It was composed in Hightstown, N.J.

Printed and bound by R. R. Donnelley & Sons Company.

McGraw-Hill books are available at special quantity discounts to use as premiums and sales promotions, or for use in corporate training programs. For more information, please write to the Director of Special Sales, McGraw-Hill, 11 West 19th Street, New York, NY 10011. Or contact your local bookstore.

Contents

Part 5 Advanced   257

Acknowledgments

I'd like to thank all those people who helped during the development of this manuscript, by reviewing parts of the manuscript, by general feedback, or by other assistance. Those people include T. W. Cook, Jim Dutton, and Boyd Hays of ParcPlace-Digitalk, Dave Farmer, Clark Hobbie, Mike Latta, Dave Muirhead, Dave Myers, and Bill Wright. I also received valuable contributions from those anonymous reviewers of an early draft whose favorable opinions were vital to getting this manuscript published. To all of these people: Your comments and suggestions have helped make this book considerably better than it might have been. To the anonymous reviewers: Thanks for the favorable opinions!

Thanks also to all the people I worked with at McGraw-Hill who helped bring this book from concept to reality—in particular, Scott Amerman, Michael Christopher, Jennifer DiGiovanna, and John Wyzalek.

I also want to thank all those people who have contributed to whatever knowledge I have of object-oriented thinking and Smalltalk programming. Many people have contributed to my education, including the authors of various books and magazine articles. From this group I'd like to acknowledge Kent Beck and Alan Knight for their wonderful articles in *The Smalltalk Report*. Of the people I have worked with, I'd like to particularly thank the following: Rob Forbes, Boyd Hays, Clark Hobbie, Mike Latta, Alan Wostenberg, Bill Wright, and the Daves (Bond, Farmer, Muirhead, Myers, and Vowels).

In particular, I'd like to thank three friends for special contributions. Dave Farmer for all the fun we had learning Smalltalk and working on our first Smalltalk project together. Boyd Hays for the philosophy and information he imparted when he came in as a consultant to review the design and progress of our first project. Scott Allen, my manager at StorageTek, who had the courage to bring in Smalltalk and commit to doing a key project in it. To these three people: Thanks.

Most of all, I want to acknowledge and thank the people whose lives were most affected by this book: My daughter, Nikki, who had less of a father during the evenings and weekends I worked on the book, and my wife, Muriel, to whom I offer the greatest thanks. On top of her own busy life she took on many additional household and child-minding duties as I spent long hours at the computer. Thanks; I couldn't have done it without you.

Introduction

This book is the book that I wanted when I started programming in Smalltalk. None of the books on the market seemed quite right; they all lacked some of what I needed to get my job done. Some were more like reference books, making sense if one already understood the material but not very good if one lacked the basic knowledge. Others simply went over material that I could easily get by looking at the system classes, using a Browser. The bottom line was that none of them seemed to provide answers to the questions I had. How do I use these capabilities when writing my application, how could I do the specific things I wanted to do, which was the best approach to take, how could I modify my development environment to make it more productive?

In short, I wanted information that would steer me in the right direction and none of the books seemed to give that. This book is written for people who have similar questions and needs, who want to become productive in Smalltalk programming in as short a time as possible.

A lot of the material describes standard Smalltalk, but some material is specific to VisualWorks from ParcPlace-Digitalk. The book assumes that the reader is using VisualWorks 2.0 or VisualWorks 2.5, and where appropriate it explains the differences between these two releases. All the examples have been verified on both VisualWorks 2.0 and VisualWorks 2.5. Note that in most examples, to save space, I have not shown the temporary variable declarations, so you will be prompted when you try to run or accept the code.

Approach

Example is the school of mankind, and they will learn at no other.

Edmund Burke

Like Edmund Burke and many other people, I learn best from example. People generally find it difficult to take a theory and apply it to create a practical example. They usually find it far easier to take a concrete example, work with it, and extrapolate the general behavior.

Because of this, I've tried to include plenty of examples in the book, practical examples that the reader can use when developing applications. My goal has been to make this book different by focusing on practicality, on helping developers solve the real programming problems they face. The book includes an attached diskette that contains the code for most of the examples.

I have tried to include the information the reader will need to understand the concepts and the capabilities of Smalltalk. The book then goes a step beyond and gives practical examples of how readers would use the capabilities when developing products. The book starts with the basic concepts of object-oriented development, specifically in the context of Smalltalk programming. It builds on this and talks about control structures, Collections, Streams, and other useful building blocks. Then it extends the basics and shows how the reader can use the Smalltalk classes when writing application programs. For example, Chapter 20 looks at the Signal and Exception mechanism that Smalltalk provides, then shows how you might use this mechanism when writing your application. Chapter 30 shows how you might test your application. Chapter 33 shows how you can track your changes, make sure that your image has the latest changes, and then build a production image from the latest changes.

Layout of the Book

The book is split into five sections: Basics, Basic System Classes, Skills and Techniques, User Interface, and Advanced.

Part 1 talks about the basics of Smalltalk—objects and classes, messages and methods, and variables and language syntax. It covers creation of instances of classes and control of program flow with the various conditional and looping structures. It ends with a chapter on thinking in terms of objects.

Part 2 goes over some of the fundamental classes that you will use. Because everything in Smalltalk is an object, and all objects are instances of a class, we will talk about classes in every section. However, Section 2 is more information-oriented and less technique-oriented than some of the other sections.

Part 3 also talks a lot about the system classes but covers techniques in using the classes. It shows how you work with Processes, how you can implement error-handling code, and how to debug in Smalltalk. The section covers a lot of skills and techniques that you will use when developing your application.

Part 4 focuses on user interface issues. It gives a lot of attention to the Model-View-Controller paradigm, then talks about how you can modify user interfaces at run time. Because the user interface mechanisms differs widely among the different flavors of Smalltalk, this is the section most specific to VisualWorks.

Part 5 is an advanced section, not because the topics are esoteric but because the chapters tend to use advanced techniques or knowledge. In fact, some of the material in this section might be very useful, covering such topics as testing, adding methods to system classes, and customizing your development environment.

The book includes a comprehensive index. I've always been frustrated when I know a book contains the information I want, but I can't find it. So I hope this index proves to be less frustrating than some. However, some chapters, such as those on Collections, Streams, Object, and Meta-Programming, make passing references to a lot of messages, and I will not always duplicate those references in the index.

Examples

The book contains many examples of Smalltalk code to illustrate points made in the chapters. There are two flavors of code: code that you can type into a workspace, highlight, and evaluate or inspect, and code that consists of classes and methods. The accompanying diskette contains all the code shown in the book. The two types of code are separated into two types of file. Files with an extension of .ex contain example code to be selected and evaluated. Files with an extension of of .st contain classes and methods that can be filed into the image. Appendix A, Source files, describes which files relate to which chapters.

(Note: When highlighting and selecting code in a Workspace, you will sometimes find that, when you click to the right of the code, the following line is highlighted rather than the line to the left of where you click. By ending the statement with a period you can prevent this problem.)

Target Audience

Based on a categorization of Smalltalk programmers into three categories—beginner, intermediate, and expert—this book is aimed at beginning to intermediate Smalltalk programmers. Expert programmers might get some useful new information from the book, but they will also already know a great deal of what it contains.

Beginning and intermediate programmers should find that the book answers a lot of questions about how to program in Smalltalk, how to use the system classes, and how to incorporate the Smalltalk mechanisms into application programs. It is a beginner's book in the sense that it goes over the basic concepts, talking about classes, instances, messages and methods, then building on these to look at Collections, Streams, Processes, and so on. However, it doesn't spend as long on the basics as would a book written totally for beginners. My feeling is that it doesn't take too long to understand the basics, and I wanted this book to be useful for longer than just a few weeks. It is an intermediate book in that it gives suggestions on how the reader might write better applications, eliminate procedural code, implement more effective error-handling mechanisms, and better test software. It also contains many tips and hints that often take years to discover.

The book assumes some amount of programming experience on the part of the reader, whether in procedural or object-oriented programming. A complete novice will get some use from this book, but doing so will take more effort. While no significant knowledge of object-oriented programming, or of Smalltalk, is required, I do assume some basic knowledge of the VisualWorks tools, including how to use the Browsers to define classes and write code (when the book refers to a tool, it is referring to the VisualWorks functionality).

About Smalltalk

Smalltalk has been around a long time. It dates back to the early 1970s, when Alan Kay, then at Xerox PARC, wanted to create a language that children could program in. Kay's classic article, "The Early History of Smalltalk," published in the ACM SIGPLAN Notices, Volume 28, No. 3, March 1993, talks about the evolution of early Smalltalk and about the influences of other languages on it.

Smalltalk was the original object-oriented (OO) language, and is still among the purest of OO languages. Unlike hybrid languages such as C++, Smalltalk forces you to think and program in OO terms. When it was originally developed it ran on its own hardware and was basically the operating system for the hardware. Perhaps due to that heritage, it contains a lot of useful process control features that one would normally associate with an operating system, such as forked processes, semaphores, and mutual exclusion semaphores.

For most of its life, Smalltalk has been associated with research and prototyping. However, it is now among the fastest growing OO languages. The success of C++ popularized and legitimized OO programming, but over time people have become frustrated with the difficulties inherent in C++ development, so a lot of attention has turned to Smalltalk. It has been further legitimized by IBM, which has made Smalltalk an important part of its development language strategy.

Smalltalk is often used for business applications, but it is also used for applications with a stronger engineering orientation. Texas Instruments used Smalltalk to control an entire state-of-the-art wafer fabrication plant, adding extensions to allow distributed objects.

Hewlett-Packard created Distributed Smalltalk, an extension to ParcPlace's VisualWorks that allows objects to communicate transparently over networks. Back in the 1980s, Tektronix began to use Smalltalk to run its logic analyzers and datascopes.

Features of Smalltalk

Smalltalk is a wonderful language to work with—in fact, it's hard to imagine a serious programming language being more fun than Smalltalk. Certainly, I've had more fun programming in Smalltalk than any other language I've worked with; so much fun that at times it's seemed incredible that I've also been paid to enjoy myself. If Smalltalk is so great, what makes it this way? I think it's a combination of things. In no particular order, here are some of them.

Interpreted language

Smalltalk is conceptually an interpreted language. This means you can make changes to code and immediately execute them without having to go through a lengthy compile-and-link process. In fact, you can make code changes to an application that is actually running and have the changes take effect next time that piece of code is executed. You can also write short code segments (in any window) and execute them immediately.[1]

Browsers

Smalltalk is a very well-thought-out environment, with a rich set of browsing tools. Because it was designed with children in mind, it is very easy to use. You can look at classes and their methods and you can see just the local methods, or you can also include inherited methods. From within a method you can ask to see all the methods that invoke it (the senders of the message), all the implementors of identically named methods (polymorphism), or you can browse the code of any of the methods invoked by the method you're in. From any of these displays you can modify code.

---

[1] While Smalltalk is conceptually interpreted, the actual implementation is rather more sophisticated. When you accept a method, the compiler checks it for correctness, complains about syntax errors, gives you warnings about semantic errors, then compiles your text into byte codes. Having pre-compiled byte codes to interpret at run time is a lot faster than interpreting the text each time. On top of that, VisualWorks caches the machine instructions. When the byte codes are interpreted, machine instructions are generated and executed. VisualWorks caches the machine instructions so that it doesn't need to interpret the byte codes next time it executes the method. Of course, as in any cache, infrequently used methods may be swapped out.

The debugger

The debugger gives you a stack trace of where you are, allowing you to look at any of the methods in the stack and to inspect any of the variables. The inspection capability is excellent, allowing you to easily follow through objects and their own instance variables using just the mouse. As well as inspecting object values, you can also change them. The debugger also has the browsing capability of looking at senders and implementors of methods. Because of the interpreted nature of Smalltalk, you can evaluate code segments in the debugger and also change the methods that are stopped in. Being able to change a method, then continue execution, is one of the best features of the debugger. In fact, I often consciously program using the debugger. If I don't know exactly how to program a method, I'll simply ask the method to bring up a debugger by writing self halt. Then I'll write the method in the debugger, using it to inspect variables and evaluate code snippets as I write.

The class library

One of the big productivity gains comes from reusable software. Smalltalk provides a class library of around one thousand classes, all of which make life a lot easier and a lot more productive for programmers. (In a new VisualWorks 2.5 image with no additional tools or classes loaded, there are 960 classes and 23,131 methods. With the Advanced Tools loaded, the counts are 1,014 and 24,529.) It's nice to be able to use an already existing class to manage a queue. It's also nice to be able to convert it to a sorted collection with a single message send. Most of the classes are conceptually simple; they have a well defined role and perform it well, which allows you to easily combine and reuse objects.

The system class code is all there for you to peruse, which gives you three benefits.

1. First, you can figure out exactly how to use it instead of having to rely on usually incomplete or hard-to-understand documentation.

2. Second, you can learn new techniques from reading the system classes.

3. Third, it makes it a lot easier to subclass from the system classes. For example, some applications using forked processes might find that a simple SharedQueue will suffice for passing objects between processes. Other applications might need a priority-based shared queue, and having a visible class library makes this very easy.

The bottom line is that having an extensive class library means that you have a huge amount of high quality code available, which means you can put together applications very quickly.

The garbage collector

One of the features of Smalltalk that makes writing code much easier is the garbage collector. When objects are no longer needed, you don't have to explicitly destroy them as in many other object-oriented languages. Instead, they are automatically garbage collected when they are no longer referenced by another object. This garbage collection makes it possible to concentrate on the application problem, not worrying about what will happen to your objects. When they are no longer needed they will simply disappear and the memory will be reclaimed.

Object-oriented thinking

Smalltalk is one of the pure OO languages. Unlike C++, in which it's easy to write procedural code, Smalltalk makes it difficult to write procedural code. It usually takes eight to twelve months for experienced procedural programmers to become fairly automatic in their object-oriented (OO) thinking. To use a language that doesn't help that process makes it much easier to remain in a halfway schizophrenic state.

OO thinking is fun and different. One difference is that OO development tends to be more iterative than procedural development; more spiral. In OO development we acknowledge that we don't fully understand our objects and their interactions, and we acknowledge that they will be changed and transformed as we increasingly understand the problem.

For several reasons, Smalltalk makes it very easy to progress through the spiral of iterative development. We've talked about how easy it is to write, test, and change code. This ease of writing makes it possible to put off real work until later, so a lot of methods will do nothing but ask themselves, or another object, to do something else. This allows you to think in conceptual terms rather than worrying about the details. Smalltalk is wonderful to work with because it helps enforce OO thinking, and because it makes it very easy to do iterative, spiral development.

Modifying and extending the environment

One of the great things about Smalltalk is that, if you don't like something, you can change it. If you think it should be possible to convert characters to strings by sending them the message asString you can extend Smalltalk to add the new method to the Character class (for example, ^String with: self). If you'd like different menu options available from your Launcher window, or you'd like different keyboard mappings, it's easy to change the code. We'll see some examples of this in Chapter 31.

Smalltalk is reflective

The Smalltalk system can reflect on itself; that is, it can look at itself. Because all the system code is available you can use the system classes to examine how the system classes work. You can write methods that use knowledge of how methods work. And, because you have the ability to find out about the nature of classes and objects, you can write code that makes use of this information. Not all applications need this knowledge, but sometimes knowing how classes and objects are put together can help you create a better solution.

Summary

In the end, no amount of intellectual discussion can really give you a feeling for the power and beauty of Smalltalk. Feelings have to be experienced, not rationalized. So, with this book in hand, get programming!

Basics

1

Basic Concepts

In traditional programming, we start with a problem to solve. We figure out how to break the problem into smaller parts, then each part into smaller parts still. At each stage we think about how to *do* things. To do something means first doing one thing, then another, then yet another. So, we divide and conquer with an emphasis on *doing*.

In the object-oriented approach, we again start with a problem to solve. We then try to figure out what objects the system has, what their responsibilities are, and how they interact. We still divide and conquer, but the emphasis is now on objects and their interactions.

Objects

What is an object? In the real world, we often think of objects as *things*: an apple, a car, a person, a house. In the world of programming, we have objects that *model* real-world objects, and we also have objects that exist to make our life easier, such as an *input field*, a *text string*, a *collection*, a *number*, a *file*, a *window*, or a *process*. The main qualifications for an object are that it can be named and that it can be distinguished from other types of objects. Let's look at the example of a stock that is traded on a stock exchange.

What are the properties of an object? An object usually has some data, and it usually has some behavior; that is, it can do things. Our stock object has some data: It holds the name of the stock, its symbol, the current trading price, the number of shares traded in the most recent trade, and the total number of shares traded today. It also has behavior: It can tell you the most recent trading price and it can accumulate the total of shares traded.

A stock exchange application will have many, many stock objects, one for each symbol traded on the exchange. It will interact with the stock objects by sending them *messages*. For example, if it wants to know the current price of a stock, let's say the XYZ stock, it would send the price message to the XYZ stock object. In response, the stock object looks in its data and returns the current price.

If the Stock Exchange gets information across the wire about a trade involving XYZ stock, it sends the message traded: aCount price: aPrice to the XYZ stock object (we'll talk a lot more about messages in Chapter 2). When the stock object receives the message, it will update its data; in this case it will update the current price, the number of shares most recently traded, and the total traded for the day.

So, *an object consists of its data plus the messages it understands.* Our stock object consists of stock name, symbol, current price, most recent trade volume, and trade volume for the day, and the messages: stockName, symbol, price, lastTraded, totalTraded, and traded:price: (plus a few more).

The data is stored in *instance variables*. Each stock object has its own copies of the instance variables, so it can store different values for price, symbol, and the other messages.

Encapsulation

When you send the message traded: aNumberOfShares price: aPrice to a particular stock object, it updates its instance variables price, lastTraded, and totalTraded. There is *no* other way to change these variables.[1] No other object can see or modify our XYZ stock object's data, except by sending messages. Some messages will cause the stock object to update its data, and some messages will cause it to return the values. But no other object can access the data directly. The data is

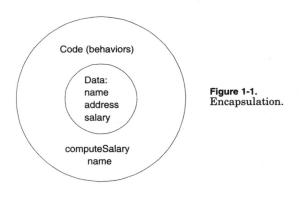

Figure 1-1.
Encapsulation.

---

[1]Actually there is, but it involves meta-programming.

encapsulated in the object. Figure 1-1 shows a representation of this encapsulation.

The fact that the data is encapsulated means that we can change the way it is stored. As long as we retain the public interface that we have defined — that is, the messages to which the object responds — we can do what we like internally. One day we might decide to store the price in dollars and cents, the next day in cents, the next day in eighths of a dollar, and so on. As long as we also modify the way that price manipulates the data before returning it, we have maintained the public interface despite changing the object internals.

Classes

The class as code respository

Suppose our program makes use of two *OrderedCollections*, or collections that store items in the order they were added. One keeps track of phone messages that we have received but have not dealt with, and the other keeps track of things we must do — action items. Among others, we will need messages to add items to our collections, and to get the first item from a collection.

We don't want to write add: and first twice, once for each object. Instead, we need a mechanism to write the code once so that it can be used by both OrderedCollections. This is where the concept of a *class* comes in. A class is basically a blueprint or a template for what the object looks like — what variables it has and what messages it understands. We define an OrderedCollection class and that's where we write the code for add: and first. So you can consider the OrderedCollection class to be a repository for the code that is executed when you send these messages. Write the code once, and all OrderedCollections (in our case, the two examples above) can execute the code.

The code is stored in a *method*. When an object receives a message, it executes a method with the same name. So, we write methods and the methods are stored with the class. Figure 1-2 shows an example of an Employee class, showing how the class acts as a template and as a code repository.

The class as factory

The next question is how our OrderedCollections are created. After all, they don't appear by magic. The answer is that we ask the OrderedCollection class to create our two *instances* of an OrderedCollection. The following code shows two instances of OrderedCollection being created and assigned to variables (:= is the assignment operator).

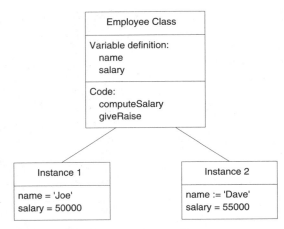

Figure 1-2. The class as code repository.

```
phoneMessages := OrderedCollection new.
actionItems := OrderedCollection new.
```

So, besides being a repository for the code, the class is also a factory. Just as a car factory produces cars, an OrderedCollection factory (class) produces OrderedCollections. The factory contains blueprints for creating objects, and a template for what the object looks like; that is, for the data it contains.

Now let's step back a moment and look at the code above, which creates the instances of OrderedCollection. Notice that we send the new message to OrderedCollection. Remember that we get objects to do things by sending them messages. It looks remarkably like the OrderedCollection class is also an object, and in fact, this is the case. Not only are our individual instances of an OrderedCollection objects, but so is the factory that creates them. We give the name *class* to the factory object, and the name *instance* to each object that the factory creates. So in our example we have an OrderedCollection class, which creates two instances of an OrderedCollection.

Because the class contains a template for individual instances of OrderedCollection, each OrderedCollection has its own copies of the instance variables firstIndex and lastIndex. And because the class is the repository for the code, each instance of OrderedCollection uses the code from the class.

The class as abstractor

A class abstracts out the common behavior and common data of the objects that it creates. It provides a place where the common behavior and common instance variables can be defined. The instance variables are simply slots; no data is contained in them until instances of the class are created. *A class is a factory with blueprints for the instances it creates. It is also a code repository.*

Inheritance

Now let's look at another type of collection — a *SortedCollection*. Our action item list is better represented by a SortedCollection because we'd prefer to have all the high priority items appear before the low priority ones.

The big difference between a SortedCollection and an Ordered-Collection is that, in the former, the items are sorted based on rules that you can specify. However, a lot of behavior is similar, and therefore a lot of the code should be identical. It would be a shame to have to duplicate all the OrderedCollection code for a SortedCollection. Not only would it be a lot of work, but it would be a maintenance nightmare to also update the SortedCollection code if you make changes to OrderedCollection.

We would like an instance of SortedCollection to use the code that is already written for OrderedCollection so that, if the code changes, SortedCollections also get the changes. We would like to share the code where it makes sense to share, such as finding the first or last item in the collection. We'd like to have different code where the behavior is different, such as when adding an item to the collection. We would like a SortedCollection to *inherit* the behavior of an OrderedCollection where they are similar.

Fortunately we can do this by setting up an inheritance relationship between the classes. In the object-oriented world, we can say that one class is a *subclass* of another class. So in our example, SortedCollection is a subclass of OrderedCollection. This allows SortedCollection to inherit all the code and instance variables of OrderedCollection. For example, if you want to loop through (iterate over) all the items in a SortedCollection, you send it the do: message, which is defined in OrderedCollection. SortedCollection inherits the code, and its instance does exactly what an instance of OrderedCollection would do.

If you didn't write any specific code for a SortedCollection, it would inherit everything that was written for OrderedCollection. In fact, if we don't change some behavior there's no point in having a new class at all. Fortunately, SortedCollections do have some different behavior. There are two types of different behavior. First, some messages need to do different things. For example, sending the add: message should add an object to the end of an OrderedCollection, but a Sorted-Collection should add the object in a position based on the sorting rule for the collection. If we do:

```
orderedCollection := OrderedCollection new.
orderedCollection add: 'xyz'.
orderedCollection add: 'def'.
orderedCollection add: 'abc'.
```

and inspect the collection, the strings will be ordered 'xyz', 'def', 'abc', in the order we added them. On the other hand, if we do:

```
sortedCollection := SortedCollection new.
sortedCollection add: 'xyz'.
sortedCollection add: 'def'.
sortedCollection add: 'abc'.
```

and inspect the collection, the strings are ordered 'abc', 'def', 'xyz', in the correct sort sequence for strings. So, in a SortedCollection we don't want to inherit our superclass's code for add:. Instead, we write our own add: method and override the one defined in OrderedCollection.

The second way we want different behavior is to add behavior to do something that our superclass doesn't do. For example, we need to be able to specify the sorting algorithm that should be used by an instance of SortedCollection. We add behavior very easily, simply by writing a new method for SortedCollection. In the example of a sort algorithm, we write the sortBlock: method, which stores the new algorithm for future additions and also resorts the collection according to the new algorithm. Figure 1-3 shows an example of inherited, overridden, and added methods.

Polymorphism

Remember the add: message that is different for OrderedCollection and SortedCollection? There are other types of collection, such as Set, Bag, and LinkedList, each of which implements its own version of add:.

This means that you can have a collection and not care much what type of collection it is; you simply send it the add: message and it will add an object to itself in the appropriate way. Another example might be a window that displays graphical objects. Rather than have the window know how to display a circle and a square, the window would

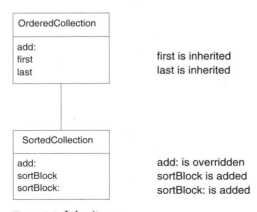

Figure 1-3. Inheritance.

simply send a message to the graphical object (for example, graphicalObject displayYourselfOn: self). The graphicalObject might be a square or circle, but the window doesn't care. It simply sends the same message regardless, and relies on the graphicalObject knowing how to display itself. In a procedural language you might write something like:

```
if (graphicalObject isSquare)
    displaySquare (graphicalObject)
else if (graphicalObject isCircle)
    displayCircle (graphicalObject)
```

Using polymorphism, we might simply write:

```
graphicalObject displayYourselfOn: self.
```

To use another example, we might have an Office object, which sees Person objects coming in to work. One approach would be for the Office object to ask the Person object what kind of person it is. If it is a Programmer object, the Office object would tell it to start programming (programmer startProgramming). If it is a Receptionist object, the Office object would tell it to answer the phones (receptionist answerPhones). If it is a Manager object, the Office object would tell it to shuffle papers (manager shufflePapers).

This approach has the disadvantage of having a lot of code whose sole purpose is to check what type of Person object just walked in, then having to modify this code when a new type of person is added to the program. The better approach is for the Office object to have no interest in the type of person that walked in, and to simply tell the person to get to work (person getToWork). If a Programmer object receives this message, it will start programming; If a Receptionist object gets the message, it will start answering phones; if a Manager object gets the message, it will start shuffling papers. Now when you add a new type of person object, you just have to make sure that it responds to the getToWork message and does the appropriate thing. We have put the responsibility where it belongs. Figure 1-4 shows an example of polymorphism.

This ability to have the same message understood differently by many objects means that we can get out of *decision making* mode and into *commanding* mode. This is a fundamental difference between procedural thinking and object-oriented thinking. Interpreting the the same message differently is called *polymorphism*. It works because of the difference between a *message* and a *method*. When a message is sent to an object, the object looks up the message name (*selector* in Smalltalk terms) in the list of messages it responds to. Associated with the message selector is a method — some lines of code that will be executed. So, the same message selector will be associated with different code for different classes.

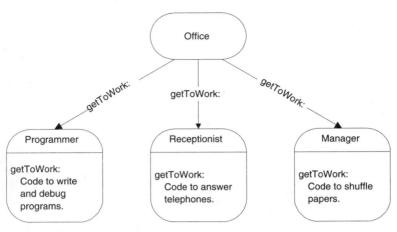

Figure 1-4. Polymorphism.

To me, the defining feature of object-oriented programming is the ability to simply tell an object to do something, rather than to get information then do different things based on the information. Polymorphism is a key part of this ability. We'll go into some explicit techniques in Chapter 28.

Abstract superclasses

Now let's extend the idea of inheritance. OrderedCollection is a subclass of SequenceableCollection. Other subclasses of SequenceableCollection include ArrayedCollection and LinkedList. OrderedCollections, Arrays, and LinkedLists have some common behavior, which has been coded in the class SequenceableCollection. However, you can't actually create an instance of SequenceableCollection. (Well, you can, but you'll get errors if you try to do anything with it!)

The class SequenceableCollection exists as a place to put the code that is common to the classes just mentioned. The common behavior has been abstracted out and placed in an abstract superclass, one that should not be instantiated - that is, should not create instances of itself. For example, the methods copyFrom:to: and occurrencesOf: are both written in SequenceableCollection and are inherited by its subclasses.

So, an *abstract superclass* is a class that has no instances of itself, but which exists as a respository for common code. The abstract superclass SequenceableCollection itself has an abstract superclass, Collection. Collection is also the superclass for Set and Bag, collections that don't have the concept of a sequence. Collection provides behavior that is common to all collections, such as isEmpty, collect:, do:, and includes:. (Some of the subclasses override these methods to provide a

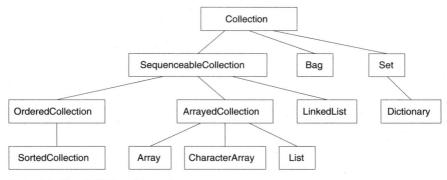

Figure 1-5. The Collection hierarchy.

more appropriate implementation for themselves. However, many of the subclasses inherit the behavior directly.) Figure 1-5 shows a small part of the Collection hierarchy.

Summary

■ Objects encapsulate data and behavior (code).

■ Classes are factories that have blueprints for creating instances. They are repositories for the code that is executed by their instances.

■ Classes are arranged in an inheritance hierarchy that allows objects to inherit behavior (and code) from other classes up their hierarchy chain.

■ Work gets done by objects sending messages to other objects, telling them to do something or to return something.

■ Many different objects understand the same message but do different things when they receive the message. That is, they execute different methods (polymorphism).

2

Messages

As we said in the previous chapter, we send messages to objects to get them to do things. There are three flavors of message in Smalltalk.

Unary Messages

A *unary* message is a message with no arguments. For example, to negate the sign of an integer we would send the unary message, negated.

Binary Messages

A *binary* message looks just like an arithmetic operator. It gets the name binary because there are exactly two objects involved. For example, 5 + 3.

Here we are sending the + message to 5 with 3 as the argument. Unlike most languages where +, -, *, etc., are operator symbols associated with algebraic operations, in Smalltalk they are messages with exactly one argument. The binary messages are:

```
+ - * / ** // \\ < <= > >= = ~= == ~~ & | , @ ->
```

Many of these are obvious, so I'll just explain the not so obvious ones.

**	Exponentiation.
//	Integer division, rounding to the next lowest number.
\\	Modulo, returning the remainder after the division.
~=	Not equal.
==	Identically equal; that is, the same object.
~~	Not the same object.
&	Logical AND, returning true if both the receiver and the argument are true. The receiver and argument are both evaluated, so it might be better to use and:, which only evaluates as much as is necessary and is also compiled in-line. Note that for both

& and and:, if the receiver is true, the argument is returned, which might or might not be a Boolean.

| Logical OR, returning true if either the receiver or the argument are true. The receiver and argument are both evaluated, so it might be better to use or:, which only evaluates as much as is necessary and is also compiled in-line. Note that for both | and or:, if the receiver is false, the argument is returned, which might or might not be a Boolean.

,   Concatenate two collections. Usually used to concatenate strings.

@   Used to create an instance of the Point class.

->   Used to create an instance of the Association class.

Keyword Messages

We still need to be able to send other types of messages with one argument and messages with more than one argument. The *keyword* message lets us do this. For example:

```
'elephant' copyFrom: 3 to: 5
```

gives the string 'eph' (Smalltalk collections are 1 based rather than 0 based as in C and C++; that is, the first element in the collection is referenced by index 1). The colons separate out the keywords in the message, where each keyword takes an argument. (In strict terms, copyFrom: 3 to: 5 is the message and copyFrom:to: is the message selector, but we will also refer to copyFrom:to: as the message.)

Message Chaining

Methods always return an object (more on this later). This means that you can *chain* messages together, because there is guaranteed to be an object to send each message to. For example, the following returns -3.

```
3.14 truncated negated
```

When the floating point number receives the truncated message, it returns a SmallInteger, which in turn returns another SmallInteger when sent the negated message. Another example might be a string that contains a number. We want to change the sign on the number and convert it back to a string. One option would be to say:

```
number := '42' asNumber.
negatedNumber := number negated.
string := negatedNumber printString.
```

However, because each method returns an object, we can write this as:

```
string := ( ( '42' asNumber ) negated ) printString.
```

Or we can leave out the parentheses because we are dealing only with unary messages, all of which have the same precedence.

```
string := '42' asNumber negated printString.
```

Message Precedence

Unlike C++, which has very complicated rules of precedence, Smalltalk has very easy rules.

1. Evaluation is done left to right.

2. Unary messages have the highest precedence.

3. Binary messages have the next precedence.

4. Keyword message have the lowest precedence.

5. You can alter precedence by using parentheses.

One thing that is immediately different from most languages is that there is no algebra. + and * are not algebraic symbols; they are simply messages. Using the precedence rules above:

```
1+ 2 * 3
```

equals 9, not 7. To get the result you would expect you have to use parentheses to specify the precedence.

```
1+ (2 * 3)
```

To give two more examples, 2 + '4' asNumber max: 5 gives 6, because, by the above rules, the unary asNumber is sent first, giving 2 + 4 max: 5. Then the binary + is sent, giving 6 max: 5, which returns 6.

The computation 30 max: 3 + 4 * 5 gives 35. There are no unary messages, so the binary messages are sent in left to right order. With the first message sent, we get 30 max: 7 * 5. With the next binary message sent, we get 30 max: 35, which returns 35. To get an answer of 30, as you would expect from normal algebra, you would have to use parentheses such as 30 max: 3 + (4 * 5).

What Happens When a Message Is Sent

Whan a message is sent to an object, the Smalltalk system looks to see if a method with that name exists for that type of object (in other words, has been written and stored in the class of the object). If there is a method, it is executed. If no method of that name is defined in the object's class, the system looks in the method dictionary for its immediate superclass. If there is no method with that name in the superclass it looks in the superclass's superclass. Figure 2-1 illustrates this.

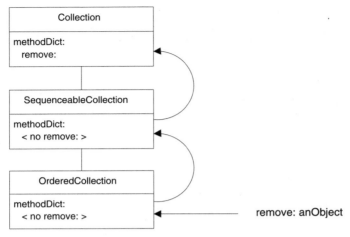

Figure 2-1. The method lookup mechanism.

The method lookup keeps working its way up the superclass hierarchy until it finds a method with that name, which it then executes. If it reaches Object and still doesn't find a method, it displays a Notifier window that gives you an opportunity go into a Debugger and figure out what went wrong.[1]

The Receiver of the Message

All messages have to be sent to an object — there's no such thing as a message in isolation. If you create an object in a method, it's easy to send a message to the object. For example:

```
MyClass>>doThis
    array := Array new: 3.
    array at: 1 put: 2.
```

(The generally used notation to show instance side method names is ClassName>>methodName. For class side methods, the notation is ClassName class>>methodName.)

self

Smalltalk methods average about seven lines, so for an object to do any serious work there's a good chance that you will have split the work

---

[1]What actually happens is that, if a method is not found, the doesNotUnderstand: message is sent. Unless this has been overridden, the doesNotUnderstand: method tells Object messageNotUnderstoodSignal to raise an exception. Unless you have a handle:do: block to trap this exception, the exception is unable to find a signal handler and it gets converted into another exception (an unhandled exception exception), which invokes the EmergencyHandler. Unless you have overridden the behavior of the EmergencyHandler, it opens a Notifier window.

into several methods (assuming you want to have short methods). How does a method invoke another method defined on the same object? The object sends a message to itself. Smalltalk has a special variable for just such use — self — which always refers to the object that is executing the code — the message receiver. Note that self refers to the receiver even if the the code was defined on a superclass of the receiver's class.

```
MyClass>>processObject: anObject
    self doThisWithObject: anObject.
    self doThatToObject: anObject.
```

If a method needs to call on a support method to do some work, send the message to self. In fact, a good rule of thumb is, if you can't figure out what object to send the message to, send it to self.

super

Remember how message lookup works. Smalltalk looks for the method first in the object that is receiving the message. If it can't find a method there, it next looks in the superclass, and so on. But what do we do if we explicitly want to start looking in our superclass? Smalltalk provides another special variable, super. So, if you want to start at your superclass, send a message to super.

When would this be useful? One common example is during instance creation. If you want to initialize some instance variables you usually write an initialize method on the instance side. You can no longer inherit new because it doesn't send initialize, so you have to write your own new method, which will inherit the behavior of new from a superclass. Note that the caret (^) shown below means return.

```
MyClass>>initialize
    ... set some variables ...

MyClass class>>new
    ^super new initialize
```

In fact, super does *not* refer the the superclass of the object that received the message. Instead, it refers to the superclass of the object that defined the code being executed. It's a subtle difference but an important one, because if it were not this way it would be easy to end up in infinite recursion.

Let's look at why. Let's say we have a class hierarchy with ClassTwo subclassed off ClassOne, and ClassThree subclassed off ClassTwo as shown in Figure 2-2.

All three classes have instance variables that must be initialized, and the initialization code looks like the following.

```
ClassOne>>initialize
    ... set some variables ...
```

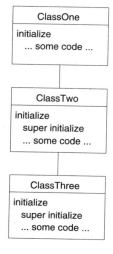

Figure 2-2.
The ClassOne, ClassTwo,
ClassThree inheritance
hierarchy.

```
ClassTwo>>initialize
    super initialize.
    ... set some variables ...

ClassThree>>initialize
    super initialize.
    ... set some variables ...
```

When we create an instance of ClassThree and execute the ClassTwo initialize code from the ClassThree object, what does super refer to? If it refers to the superclass of the class *executing* the code, then super will be ClassTwo and the initialize message will be again sent to ClassTwo. That is, we'll end up in an infinite loop. On the other hand, if super refers to the superclass of the class *defining* the code, the message will be sent to ClassOne and everything will work fine.

A key point to note is that self has an identity of its own and can be inspected, assigned to a variable, and passed as a parameter. However, super has no identity and you cannot inspect it or assign it. When you accept a method, the compiler compiles the method text into byte codes. When it comes across the word super it generates byte codes that instruct the run-time engine to start the method lookup in the superclass of the class defining the method. Thus super is simply a mechanism for telling the compiler how to generate byte codes.

3

Methods

Methods contain code that is executed in response to message sends. Unlike functions in C or C++, which can be void functions, in Smalltalk all methods return a value. If there is no explicit return value, the method will return self, the object executing the method.

Method Types

There are two basic type of methods, ones that return an object other than self and ones that cause an effect. Examples of the first type are asSortedCollection, which converts a collection into a sorted collection and returns this, and printString, which returns an object that is a printable representation of the object receiving printString. Examples of the second type of method are printing to the Transcript (e.g., Transcript show: 'hello'), and updating a file with data.

As a general philosophy, it's better to try and make your methods one type or the other. Try to avoid methods that both do something and return a meaningful object. Sometimes it will be unavoidable, but less often than you might expect. Unlike languages in which you have to check the status returned from a function call, Smalltalk provides an exception-handling mechanism that allows you to bypass the whole status checking aspect of error-handling.

Method Length

In the VisualWorks class library, the average Smalltalk method length is reputed to be seven lines. A short method is a good method because it makes it easy for programmers to understand what the method is doing. A short method is also easier to reuse and easier for subclasses to override in order to modify the behavior. For these reasons it is a good idea to define a "standard" sized browser and have a guideline that all methods should fit in the browser window. If a method is larger, it's usually possible to break it into smaller methods by abstracting out the concepts of what you are doing and putting each concept in its own method. For example, a long method might end up as a short method such as:

```
MyClass>>myMethod
    self myDoConceptOne.
    (someCondition)
        ifTrue:
            [self myDoConceptTwo]
        ifFalse:
            [self myDoConceptThree.
            self myDoConceptFour]
```

Method Names

Because short methods that fit in a screen can be more easily understood, it doesn't make sense to compromise or prevent that understanding with poor names. Use method and variable names that are as explicit as possible. Don't abbreviate words unless they are standard abbreviations understood by everyone working on the project. Because you don't type names very often in Smalltalk, it doesn't hurt to make them long enough to be very explicit and understandable.

Method names should say exactly what the method does. Don't be stingy with the number of characters; it's more important to be understandable than short. A programmer should be able to pick up someone else's code and immediately know what the method does, just by reading the name. However, it's not always easy to come up with a great method name when you are looking at the method itself. It's when the method is being invoked, when you are doing the message send, that you'll find out how good the name is. If it makes sense in the context in which it is sent, then you've probably got a good name. So, while it's okay to name the method when you are writing it, be prepared to go back and change the name after you use it in other methods.

Stupid Methods

If a method is short, has a good name, and has well thought-out names for its variables, it will be fairly understandable. If class comments describe the general behavior of the object and describe the instance variables well, a good method doesn't need much comment. I really like the idea of *stupid methods*. (I'd like to give credit to the creator of the term, but unfortunately I can't remember where I read about the idea.)

A stupid method is one that is so obvious it doesn't need any documentation. The problem with documentation is that it makes a method longer, so if you have a method that is long enough to need some serious documentation you compound the problem by making it longer and less able to fit on a screen. And because it does not fit on a screen it is less readily grasped by a programmer. The ultimate compliment for a method is, "That method is really stupid."

Method Formatting

The formatter does a pretty good job of formatting methods for you. My rule is to ignore formatting when I'm creating a new method, then to run the formatter. If I don't like what the formatter does I'll reformat the code by hand. Here are a few examples of how I might reformat when I don't like the formatter results. To save space I won't show the original formatting; to see it, you'll have to type in the code and run the formatter.

```
myMethod: aParameter
    aParameter
        doThis;
        doThat;
        doSomethingElse

myMethod: aParameter
    self errorSignal
        handle: [ :ex | ex return]
        do:
            [aParameter doThis.
            aParameter doThat]

myMethod: aSource and: aDestination
    (aSource location = aDestination location)
        ifTrue: [self errorSignal
            raiseWith: #sourceEqualsDest
            errorString: 'This is an error string'].
```

Some people find the formatter's format too difficult to read, especially in the case of complex, nested code. An approach preferred by some is to put each closing square bracket on its own line. The trade-off is that it becomes less likely that a method will fit into one screen, which is a strong goal of mine. One answer is that if the code is difficult to read, the method is very likely too long, too complex, or both. So you might call the formatter a benefit if it forces you to refactor your code to make it more elegant and comprehensible.

To improve clarity it's often worth putting in redundant parentheses. A programmer looking at code and working through the message precedence rules can always figure out what is happening, but you can shorten the process if you add parentheses to group things. Because the formatter removes redundant parentheses but leaves required parentheses, you can also use it to tell you where parentheses should be. For example, the first conditional below causes an exception, the second conditional shows what you intend, and the third conditional is what the formatter gives you when you format the second conditional. If you had something more complex, it might be worth leaving the extra parentheses in.

```
a < b | c < d
(a < b) | (c < d)
a < b | (c < d)
```

Public and Private Methods

In C++ there is the notion of public and private fuctions. Public functions are ones that any object can invoke. Private functions are ones that are accessible only to instances of the class that defines them, or its subclasses (actually, protected functions in the latter case).

Smalltalk does not have such a concept. All methods are accessible to all objects; they only have to send the correct message. However, the notion of public and private methods is useful; you really don't want other objects sending messages that exist only to help with the implementation details. Suppose you decide to change the way something is implemented. You don't want to have to preserve all the private interfaces. You want to be able to encapsulate behavior so that other objects can use the public interface and you can be free to change the implementation details.

Because there are no private methods in Smalltalk, any distinction between private and public methods has to be made using standards. One standard is to use the word private in the protocol names for private methods. You might see a protocol named private or private-accessing. The disadvantage of this scheme is that you don't always notice the protocol name. If you are browsing methods using senders, implementors, and messages, you are not told the protocol so you might easily decide to use a particular message.

The technique I like is one described by Bob Brodd in *The Smalltalk Report, Nov-Dec, 1994*. All private methods are prefixed with my. Now you use commonsense English to prevent the public use of private methods. Basically it looks strange to see something like anObject myDoThis, whereas it looks reasonable to say self myDoThis. If you ever see a my message sent to anything other than self, be suspicious. You are probably seeing a private method being used as if it were public. Here's an example of using the my prefix for private methods.

```
ImageCreator>>createImage
    self myRemoveSelfAsDependent.
    self myFileInApplication.
    self myRunStripper.
    self myOpenApplication.
    self myCloseLauncher.
    self myInstallEmergencyHandler.
    self mySaveImageAndQuit
```

If you use the my technique, there are two basic approaches you could take. One is to make everything public unless you know it is a support method that shouldn't be invoked in isolation. The other is to start by making all methods private, then making them public as you come across a message that needs to be sent by another object.

The advantage of the first approach is that you can't predict how other people will want to use your class, and if you make methods private by default, you don't give people the opportunity to be fully creative. The advantage of the second approach is that, by making methods private by default, you define a public interface to your object and don't open up the implementation details to other objects. I generally follow the latter philosphy, because I want my objects tightly encapsulated. However, I also make the distinction between domain-specific objects and general reusable objects; the latter usually have more public methods.

We can extend the concept of my methods to include *friend* methods. A friend message is one that can be sent between friend objects. Suppose you have a nicely encapsulated subsystem that consists of several collaborating objects. None of these objects has a life outside the subsystem, and they don't expect to receive messages from objects outside the subsystem. We can consider these objects all friends of each other and define a prefix, such as fr to denote messages that can only be sent by a friend. Each class that defines friend methods would have to provide documentation in the class comments, describing exactly which classes were friends. Any programmer wanting to use a message starting with fr would have to look at the class comments to find out if the sending object were actually a friend.

In Chapter 29, we will show an extension to Class that automatically creates both public and private accessors for all our instance variables when we define a class.

Returning from a Method

In Smalltalk, all methods return a value. There is no such thing as C++'s void function. By default, all methods return the object the message was sent to. So, if there is not an explicit return in a method, in effect the last line of the method looks like:

```
^self
```

^ is the return symbol and self refers to the message receiver — the object executing the method. Most methods implicitly return self. In the VisualWorks Browser, if you hold the shift key down while selecting a method with the mouse you will see the decompiled code, which actually has a ^self at the end. The return (^) is executed after all other message sends and assignments in the statement have been done.

Return Object Defined by Method Name

Often the method name will tell you what type of object will be returned. For example, method names that start with is will usually return a Boolean, true, or false. For example, isEmpty, isNil. Messages that start with as will usually return the thing specified. For example, asSortedCollection sent to a collection will return a SortedCollection. The asNumber message, sent to a string, will return a number of the appropriate type. (However, asString is not implemented by numbers so you should use printString or displayString instead.)

Methods that add objects to collections, such as add: and at:put:, return the object that is added. Methods that remove single objects from collections, such as remove: and removeFirst, return the object that was removed. Because of this it's worth knowing about the yourself message. The following example illustrates how the use of yourself ensures that collection contains the list rather than the last object added (the example makes use of message cascading, which we will talk about in Chapter 6).

```
collection := List new
    add: thisObject;
    add: thatObject;
    yourself.
```

Consistency and predictability are great virtues, so when adding these types of methods to your own classes, follow the common usage patterns. Otherwise, you'll confuse every programmer who looks at or uses your code.

Return Object Defined by Last Statement

If a method returns something other than self, the last line or the last statement in the method will specify what is being returned. The assumption when you see an explicit return at the end of the method is that the message sender will care about what is being returned. For this reason, don't do ^self at the end of the method unless this has an explicit meaning for the sender.

Guard Clauses

If you wish to execute the method body only if some condition is true, the obvious way to do this is:

```
MyClass>>someMethod
    (some condition) ifTrue:
        [self doThingOne.
        self doThingTwo.
        self doMoreLinesOfCode]
```

However, it is often better to return self from an iffalse: block, then execute the main code. Thus we have a *guard clause* protecting entry to the method.

```
MyClass>>someMethod
    (some condition) ifFalse: [^self].
    self doThingOne.
    self doThingTwo.
    self doMoreLinesOfCode]
```

This makes the code a little easier to follow, because it's all straight line code rather than conditional. This approach goes against the structured programming adage of one entry point, one exit point. The rule was created to solve the understandability problem of long functions with multiple entry and exit points. However, Smalltalk methods are usually short, so it's easy to see exactly what is happening.

Consistency in Objects Returned

If your methods implicity return self at the end, use ^self to return earlier. Don't return a different value, such as nil, unless nil has a specific meaning to the sender.

Misplaced Methods

If a method doesn't reference any instance variables and simply operates on parameters, you might ask if the method is defined in the right place. If the method is manipulating a parameter, perhaps the code should be defined by the class of the parameter. For example, when working with a string, you might decide you need to remove the leading and trailing white space. So you write a new method for your class that trims the white space.

```
MyClass>>removeWhiteSpaceFrom: aString
    ... remove leading and trailing white space...
    ^newStringWithWhiteSpaceRemoved
```

However, this is a very procedural way of writing code. If you are thinking in terms of objects, you figure out where the responsibility really lies and tell objects to do things. Because MyClass really is not responsible for removing white space from strings, where should that responsibility lie? The most obvious place is the class String (or one of its superclasses). You can then tell your string to strip itself of white space.

```
trimmedString := aString trimWhiteSpace.
```

Number of Methods

There is no rule for how many methods an object should have, but if you find that one object has many more methods than other objects, it might be that you are not distributing the workload well. In a good object-oriented system, you don't have super intelligent objects. Instead, you have many peer-type objects cooperating. For more information, see Chapter 9.

Defaulting Parameters

In C++, you can leave out parameters in function calls and the parameters will be defaulted (assuming the function is written this way). In Smalltalk, no such capability exists. Instead, you often see a method do nothing other than invoke another method with an additional parameter.

A good example of this is the changed message. When you invoke the dependency update mechanism, you use changed to specify that something has changed. You use changed: to specify what has changed, and changed:with: to specify the new value.

```
Object>>changed
    self changed: nil

Object>>changed: anAspect Symbol
    self changed: anAspectSymbol with: nil

Object>>changed: anAspectSymbol with: aParameter
    self myDependents
        update: anAspectSymbol
        with: aParameter from: self
```

Method Template

The method template (what you see when you are looking at methods but don't have a method selected) is defined in Behavior>>sourceCodeTemplate. If you don't like it you can change it. For one example of how you might change it, see Chapter 31.

4

Variables

In this chapter we'll look at the different types of variable that are available in Smalltalk: instance, class, class instance, parameter, and temporary. Global variables are a big enough topic in themselves to merit their own discussion in Chapter 7. Smalltalk also has a few special variables that we will see in Chapter 6.

Variable Names

Code is easier to understand when all method names and variable names are meaningful. Make variable names explicit and obvious so a reader will immediately know the purpose of the variable. Don't abbreviate names; spell them out in full except for abbreviations that are accepted by all programmers or are part of the project vocabulary. Your goal should be to produce code that a programmer can look at and immediately understand, even without comments in the code itself. Part of this involves a good division of responsibility in the code, and part involves well-thought-out names for methods and variables.

Variable names consist of one or more words strung together. The first letter of each word should be capitalized, and the rest of the letters should be lowercase. The exception to this is the first letter of the name for which the following rule applies: Instance, parameter, and temporary variables should start with a lowercase letter. Class, class instance, and global variables should start with an uppercase letter. Some people leave acronyms as uppercase; I try to avoid having two capital letters in a row as it makes it just that little bit harder to break the name into words. Here are some examples of variable names:

```
"Instance or temporary variables"
employeeName
collectionOfStrings
upperLeftCornerOfBox
```

```
"Parameter"
aNumber
aCollectionOfEmployees

"Class, Class instance, or Global variables"
Employee
DaysInMonth
MonthNames
```

I've always found it useful to prefix class names with an application or component prefix because I like to know where a class comes from when I see it in the code. For example, if you have an accounting application with payroll, accounts payable, and general ledger components, you might have prefixes such as Pr, Ap, Gl for the components, then something like Aac for the classes used for the communication between components (Accounting Application Communication). General support classes that will be used across applications or components get a general company prefix, or a prefix such as Sup.

Instance Variables

Suppose we have a class called Friend. Each friend in our application has a first name, a last name, and a phone number. The class definition for Friend specifies that each instance of Friend has three variables: firstName, lastName, and phone. We specify these *instance variables* in the class definition.

```
Object subclass: #Friend
    instanceVariableNames: 'firstName lastName phone'
    classVariableNames: ''
    poolDictionaries: ''
    category: 'MyCategory'
```

When we create a new instance of Friend, it will have its own values in the instance variables. We might create an instance of Friend by sending the following instance creation message to the class Friend.

```
friendOne := Friend
    newLastName: 'Doe'
    firstName: 'John'
    phone: '555-5555'
```

If we then create another friend, friendTwo, it has no effect on friendOne, because friendOne has its own values in the instance variables.

```
friendTwo := Friend
    newLastName: 'Smith'
    firstName: 'Jane'
    phone: '111-1212'
```

The two instances of Friend have their own values in the instance variables, independent of the values in the other instance. If we change the value of one instance variable it has no effect on the other friend.

For example, we can change the phone number for John Doe without affecting the phone number of Jane Smith.

Class Variables

Suppose we have several instances of class Date. Each instance will be unique, and will have its own values for the instance variables defined by Date (these are year, the year, and day, the number of days since the beginning of the year). We want to know the name of the month for each of these instances. Something has to keep track of the names of the months, and since month names are associated with dates, we might as keep track of the names somewhere in the Date class. However, we don't need to waste space by having each instance of a Date keep this array. Instead, we put the array of month names in a *class variable*. This lets the Date class keep track of the array, so we only have one copy of the array. All instances have access to the class variables of their class, so each instance of Date can access the month name array. In fact, Date has many class variables, as shown in the following class definition:

```
Magnitude subclass: #Date
    instanceVariableNames: 'day year '
    classVariableNames: 'DaysInMonth FirstDayOfMonth MonthNames SecondsInDay WeekDayNames '
    poolDictionaries: ''
    category: 'Magnitude-General'
```

Here are a two examples where instances of Date reference some of the class side variables. The messages monthName and daysInMonth look at the arrays held in the class variables MonthNames and DaysInMonth.

```
(Date newDay: 115 year: 1960) monthName.     #April
Date today monthName.                        #October
Date today daysInMonth.                      31
```

All instances can directly reference their class variables, although it might be preferable to reference them through *accessors*, which we'll look at later in this chapter. Although instances have access to the class variables of their class, the class itself does not have access to any instance variables of its instances, and in fact, the class doesn't usually even know that it has instances. You can inspect the class variables of a class by inspecting the class then inspecting the classPool variable.[1]

---

[1]Alternatively, you can send the classPool message to the class (e.g., Date classPool). If you know the name of the class variable, you can do something like Date classPool at: #DaysInMonth. (Interestingly, you can inspect the class variables of Object directly, just by typing the variable name in a text window, such as a workspace or a Browser, then inspecting the name. This works because in a text window, self is either nil or the class that you are browsing. Because of inheritance, both of these objects have direct access to the class variables of their superclasses, and so can see the class variables of Object.)

Classes referencing their instances (advanced)

Even though classes don't by default know about their instances, you will sometimes find that classes manage their instances. You might also find that there is a concept of the *current* instance of a class. Combining these concepts (which doesn't usually happen), you might see something like the following in a class definition. Note that what we describe here is very simplistic and is just designed to point out the concepts.

```
Object subclass: #MyClass
    instanceVariableNames: 'instVar1 instVar2 '
    classVariableNames: 'Instances Current '
    poolDictionaries: ''
    category: 'MyCategory'
```

When a new instance is created, it is stored in a collection of instances held by the Instances class variable. There is also a method to retrieve and set the current instance so that the rest of the system knows which instance of MyClass they should be working with.

```
MyClass class>>initialize
    "self initialize"
    Instances := OrderedCollection new.

MyClass class>>new
    "This shows the concepts"
    newObject := super new initialize.
    Instances add: newObject.
    ^newObject

MyClass class>>new
    "This shows a tighter implementation"
    ^Instances add: super new initialize.

MyClass class>>current
    ^Current

MyClass class>>current: anInstance
    "Set the current instance and inform dependents, telling them the old value"
    old := Current.
    Current := anInstance.
    self changed: #current with: old
```

This last method shows some code associated with the Smalltalk dependency mechanism. We'll see more about this in Chapter 19, but for now we'll simply remark that it provides a way for other objects to be told when the current instance has changed, and gives them a chance to take whatever actions are meaningful for them as they change to the new current instance.

Class Instance Variables

Besides class variables and instance variables, Smalltalk provides a variable called a *class instance variable*. It's a variable defined on the *class* side, and provides a way to hold a value that is potentially different for each subclass of the original class. Instances of each subclass all have access to the variable, but instances of one subclass will see a different value than will instances of another subclass.

It's not very common to see examples of class instance variables, but they can be useful. Here's an example of one such use. Suppose that your application has a centralized error message facility (we talk more about this in Chapter 20). However, each component of the application wants to have its own error messages and its own numbers, each prefixed by the appropriate tag. By having separate subclasses for the different components, programmers can work on the components in isolation without having to worry about message symbol or number conflicts. The component error messages classes are subclassed off ErrorMessages. Note that all the definitions and methods below are on the class side.

```
ErrorMessages class
    instanceVariableNames: 'Messages'

ErrorMessages class>>initialize
    Messages := Dictionary new.

ErrorMessages class>>number: aSymbol
    ^(Messages at: aSymbol ifAbsent: [self notFoundError: aSymbol]) key printString

ErrorMessages class>>notFoundError: aSymbol
    ^0->('Symbol <', aSymbol, '> not found')

ComponentOneErrorMessages class>>initialize
    super initialize.
    Messages
        at: #notFound        put: 1 -> 'Account not found';
        at: #duplicate       put: 2 -> 'Duplicate account'.

ComponentOneErrorMessages class>>number: aSymbol
    ^'C1-', (super number: aSymbol)

ComponentTwoErrorMessages class>>initialize
    super initialize.
    Messages
        at: #duplicate       put: 1 -> 'File already exists';
        at: #notFound        put: 2 -> 'File not found'.

ComponentTwoErrorMessages class>>number: aSymbol
    ^'C2-', (super number: aSymbol)
```

To sum up, class instance variables are used when you need a class variable to store information that might be different for each subclass. We show another use of class instance variables in Chapter 30, where we use them to hold the display name of the test case subclasses.

Parameters

Parameters (or arguments) are objects that are passed into a method or a code block. Smalltalk doesn't have type checking, so you can pass any object as a parameter to any method. Of course, when you send a message to the parameter object, there will be problems if the object doesn't understand the message — if the object is not of the appropriate type. (Some people jokingly say that Smalltalk is very strongly typed — all arguments must be objects!) Unlike what happens with the other types of variable, you can't assign a different value to a parameter variable. Fortunately, the compiler will catch this so you won't even be able to accept the following:

```
MyClass>>doSomethingWith: anObject
    anObject := 3.
```

However, you can modify the contents of a parameter, so it's perfectly legitimate to do the following, although not necessarily good style:

```
MyClass>>modifyCollection: aCollection
    aCollection add: 3.
```

Method parameters

In the code shown above, we've seen various examples of messages and parameters. Shown below are a few examples of method and parameter names as shown in the various definitions.

```
Date class>>newDay: dayCount year: referenceYear
Object>>changed: anAspectSymbol with: aParameter
OrderedCollection>>add: newObject
Dictionary>>at: key put: anObject
MyClass>>modifyCollection: aCollection
```

The objects after the colons are the parameters. Why do the parameters have these names? There are two types of naming schemes: you can name the parameter according to its *content (e.g.,* lastName, salary, price, quantityOnHand), or according to its *type (e.g.,* anInteger, anArray, aSymbol) As a general rule, you'll find instance and temporary variables named according to their content, while method parameters are named according to their type. You'll often see methods that have parameters with names such as aString, aCollection, anEmployee, aRobot. This type of information tells the programmer a lot about the messages that can be sent to the object. Sometimes, however, *type* information is not enough.

In the examples above, the parameter to newDay: could have been anInteger, but this would provide very little information about what the content of the integer should be. So, the parameter is named dayCount. Similarly, we might have a method that creates a new instance of Employee as follows:

```
Employee class>>firstName: firstName lastName: lastName
```

It makes more sense to give the parameters names such as firstName and lastName rather than aStringOne and aStringTwo. Even names such as aFirstNameString don't add a lot of information, especially since the method will probably not do anything with the parameters other than store the values in instance variables.

To summarize, method parameters are often named according to their *types*. However, there will be situations in which naming them according to their content makes more sense, and situations in which naming them according to a mixture of type and content makes sense.

Block parameters

Code blocks contain code that is not executed until the block is sent a message from the value family. To pass a parameter to a block, the message will have to be one that has a parameter, such as value: or value:value:. For example, we might have something like the following:

```
block := [ :nameString |Transcript cr; show: 'The name is ', nameString ].
block value: 'Alec'.

block := [ :nameString :age |
        Transcript cr; show: 'The age of ', nameString, ' is ', age printString].
block value: 'Dave' value: 12.
```

You probably won't often use blocks with more than one or two parameters, but if you do, you can send value:value:value: for blocks with three parameters, or valueWithArguments: anArray if you have more than three. For example, a block with five parameters might look like the following (if the number of array elements doesn't match the number of parameters, you'll get an exception):

```
[ :parm1 :parm2 :parm3 :parm4 :parm5 | self doSomething ]
    valueWithArguments: #(99 88 77 66 55).
```

You'll see block parameters used in the enumeration methods of collections. For example:

```
aCollection do: [ :each | Transcript cr; show: each printString].
aCollectionOfNumbers collect: [ :each | each * 30].
aCollectionOfNumbers inject: 0 into: [ :subtotal :each | subtotal + each ].
```

When naming the parameters of a block that is used when iterating over a collection, one convention is to use the parameter name each. This tells you instantly that the variable is the current element of the collection. Alternatively, use the name index if you know that the variable is an index, or the name char if the variable is a character in a string.

```
1 to: 5 do: [ :index | self doSomethingUsing: index ].
'now is the time' do: [ :char | self doSomethingUsing: char ].
```

Generally, I would use a name other than each, index, or char for the collection element only if there were nested collection iterations and I couldn't use the same name in both of them. For example:

```
#('cat' 'dog' 'gerbil')
    collect: [ :pet | #('milk' 'water' 'oj')
        collect: [ :drink | pet -> drink]]
```

Temporary Variables

Temporary variables are variables that exist for only a short time, for the duration of a method or the duration of a block of code. There are several reasons to use a temporary variable. The most important reason is to *capture a value that can't be regenerated*. For example, if you are reading an object from a stream or a shared queue and you want to use that object several times, use a temporary variable to capture it. For example:

```
request := sharedQueue next.
originator := request originator.
requestTime := request creationTime.
```

Another reason to use a temporary variable is to *avoid having to repeat expensive operations*. For example, if you are comparing a variable with a value from a database, it's appropriate to store the database value in a temporary variable. Compare the two examples here:

```
aCollection detect: [ :each | each = self myValueFromDatabase ] ifNone: [nil].

databaseValue := self myValueFromDatabase.
aCollection detect: [ :each | each = databaseValue ] ifNone: [nil].
```

A third reason to use a temporary variable is to *increase performance by reducing the number of message sends*. For example, in the first example below, we have to do several identical message sends several times. It saves a lot of message sends if we do them the way shown in the second example:

```
self checkAddress: (employeeCollection at: employeeId) address.
self validateSalary: (employeeCollection at: employeeId) salary.
self printCheck: (employeeCollection at: employeeId).

employee := (employeeCollection at: employeeId).
self checkAddress: employee address.
self validateSalary: employee salary.
self printCheck: employee.
```

A fourth reason to use a temporary variable is to *make it easier to understand the code*. Sometimes it can be difficult to understand what object we have as a result of a complex sequence of message sends. While we might not need to use a temporary variable if we only do this sequence of message sends once, it can make the code more readable to store the result of this sequence in a well named temporary variable. (An alternative approach is to compute the complex result in another method and replace the complex message sends with a single message send.) For example, the code below makes it easy to see what is going on without having to read through the sort block code:

```
MyClass>>mySortByBirthday: aCollection
    | birthdaySortBlock |
    birthdaySortBlock := [ :first :second | first birthday <= second birthday ].
    ^aCollection asSortedCollection: birthdaySortBlock.
```

Temporary to the method

Temporary variables are named between vertical bars before any code in the method. For example:

```
copyWith: newElement
    | newCollection |
    newCollection := self copy.
    newCollection add: newElement.
    ^newCollection
```

You can type in the temporary variable name between the vertical bars, or you can let the compiler generate the name between the bars. The compiler will generate the names of temporary variables in the order in which they occur in the method. I usually let the compiler generate the names, but this sometimes leads to problems. If you give a temporary the same name as an instance variable, the compiler will assume that you are referring to the instance variable and will not generate the name for you. (If you type the name in yourself, you will be warned that a variable of that name already exists, perhaps in an outer scope.) On the class side, if you name a temporary variable name and don't put it between vertical bars yourself, the class itself will be given a new name when the code is run!

Temporary to the block

Temporary variables in blocks are enclosed between vertical bars, just as method temporaries are. For example:

```
[ | result |
result := self myDoSomething.
... ]
```

If you have block parameters and block temporary variables, they are defined as follows. Note that a vertical bar appears after the parameters, and the temporary variables are defined between their own vertical bars. So there are two vertical bars.

```
myMethod
    aCollection do: [ :each |  | result |
        ....
```

BlockClosures have better performance if all the variables they reference are local to the block. So, rather than letting the compiler generate temporary variable definitions at the top of the method, look to see if it is possible to make all block references internal to the block.

Global Variables

Chapter 7 covers global variables, so we won't discuss them here.

Variables as Slots

Variables are simply slots which hold an object. The object itself exists somewhere in computer memory, but it is *bound* to the variable. If we bind a different object to the variable, the first object might no longer be bound to any variable. When an object is not bound to any variable (i.e., it is no longer referenced), the object is available to be garbage collected. In concept it is floating somewhere in memory with nothing attached to it, and the garbage collector comes along and sweeps it up.

Because an object exists separately and is just bound to a variable, there's no reason that an object can't be bound to many variables simultaneously. We could easily have a situation such as the following. When you inspect d you'll see that it contains three items, the numbers 1 and 2, and 3. Multiple assignments, as shown in the example, are legal but bad style.

```
a := b := c := d := OrderedCollection new.
a add: 1.
b add: 2.
c add: 3.
d inspect.
```

In this example, we assign the same instance of OrderedCollection to all the variables. When we modify the collection via one variable, its contents are changed and that change is visible to all variables that have been bound to it. This is illustrated in Fig. 4-1.

On the other hand, if we were to do the following, we would find that b contains the number 2, while d contains the numbers 1 and 3.

```
a := b := c := d := OrderedCollection new.
a add: 1.
b := 2.
c add: 3.
b inspect.
d inspect.
```

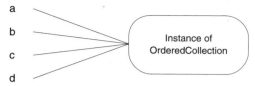

a

b

c

d

Instance of
OrderedCollection

Figure 4-1. All variables holding same object.

In this example, we assign a different value to b and bind it to the object 2 instead of the instance of OrderedCollection. This is illustrated in Fig. 4-2.

Accessors

Accessors are methods that allow you to get and set the values of instance variables and class variables. Since instance variables are more heavily used than class variables, you will see accessors most often used with instance variables. Because they get and set variables, accessors are sometimes known as *getters* and *setters,* and when you write accessors you will usually write both a getter and a setter. The convention is to name them the same as the instance variable. For example:

```
Employee>>salary: aNumber
    salary := aNumber

Employee>>salary
    ^salary
```

If you choose to use lazy initialization (initializing a variable only when it is first needed) rather than to initialize instance variables in an initialize method, the salary accessor would look something like:

```
Employee>>salary
    ^salary isNil
        ifTrue: [salary := 0]
        ifFalse: [salary]
```

Lazy initialization is a reasonable approach when variables are accessed infrequently or not at all, and the cost of initialization is high. Otherwise, it's probably worth initializing variables in an initialize method.

Accessors for collections

If your variable contains a collection, what should the getter return? The usual answer is to return a *copy* of the collection. Other classes will be able to take actions based on the contents of the collection, but they won't be able to directly add to or remove from the collection. As well as providing accessors, you would also provide methods to add to and remove from the collection. For example:

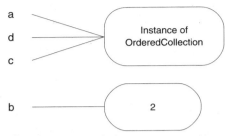

Figure 4-2. Variables holding different objects.

```
Employee>>skills
    ^skillsCollection copy

Employee>>addSkill: aSkill
    ^skillsCollection add: aSkill

Employee>>removeSkill: aSkill
    ^skillsCollection remove: aSkill ifAbsent: [nil]
```

However, you might want to consider not providing *any* direct public interface to your collections. After all, you might decide to change the collection from an OrderedCollection to an Array or a Dictionary, and you don't want to be concerned about how other software is accessing the collection. By providing a few accessing methods, such as the addSkill: and the removeSkill: methods shown above, you don't have to expose the actual collection at all. (Another approach would be to provide a getter that always converts the actual collection into an OrderedCollection and returns this.)

The five accessor approach

I have a friend who uses what he calls the "fascist" approach to instance variable accessors. For each instance variable, there are five accessors. Using a variable called salary as an example, we would have the following accessors in this scheme. The only two public accessors are salary and salary:. The others are all private. The public accessors are allowed to have side effects (for example, establishing connections), while the private methods are not allowed to have side effects.[2] Not many people use a technique this strict, however.

---

[2]Jumping well ahead of ourselves, subclasses of ValueModel provide two setters, value: and setValue:. This allows objects to use value: when they want to notify dependents of changes, and setValue: when they want to make a change without notifying dependents. This latter option helps avoid infinite loops when updating a value as a result of a change notification from a dependent. Don't worry if this doesn't make any sense now — we'll cover dependencies later. Below (bottom page 39) are examples of both methods:

```
Employee>>salary
    "Answer salary. This accessor is allowed to have side effects."
    self myGetSalary == nil
        ifTrue: [self mySetSalary: self myComputeSalary]
    ^self myGetSalary

Employee>>myGetSalary
    "Answer salary. No side effects are allowed."
    ^salary

Employee>>myComputeSalary
    "Answer the initial value for salary, possibly computing it"
    ^self baseSalaryForGrade * self locationFactor

Employee>>salary: aValue
    "Set the salary. This accessor is allowed to have side effects"
    self mySetSalary: aValue.
    self informPayrollSupervisor

Employee>>mySetSalary: aValue
    "Set the salary. No side effects are allowed"
    salary:= aValue
```

Accessors or Direct Referencing

There are schools of thought about how instances should reference their instance variables. One school says that instance variables should *always* be referenced indirectly, through accessor methods. The other school says that *sometimes* instance variables should be referenced directly. Let's look at these two ideas.

Direct referencing

The advantages of referencing instance variables directly are threefold:

1. You don't have to write accessor methods (although the VisualWorks CodingAssistant helps you with this).

2. It's a little more efficient to access them directly, because you save a message send on each access (although not much, since the compiler can optimize these message sends).

```
ValueModel>>value: newValue
    "Set the currently stored value, and notify dependents."
    self setValue: newValue.
    self changed: #value

ValueHolder>>setValue: aValue
    "Just initialize the value without notifying dependents of a change. "
    value := aValue
```

3. The most significant advantage of referencing variables directly, is that you preserve the encapsulation of the object. Anytime you write an accessor the whole world has access to the instance variables, which violates the principle of encapsulation. Sometimes you want to give access to instance variables, but much of the time you'd like to keep private the internal details of how the class works. In *Celebrating 25 Years of Smalltalk*, Ward Cunningham says, "But if I could change anything... I'd like to see people stop giving away all their instance variables with accessing methods."

Referencing through accessors

Requiring all access to go through accessors makes it easier to preserve the public interface to an object when the underlying implementation changes. You might get rid of instance variables or combine them in some way, but as long as you can compute the information that was returned by a getter, and as long as you can make use of the information that was given to a setter, you can preserve the same interface to the world. To use a trivial example, suppose we have an Account object which contains a balance instance variable. Perhaps the accessors at one time were:

```
Account>>balance: aFloat
    balance := aFloat

Account>>balance
    ^balance
```

We decide that we'd rather store the value internally in cents rather than in dollars, so we modify the accessors to look like:

```
Account>>balance: aFloat
    balance := (aFloat * 100) rounded

Account>>balance
    ^balance / 100
```

Other advantages to accessors include:

- If you want to change an instance variable, and instance variables are accessed directly, you have to look through the class and all its subclasses to find references to the variable; on the other hand, if you have accessors on all your instance variables, all you have to do is browse senders of the accessor messages.

- If you have long methods, it can be difficult to tell what are instance variables and what are temporary variables if you don't use accessors.

- Having set accessors makes it easier to notify dependents of changes, and to mark an object as modified or dirty when it has changed. For example, combining these last two, you might have a setter that looks like:

```
MyClass>>weight: aNumber
    oldWeight := weight.
    weight := aNumber.
    self markDirty.
    self changed: #weight with: oldWeight
```

Which way to go

My view is that, when implementations change, it's usually easier to find and change the references to variables than to preserve an obsolete interface. In code I write for myself I tend to use accessors only when I want to provide public access to the variables. Sometimes this means providing a getter but not a setter. At work, I follow whatever standards prevail (which is usually to use accessors for all instance variables), because I believe it's more important to conform to the standard than to be inconsistent.

If you choose to use accessors but are concerned about violating encapsulation, you can use the my prefix described in Chapter 3. This allows you to use accessors and also preserve the encapsulation, assuming that people don't violate the rules about methods starting with my. In Chapter 29 we will show an extension to Class that automatically creates both public and private accessors for all our instance variables when we define a class.

Chains of Accessors

One thing to beware of when writing accessors is creating long chains of accessors to get hold of an object in an object in an object in an object. For example, we might have something like:

```
companyName := employee department division company companyName.
```

The problem with this approach is that it violates encapsulation in a big way. Not only do you know the implementation details of the employee, but you also know and rely on the instance variables for the department, the division, and the company. This makes the system much more fragile because you can't make a change to any of the objects without worrying about how it will affect code. Instead, it's better to encapsulate the inner details. Provide accessors on the outer object that will return inner details. In our example, we might write company and companyName accessors on the employee, so we can now write:

```
companyName := employee companyName.
```

This means that we can restructure how the company is organized, perhaps removing the division layer or perhaps adding a country layer, without having to change the code that needs the company name for the employee. Similarly, we would probably write company and companyName methods on Department and on Division for the same reason. Our accessors on Employee might look like the following:

```
Employee>>companyName
    ^self company companyName

Employee>>company
    ^self department company
```

This leads to the idea that to maintain loose coupling between classes, a method should send messages only to self, super, to its class, to instance or class variables, to a parameter, or to an object it creates. If the method sends messages to any other object, it is either referencing a global variable or it knows something about the internal details of the object. This is illustrated in Figure 4-3.

Documentation on Variables

All instance, class, and class instance variables should be documented in the class comments. You should describe at least the type of the variable, its purpose, and any special information that will be useful to other programmers. For example, here is part of the class comment for Date:

```
Instance Variables:
    day       <Integer>    from 1 to (365 | 366)
    year      <Integer>    typically after the year 1900

Class Variables:
    DaysInMonth            <Array of: Integer> the number of days in each month
    MonthNames             <Array of: Symbol> the names of the 12 months
```

Once you have decided what information your project requires to be in a class comment, you can customize the class comment template by modifying the commentTemplateString method in ClassDescription.

self	someMethod: aParameter
super	self foo.
self class	super foo.
self instVar	self class foo.
self classVar	self instVarOne foo.
aParameter	instVarTwo foo.
SomeClass new	self classVarOne foo.

```
someMethod: aParameter
    self foo.
    super foo.
    self class foo.
    self instVarOne foo.
    instVarTwo foo.
    self classVarOne foo.
    classVarTwo foo.
    aParameter foo.
    thing := MyThing new.
    thing foo.
```

Figure 4-3. Message sends for loose coupling.

5

Instance Creation

We've now covered enough material to look more closely at creating instances of a class. The basic instance creation message is new, which returns a new instance of the class. For example,

```
employee := Employee new.
collection := OrderedCollection new.
```

If you send new to a collection class it will return a new collection.[1] The size will always be zero because the collection is empty, but the capacity will be the default capacity for that class. The capacity is the number of items you can put in the collection before it has to grow. For example, printing the following expressions gives the capacity shown on the right in the following table:

```
Array new capacity              0
Bag new capacity                0
Dictionary new capacity         3
Set new capacity                3
List new capacity               5
OrderedCollection new capacity  5
```

Growing a collection is quite expensive, because the growing code creates a new collection with a larger capacity, copies over all the elements of the collection, then becomes the new collection. If you know how big the collection should be, or have an idea for the starting capacity, it's more efficient to create the collection by sending the message new: with the starting capacity as a parameter. Some collections, such as instances of Array, don't grow automatically, so it's important to specify their capacity (for collections that don't automatically grow, the size and capacity are the same). For example:

---

[1]Sending new: to a class that is not variable-sized will generate an exception.

```
array := Array new: 10.
collection := OrderedCollection new: 20.
stream := (String new: 100) writeStream.
```

The new and new: methods are implemented by Behavior, although they are overridden by many other classes. Because your class will inherit new and new:, you don't need to override them unless your class has data that needs to be set when an instance is created. There are two types of data setting that can be done: setting variables to a default initialized value, and setting variables to data that is specific to the instance. Let's take a look at each of these.

Setting Default Values

Suppose we have an Employee object that tracks the number of hours of vacation and sick time allowed and taken. When an instance of Employee is created, we want to initialize these instance variables to the appropriate values, regardless of the name or salary of the employee. There are two ways of doing this. First, we can use lazy initialization as we saw in Chapter 4. For example:

```
Employee>>sickHoursUsed
    ^sickHoursUsed isNil
        ifTrue: [sickHoursUsed := 0]
        ifFalse: [sickHoursUsed]
```

Alternatively, we could initialize all the data in a single initialize method. Lazy initialization is useful if you have objects where the data might never be accessed, and where it's expensive to initialize the data, but it has a cost of an extra message send each time the data is accessed. If you will be accessing the data a lot, it's worth doing the initialization in an initialize method. For example, for our Employee object we might have the following (although we wouldn't have hard coded values for the allowed variables).

```
Employee>>initialize
    self sickHoursUsed: 0.
    self vacationHoursUsed: 0.
    self sickHoursAllowed: 80.
    self vacationHoursAllowed: 80.
```

To invoke the initialize method you'll have to override new because the inherited new doesn't invoke initialize (at least, not if Employee is sub-classed off Object). The usual way to override new is as follows. (Note: one of the most common errors of beginning Smalltalk programmers is to leave off the ^, which means that the class itself will be returned, rather than the newly created instance)

```
Employee class>>new
    ^super new initialize
```

Before you override new like this, you need to be aware of what super new does. If the new method in the superclass sends initialize, your initialize method will be invoked twice, first by the superclass new method, then by the Employee new method. In this situation you don't need to override new because you can inherit it from your superclass. Because the superclass has an initialize method that presumably initializes superclass data, your initialize method should start with super initialize.

For example, suppose we have an Employee class, with subclasses of HourlyEmployee and SalariedEmployee. Let's assume that hourly employees get two weeks of vacation while salaried employees get three weeks. We might have the following:

```
Employee class>>new
    ^super new initialize

Employee>>initialize
    self sickHoursUsed: 0.
    self vacationHoursUsed: 0.

HourlyEmployee>>initialize
    super initialize.
    self sickHoursAllowed: 80.
    self vacationHoursAllowed: 80.

SalariedEmployee>>initialize
    super initialize.
    self sickHoursAllowed: 120.
    self vacationHoursAllowed: 120.
```

While overriding new to be ^super new initialize is the common way of doing it, some people prefer to use the basicNew message.

```
MyClass class>>new
    ^self basicNew initialize
```

Methods that start with basic, such as basicNew and basicAt:, should not be overridden. Their purpose is to provide the basic functionality, and programmers should be able to rely on this. If you want to override the functionality, override new and at:. By using basicNew you don't have to worry about any superclass sending initialize and thus causing your initialize method to be invoked more than once. However, you still need to determine whether you should send super initialize in your initialize method.

Overriding new

It gets frustrating to have to override new just so you can invoke initialize. One solution is to have all your application classes subclassed off MyApplicationObject, which is subclassed off Object. In MyApplicationObject, you override new on the class side, and write a default initialize on the instance side. Now you can override initialize in your class without having to override new.

```
MyApplicationObject class>>new
    ^self basicNew initialize

MyApplicationObject >>initialize
    "do nothing"
```

Setting Instance-Specific Values

Often, when you create a new instance you want to give it some information. In our employee example we need at least a name. We might also need to provide a social security number, a salary, and information about gender, marital status, and number of dependents. There are two choices: To create the instance then set the variables, or to set the variables as part of instance creation. For the sake of example, let's assume that, when creating an employee object, two pieces of information are absolutely required, a name and a social security number. If we create the instance then set the variables, we might have something like:

```
employee := Employee new.
employee name: aName.
employee socialSecurityNo: aSocialSecurityNo.
```

The problem with this approach is that you are relying on all programmers to remember to set the required variables after creating the instance. This is okay if the variables are optional, but dangerous if they are required. If you need to guarantee that the data is set you are better off writing an instance creation method that forces programmers to provide the required information. For example, if we write our own instance creation method, we can create an employee like this:

```
employee := Employee name: aName socialSecurityNo: aSocialSecurityNo.
```

What would the name:socialSecurityNo: method look like? One option would be to simply pass on to an initialization method the information that needs to be set.

```
Employee class>>name: aName socialSecurityNo: aSocialSecurityNo
    ^super new initializeName: aName socialSecurityNo: aSocialSecurityNo
```

This is a reasonable approach if you need an initialization method to initialize other data, such as the vacationHoursUsed variable shown above. However, if the initialization method does nothing except set the variables passed in, you might set the data directly. For example, you could use one of the following techniques; the second one dispenses with the temporary variable.

```
Employee class>>name: aName socialSecurityNo: aSocialSecurityNo
    |instance |
    instance := super new.
    instance name: aName.
    instance socialSecurityNo: aSocialSecurityNo.
    ^instance

Employee class>>name: aName socialSecurityNo: aSocialSecurityNo
    ^super new
        name: aName;
        socialSecurityNo: aSocialSecurityNo;
        yourself
```

Overriding new **to Avoid Its Being Used**

If you require programmers to use name:socialSecurityNo: to create instances of Employee, you could override new to raise an exception. Doing this is not very common, but it does make it easier for programmers to discover that they are creating employee objects in the wrong way.

```
Employee class>>new
    self error: 'Please use name:socialSecurityNo: to create Employee instances'
```

Avoiding the Use of new:

If only the employee name is required, you might be tempted to use new: aName. Resist the temptation. The instance creation message new: is used to specify the size of a collection, and programmers reading code should be able to assume that a collection is being created when they see new:. Instead, use name: or newNamed: or newWithName:. I tend to like method names that tell me both that they are creating a new instance and what the parameter is.

Sole Instances of a Class

Some classes have but a single instance. Examples in the system classes are true, which is the sole instance of True; false, which is the sole instance of False; nil, which is the sole instance of UndefinedObject; and Processor, which is the sole instance of ProcessorScheduler. The classes UndefinedObject, Boolean, and ProcessorScheduler override new to prevent the creation of new instances.

In your own code, if you have a class that should have only one instance, the easiest way to handle this is to have a class variable that contains the sole instance. When someone tries to create a new instance after the first one, you can either raise an error or return the sole instance. For example,

```
MyClass class>>new
    Instance isNil ifFalse: [self error: 'You can only have one instance of MyClass'].
    Instance := self basicNew.
    ^Instance

MyClass class>>new
    ^Instance isNil
        ifTrue: [Instance := self basicNew]
        ifFalse: [Instance]
```

6

Special Variables, Characters, and Symbols

Smalltalk is a very small language, with a very large class library. But even though it is a small language, there are still a few things to learn.

Character Pairs

There are several character pairs that mean things when used together. The VisualWorks Browser makes it easy to manipulate text and character pairs. You can surround a block of text with a character pair by highlighting the text then pressing Esc-leftCharacter (the Escape key followed by the left character of the pair). You can select and highlight all the text between a character pair by double-clicking between the character and the text (at either end). You can remove the character pair by highlighting the text between the pair then pressing Esc-leftCharacter.

"This is a comment"

Text between pairs of double quotes is comment text and will not be compiled. You can make a block of text into a comment by highlighting it then pressing Esc-".

'This is a string'

Enclosing a sequence of characters within single quotes is a way to create an instance of String. See the section below on Automatically constructed objects.

(2 * 3)

Enclosing something within parentheses gives it higher precedence. Thus, 1 + (2 * 3) means that 2 * 3 is evaluated before adding the result to 1. Parentheses are also used to enclose literal arrays (see below).

[some code]

Surrounding code with square brackets creates an instance of BlockClosure. See the section below on Automatically Constructed Objects.

Prefixes

$

The dollar sign is a prefix for creating an instance of class Character. See the section below on Automatically constructed objects.

#

The pound/hash/number symbol is used to create a symbol or a literal array. See the section below on Automatically constructed objects. The # character is also used in documentation to denote a message. For example, if you read an article that describes sending the new message, it might refer to the message as #new. In this book we are denoting messages with (this font) rather than with a # prefix.

Special Variables

The special variable self is the receiver of the message, or the object executing the method. You use self when an object wants to send a message to itself. This is described more fully in Chapter 2.

The special variable super refers to the superclass of the class that *defines* the currently executing method. This is described more fully in Chapter 2.

The special variable thisContext is the current context that is executing. The statement thisContext receiver gives the object executing the method, while this Context sender gives the context of the method that sent the message being executed, and thisContext sender receiver gives the object that sent the currently executing message.

The most common usage of thisContext is in the debugger, because it is possible to trace through the stack using the sender message. To get a feel for thisContext, when you are comfortable writing methods, put the following in a method:

```
Transcript cr; show: thisContext printString.
```

Assignment

:= is used to assign a value to a variable. For example:

```
number := 3
```

Assignments are the last things to happen in a statement (except for returns). So, the following assigns the string '68' to the variable x:

```
x:= 67.8 rounded negated printString copyFrom: 2 to: 3
```

The assignment operator is usually called "gets" or "colon equals" in spoken English. Giving it a special name rather than "equals" means that you are less likely to type something like number = 3, which sends the = message to number with 3 as the parameter, and returns a Boolean.

Note that you can do multiple assignments in a statement, although I don't particularly recommend it because it doesn't help clarity. For example:

```
x:= y := 3
```

Return

The caret symbol (^) is the return symbol. If the line being executed says ^3, the method will exit and return a SmallInteger with the value 3. ^ is the very last thing done in the statement. In the following example, the variable instVar will be assigned the value -3, then the value of instVar (i.e., -3) will be returned from the method.

```
^instVar := 3.14 truncated negated
```

By default, a method returns self. That is, if the method gets to the end without executing an explicit ^ statement, it returns self. You can see this by holding down the Shift key when you select the method with the mouse. This shows the decompiled code, which will usually have ^self at the end.

You will sometimes see fairly complex looking return values. Two common return statements follow. In the first example, you might think of returning from the blocks or setting a temporary variable, but the example shows the more common style. In the second example, we return the results of building a new collection in one operation rather than putting the new collection in a temporary variable, then returning the temporary.

```
^objectOne > objectTwo
    ifTrue: [objectOne]
    ifFalse: [objectTwo]

^someCollection
    collect: [ :each | self manipulate: each]
```

Statement Separator

A period (.) is the statement separator. If there are two statements, the first needs a period to let the compiler know that the first statement is done and the second statement is about to start. Leaving out periods is one of the most common errors and usually results in a messageNotUnderstood exception when Smalltalk treats the first word of the second statement as a message to be sent to the result of the first statement. A good way to check for missing statement separators is to run the formatter after accepting a method. If the method looks different than you expected, you might have a missing period.

Note that the period is *not* a statement terminator. A method with one statement does not need a period. Nor is a period needed for the last statement in a method or a block. This is unlike C++, in which a semicolon is a statement terminator and is required for all statements. Putting in a period after a statement where it is not needed is okay, though. My usual mode of typing is to not worry about extra periods. After I'm done and the method compiles (i.e., it is successfully accepted) I run the formatter, which removes any unnecessary parentheses and periods.

Cascading

The cascade operator is a semicolon (;). Cascades allow you to send multiple messages to the same object (the same receiver) without having to name it every time. The most common occurrences show up when printing to the Transcript, when overriding printOn:, and when adding multiple items to collections. For example:

```
Transcript cr; show: 'this is a string'.

aCollection
    add: 'this';
    add: 'that'.

printOn: aStream
    aStream
        print: self class;
        crtab;
        print: self instVarOne.
```

If you use cascades, the generally accepted practice is to put the message receiver on a line by itself, then each cascade goes on a separate line, tabbed over one from the receiver. Short messages, such as cr or tab, are often put on the same line in short cascades. Unfortunately, the formatter destroys any indentation you specify for cascades. Because of this, I will often specify the message receiver each time, and will use a period to separate the statements. There is no performance loss by doing this.

Automatically Constructed Objects

Some objects are created automatically rather than by explicitly sending a message, such as new, to a class.

SmallInteger

4 An instance of SmallInteger can be created by simply using the integer value. One of the interesting thing about integers is that you can't get integer overflow, because if you add one to the largest possible SmallInteger, the return from the + message is a LargePositiveInteger. Try inspecting SmallInteger maxVal + 1.

Float

3.14 An instance of Float can be created by using a floating point value.

String

'here is a string' An instance of String (actually a subclass of String) can be created by enclosing a sequence of characters in single quotes. String is a funny class because, even if you do String new, you still end up with an instance of a subclass of String. To create a string with an embedded quote, use two single quotes to denote the embedded quote. For example:

'You can''t do that'.

Character

$A An instance of Character can be created by preceding the character with a dollar sign. For example, the character X is created by writing $X. You can create instances of space, tab, carriage return, and other white space characters the same way; for example, you can refer to a space as $ and a new line by typing $ followed by pressing the Return key. However, it's difficult to read white space characters created like this, so the preferred way to create them is to send the appropriate message to Character (i.e., Character space or Character cr). To see which characters can be created with message sends, look at the class side messages of Character or inspect Character constantNames.

Symbol

#notFound An instance of Symbol can be created by prefixing a sequence of characters with a #. If you want the symbol to contain space characters, you can enclose the symbol name with single quotes. For example, #'not found'. If you inspect this symbol, it will display with the quotes but when you look at the first character, you will see that it is a $n rather than a single quote.

Array

#(1.1 $a 'hi') An instance of Array can be created by enclosing other automatically constructed objects between parentheses and preceding this with a # character. Note the space between array elements. Note also that the array elements do not have to be of the same type.

You cannot use this type of contruction with objects that require message sends. So you *can't* say #(1 (Character cr)) and expect to get an array of an Integer and a Character. However, you *can* create literal arrays that contain other literal arrays, such as #(1 $a #(1.1 'hi' #(2 #symbol))).

BlockClosure

['Hi' echo] An instance of BlockClosure can be created by enclosing code between square brackets. The code will not be executed until the block is send a message from the value family. You can set up code in a BlockClosure then pass the block to another method where it will be executed. BlockClosures are often stored in Dictionaries for later access and execution. Note that the value of a block is the value of the last statement evaluated in the block. So, the value of [3. 4. 5. 1] is 1.

Blocks can have parameters, which are defined with a colon in front of them and a vertical bar separating them from the rest of the block. For example, [:parameter | parameter echo]. Blocks can also have temporary variables, which are enclosed between vertical bars. For example, [:parameter | | temp | temp := parameter * 2. temp echo].

If all the blocks used as either receivers or parameters in messages such as whileTrue:, ifTrue:, and and: are literal blocks (i.e., defined directly with square brackets and not stored in a variable), the blocks will be compiled in-line and will not be treated as blocks.

There are three kinds of BlockClosures: full, copying, and clean. In general, blocks need to maintain a reference to the method that defined them, which they store in a variable called outerScope. If the block contains an explicit return (^), or a reference to variables defined outside the block and which can change after the block is created, outerScope will contain a non-nil value and the block is a *full* block. If there is no explicit return and any outside variables are determined to be non-changing after the block is created, copies of these variables are made and stored in another instance variable called copiedValues. For obvious reasons, this type of block is called a *copying* block. A block that contains neither an explicit return or references to outside variables is called a *clean* block. So, for example:

[:parameter | parameter echo]	clean
[:parameter | | temp | temp := parameter]	clean
[:parameter | self foo: parameter]	copying (note the self)
[methodTemporary echo]	copying or full
[:parameter | ^ parameter * 3]	full

Because full blocks have to chain back through the outer scope point- ers, and this chaining is relatively expensive, it pays to avoid full blocks if possible. Create clean blocks if you can because they have the highest performance. If your block refers to self or to another outside variable, try to make it a copying block—that is, convince the compil- er that the variables will not change after the block is created.

= & ==

The two messages = and == are not special in the same way as the things described above; they are just binary messages like any other binary message. However, there are some things about them that deserve to be specifically mentioned, so here is as good a place as any.

The = message returns true if the two objects are equal, while the == message returns true if the two objects are *identically* equal. What does this mean? (The opposites of = and == are ~= and ~~. These are a sin- gle tilde and two tildes.)

Identically equal

Objects are *identically equal* when they are the *exact same* object. The way that Smalltalk knows they are the same object is that they have the same object pointer. Object pointers are 32-bit quantities, with some of the bits providing information about whether the value is a pointer or an object value. If you have an employee object, the object pointer will reference the employee object that exists somewhere in memory. Two employee objects are identically equal if the object point- ers reference the same location in memory.

On the other hand, some objects can be represented fully in 32 bits. These objects return true when sent this isImmediate message, and cur- rently are objects of class SmallInteger and Character. (The maximum value of SmallInteger is less than the maximum value of a 32-bit inte- ger because three bits are used to denote that it is a SmallInteger and not a pointer to an object.) Because of the way they are stored, identi- cally named instances of Symbol are also identically equal.

3 == 3	true
$a == $a	true
#abc == #abc	true
true == true	true
nil == nil	true
'abc' == 'abc'	false
3.14 == 3.14	false
#(1 $a) == #(1 $a)	false

If you examine the following, you will discover that x is identically equal to y. This is because assignment does not copy the value; it binds the same object to a new variable so that both variables now contain the same object.

```
x := #(1 $a).
y := x.
x == y true
```

Equal

Objects are *equal* when their values are equal. Two strings with the same character sequence will be equal. If we look at the examples above that returned false and check for simply equality, we get:

```
'abc' = 'abc'        true
3.14 = 3.14          true
#(1 $a) = #(1 $a)    true
```

If you define a new class, how does the default = method tell whether you consider two object of this class to be equal? The answer is that it doesn't. If you look at the default = method defined by Object you will see that the default implementation requires two objects to be identically equal before it agrees they are equal. That is, = simply does ^self == anObject.

If you define your own = method you should also write a hash method, and vice versa. Two equal objects should also have the same hash value. The reason that hash and = need to go hand in hand is that some collections store objects using a hashing scheme (such as Dictionary, Set, and Bag). Because hashing schemes can have location conflicts, a hash scheme uses hash to find the primary location for the object, then uses = to see if an object in the location is the object it wants. (By the way, don't try to redefine ==. First, the system will ignore your override, and second, == has a well defined meaning that should not be changed.)

If you override =, you might consider first checking that the class of the receiver is the same as the class of the parameter. The first example below checks that the classes are the same, while the second allows the parameter to belong to a subclass of the receiver.

```
MyClass>> =
    anObject class == self class ifFalse: [^false].
    ....


MyClass>> =
    (anObject isKindOf: self class) ifFalse: [^false].
```

7

Global Variables

I'll start with the standard caveat that global variables should be used sparingly, if at all, and that most information should be stored in instance variables or should be passed as method arguments. Having said that, there is a definite use for global information and objects. You might have constants that are used through your system, or you might have global objects such as configuration objects or trace log objects. Let's look at some techniques that can be used for these purposes. We'll use two examples: a configuration object and a timeout value.

Global Dictionary

The most basic technique is to put global objects in the system dictionary named Smalltalk, because objects in Smalltalk can be referenced from anywhere. For example, you might have code that does:

```
Smalltalk at: #Timeout put: 20.
Smalltalk at: #Config put: MyConfiguration new.
```

I recommend against using Smalltalk for application globals, because it's used heavily by the Smalltalk system (for example, it contains all the classes in the system, and global variables such as Transcript, Processor, and ScheduledControllers). I prefer not to clutter Smalltalk up with application objects or risk name collisions.

PoolDictionary

The next technique is to use a PoolDictionary. A PoolDictionary contains objects to which you want global access for your application. The nice thing about a PoolDictionary is that classes have to register an interest in it before they can access its objects, so it allows you a certain amount of scoping. The way a class registers an interest is to name the

PoolDictionary in the appropriate line in the class definition template. (In VisualWorks 2.0, subclasses inherit the PoolDictionary, but in VisualWorks 2.5, you have to explicitly name the PoolDictionary in each subclass that wants to reference PoolDictionary variables.) In the example below, I've called it MyPoolDictionary.

```
NameOfSuperclass subclass: #NameOfClass
    instanceVariableNames: 'instVarName1 instVarName2'
    classVariableNames: 'ClassVarName1 ClassVarName2'
    poolDictionaries: 'MyPoolDictionary'
    category: 'MyStuff'
```

Before you write code you must have done two things. First, before referencing the PoolDictionary in your class definition you have to make the name of the PoolDictionary universally known by adding it to the Smalltalk dictionary. To do this, execute the following. Note that we are using a Dictionary and not an IdentityDictionary. Because of the way an IdentityDictionary is implemented, it will not work as a PoolDictionary.

```
Smalltalk at: #MyPoolDictionary put: Dictionary new.
```

Before you write code referencing the objects in the PoolDictionary, you have to add these objects to the PoolDictionary, so the compiler can associate a variable name in your method with an object in the PoolDictionary. However, the compiler just needs to be able to refer-ence the name in the PoolDictionary and doesn't care about the type of the object. For the purpose of accepting your method, the easiest thing to say initially is:

```
MyPoolDictionary at: #Config put: nil.
```

We don't want to do these steps manually every time we file in our code (see Chapter 33 for more information on managing projects and filing in code). So, at the beginning of the file that files in our code, we add the following.

```
Smalltalk at: #MyPoolDictionary put: Dictionary new.
MyPoolDictionary at: #Config put: nil.
```

If you have code that refers to PoolDictionary variables and you cre-ate a new PoolDictionary, the code will no longer be able to find the old variables. If you get an error in a method because a PoolDictionary variable is not found, and yet a PoolDictionary exists with the appro-priate variable, recompile the method by making a small change and accepting the method. If this solves the problem, somewhere you cre-ated a new PoolDictionary while your code still references the old one.

The question that always comes up when using a PoolDictionary is, How do you find all the references to an object in your PoolDictionary, because you can't browse References To or Implementors Of? The answer is to evaluate the following code:

Browser browseAllCallsOn: (MyPoolDictionary associationAt: #Config).

It might be worth putting something like this in your Workspace and saving your image. VisualWorks 1.0 had a menu option to open the System Workspace, which, among other useful code samples, has code to find PoolDictionary variable references. The System Workspace is not obviously available in VisualWorks 2.0 or 2.5, but you can get it by executing:

ComposedTextView openSystemWorkspace.

Advantages of using a PoolDictionary are that you refer to the objects in a PoolDictionary by a name starting with an uppercase letter, which makes it very obvious that the code references a global object. And, only classes with an interest in the PoolDictionary have access to it. Disadvantages of PoolDictionaries are that you have to take specific actions to allow PoolDictionary objects to be referenced, and it is harder to find all the references to the PoolDictionary object.

Class Side Variables

The next technique is to use a class to store global data. For example, we might have two classes: MyGlobals and MyConstants. Global and constant values are referenced by sending messages to the appropriate class. For example, we might reference and define a timeout value as follows:

```
MyClass>>myMethod
    timeout := MyConstants timeout.
    ...

MyConstants class>>timeout
    ^20
```

We might reference and initialize a global value (in this case, a Log file) as fillows:

```
MyClass>>myMethod
    ...
    MyGlobals logfile log: 'salary=', salary printString.

MyGlobals class>>logFile
    ^LogFile

MyGlobals class>>initialize
    LogFile := MyLogFile on: self logFileName.
```

To find all references to an individual global, we can browse references to the message that returns the global. To see all the places that any global is used, we can browse class references for MyGlobals. Similarly, for constant values.

Unlike with variables in a PoolDictionary, we don't have to do anything special on fileIn, and we don't have to make sure that the reference contains an object when we write methods that refer to constants and globals. The only disadvantages of this approach over a PoolDictionary are that you can't restrict scope in the same way, and you have a class that does not act as a factory for instances.

Default Instances

There's one other thing to talk about while we are on the topic of class side behavior. Sometimes you have a single instance of a class that you want to access from many places. Our Configuration object might be such an example. There's a definite temptation to say that there will never be more than one instance of this class, so we might as well just dispense with the instance and put all the information and behavior on the class side. That way you can access the behavior easily, because class names are globally known.

Despite the temptation, it should be resisted. There's another way that allows similar ease of access without preventing you from creating additional instances. Suppose the class is MyClass. Define a class variable called Default. On the class side, create a class initialization protocol with an initialize method.[1] In the class side initialize method do the following:

```
MyClass class>>initialize
    "self initialize"
    Default := self new.
```

You'll probably need to initalize the instance so you'll either need to write new, which invokes initialize, or in the class initalize method do Default := self new initalize. Then on the class side write a default method:

```
MyClass class>>default
    ^Default
```

In your application code, you can now write code such as:

```
length := MyClass default length.
```

If you want to get *really* fancy, you can assume that instance side messages being sent to the class are really intended for the default instance. You'd write the last example as:

```
length := MyClass length.
```

Given that the class doesn't understand the length message, how do we make this work? We can implement length on the class side as ^self

---

[1]Class initialization is only done on fileIn, so it's a good idea to always put self initialize in comments at the start of class side initalize methods. That way you can reinitialize the class if you make changes to initialize. Of course, you can select the whole method and doIt, but having self initialize makes it more obvious that it might need to be done.

default length, or we can implement the method doesNotUnderstand: on the class side as follows:

```
MyClass class>>doesNotUnderstand: aMessage
    ^self default
        perform: aMessage selector
        withArguments: aMessage arguments
```

I don't particularly recommend this way of coding because it's not obvious how it's working, but hey, it's ideas like this that make Smalltalk so much fun! If you decide to use this technique, make sure your class comments contain explicit information about what you are doing.

Environment Variables and Command Line Arguments

Environment variables and command line arguments are not global variables, but because the information is globally available and varies depending on the environment and how the image was invoked, we'll mention them here. The following returns an array containing the command line arguments. The first element is the program name and the second is the image name. Any additional array elements will be other command line arguments you added.

```
CEnvironment commandLine.
```

You can also retrieve environment variables using getenv:. For example:

```
CEnvironment getenv: 'LOGNAME'
```

Image Version Number

The version number for your image can be discovered in one of two ways. You can send the version message to Smalltalk, or the versionId message to ObjectMemory. For example, on a VW 2.0 system, I get the following:

```
Smalltalk version          'VisualWorks(R) Release 2.0 of 4 August 1994'
ObjectMemory versionId     #[42 26 35 0 20 0 0 4 42 26 35 4].
```

In particular, element 5 of the array returned by versionId is the image major version number. VW 2.0 gives 20, while VW 2.5 gives 25. So, to discover if you are using VW 2.0 you could do either of the following.

```
(Smalltalk version findString: '2.0' startingAt: 1) > 0
(ObjectMemory versionId at: 5) == 20
```

Chapter

8

Control Structures

Modern programming languages provide ways to execute code conditionally, and to repeat blocks of code. In C, we have if () {}, if () {} else {}, do {} while (), while () {}, and for (;;) {}. These types of constructs are usually part of the language.

In Smalltalk, however, the language itself does not have any of these constructs. Instead, they are created by sending messages to objects. The result of this is that, if you don't like the way a control message works, you can change it (not recommended!). If you want a new type of control structure, you can write it. For example, Smalltalk does not come with a switch/case message, so if you feel the need for one you can write it (again, not recommended for reasons we'll see in Chapter 28). In fact, you probably won't need any control structures other than those that come standard with the Smalltalk library. Let's go through these.

Conditional Execution

The simplest type of conditional execution is to execute only a particular block of code if some condition is true (or false). In Smalltalk, there are two messages, one for when the condition is true and one for when it's false. Both messages are sent to an instance of Boolean (i.e., to true or false). Here is the general approach, with an example:

```
booleanValue ifTrue: [some code].
booleanValue ifFalse: [some code].
3 < 4 ifTrue: [Transcript cr; show: 'True']
```

We can extend this to executing some code if the condition is true, or other code if the condition is false. In Smalltalk we write one of the following. The ifTrue: and ifFalse: blocks can be in either order. For example, if the ifTrue: block is long enough to obscure a later ifFalse: block, put the ifFalse: block first.

```
booleanValue
    ifTrue: [some code]
    ifFalse: [some code].
```

```
booleanValue
    ifFalse: [some code]
    ifTrue: [some code].
```

For example:

```
3 < 4
    ifTrue: [Transcript cr; show: 'True']
    ifFalse: [Transcript cr; show: 'False'].
```

Smalltalk doesn't provide an easy way to do C's if () {} else if () {} else {} type of construct. You can do it with nesting such as:

```
booleanValue
    ifTrue: [some code]
    ifFalse: [booleanValue2
        ifTrue: [some code]
        ifFalse: [booleanValue3
            ifTrue: [some code]
            ifFalse: [some code]]]
```

However, this type of code is very procedural rather than object-oriented. If you find that you are writing code like this, it might be time to rethink how you are doing things. See Chapter 28, Eliminating Procedural Code for more information.

Looping

Smalltalk has no looping constructs in the language. Instead, it provides looping functionality by sending messages to BlockClosures. The most basic type of loop is one that continues to loop while some condition is true. As long as the block (i.e., the last statement in the block) evaluates to true, the loop will continue. This type of mechanism is similar to C's do {} while ( ); construct. Here is the syntax and an example:

```
[some code] whileTrue.
```

```
count := 0.
[Transcript cr; show: count printString.
count := count + 1.
count < 10] whileTrue.
```

The condition can be reversed so that the loop continues as long as the block evaluates to false.

```
[some code] whileFalse.
```

The next type of looping mechanism is similar to the above, but if the first block evaluates to true, a second block of code is executed. This type of mechanism is somewhat similar to C's while () {}, but is more powerful because it allows multiple statements in the first block. Again, here is the syntax and an example:

```
[some code]
    whileTrue:
        [more code]

[Dialog confirm: 'Continue']
    whileTrue:
        [Transcript cr; show: 'Continuing'].
```

As before, you can reverse the conditions so that the loop continues if the first block evaluates to false.

```
[some code]
    whileFalse:
        [more code]
```

The final straight looping mechanism is one that simply repeats. This means that the code in the block needs a way to return from the method, or to somehow stop execution or you will find yourself in an infinite loop.

```
[some code] repeat

[(Dialog confirm: 'Continue') ifFalse: [^self].
Transcript cr; show: 'Continuing'] repeat.
```

Repetition

In Smalltalk, there are three ways to repeat a block of code a fixed number of times. Two of them pass in the index, while the other one assumes that you don't care which iteration you are on. If the loop doesn't care about the index number, the simplest mechanism is to send timesRepeat:, passing the code block as the parameter. For example:

```
5 timesRepeat: [Transcript cr; show: 'hello']
```

If the loop needs to know what iteration it is on, you'll need to send one of the following two messages. If you want to loop from one number to another, incrementing by one each time, send to:do:, passing the code block as a parameter. The block expects to receive the index number as a parameter. For example:

```
1 to: 5 do: [ :index | Transcript cr; show: index printString]
```

If you need a loop like this but don't want to increment by one, you can specify the step value by sending to:by:do:. Again, this message expects the block of code as a parameter, and the block should expect to receive the index number as a block parameter. For example:

```
15 to: 1 by: -2 do: [ :index | Transcript cr; show: index printString].
```

Despite the existence of these messages, they are less useful than you might expect. Most repetitive looping is done over collections of objects, and collections have some powerful mechanisms for looping. We'll talk a lot more about looping over collections in Chapter 11.

Optimized Messages

BlockClosures are used in the above control mechanisms usually as parameters, but sometimes as the receiver of the message. The BlockClosures can be stored in variables or can be written as literal blocks—that is, as code with square brackets around it.

If all the BlockClosures involved in the control message are literal blocks, the message is compiled in-line and so no message send occurs. On the other hand, if any of the BlockClosures involved in the message are variables rather than literal blocks, the code will not be in-lined and the message will be sent. Usually these messages are compiled in-line because most blocks are literal blocks.

Object-Oriented Thinking

Smalltalk is one of the pure object-oriented (OO) languages. Unlike C++, which makes it very easy to write procedural code (i.e., use C++ as a better C), Smalltalk makes it difficult to write procedural code. Thinking in objects is very different from thinking in procedural terms, and it usually takes eight to twelve months for experienced procedural programmers to become fairly automatic in their OO thinking. To use a language that doesn't help that process makes it much easier to remain in a halfway schizophrenic state.

OO thinking is fun, and it is different. One difference is that OO development tends to be more iterative than procedural development; more spiral. In OO development we tend to acknowledge that we don't fully understand our objects and their interactions. Some objects that we thought we needed will disappear, others will come into existence as we realize we need them, while others will find their behavior and responsibilities changed or split off to other objects.

Little Steps

Because Smalltalk code is so easy to change, it's very natural to approach problems in an iterative way. When I'm faced with a difficult application problem, I don't usually know how I'm going to solve it. I do enough analysis and design to get a grasp of the problem, but the whole solution rarely appears to me. So, I just start somewhere and write Smalltalk code. The act of writing the code, creating the classes, and defining their interactions gives me new insight into the problem — and into solutions, which then allows me to write code to explore those new ideas, which leads to fresh insights, and so on.

Smalltalk makes it very easy to approach problems in an iterative manner, taking very small steps, getting things working, then taking the next small step. In working like this you really are combining the

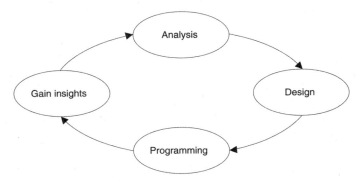

Figure 9-1. The object-oriented development cycle.

analysis, design, and programming phases, doing a bit of each, then a bit more of each. The OO cycle is very much one of do some analysis — do some design — do some programming — gain some insights — do some analysis, etc.

Write Down the Concepts

It is extremely easy to write, test, and change code in Smalltalk. This ease of writing allows you to write your design in the code, to think in conceptual terms rather than worrying about the details (which is exactly the difference between design and implementation). In a method, just write down the things that need to be done, at a fairly high conceptual level. Someone should be able to easily read the method to see what it's doing (short method, very descriptive names) without actually seeing any of the work being done. So, for example, you might write a method as follows:

```
MyClass>>doSomething
    self myDoConceptualThingOne.
    self myDoConceptualThingTwo.
    self myDoConceptualThingThree
```

You've now written down the basic design. You can implement the design by writing myDoConceptualThingOne, etc. The beauty of being able to do this easily is that, as you gain insights into the domain problem, you can easily incorporate changes. For example, it might become apparent that another object should be doing ConceptualThingTwo. However, you also need to do ConceptualThingFour. It is very easy to move myDoConceptualThingTwo to another object, then to modify your code.

```
MyClass>>doSomethingWith: anObject
    self myDoConceptualThingOne.
    anObject doConceptualThingTwo.
    self myDoConceptualThingThree.
    self myDoConceptualThingFour
```

Admittedly, this is low level design; however, this is not a book on Design with a capital "D", so we won't explore how you work on the big picture.

Put Off the Work

Because good Smalltalk methods are small, it's hard to do much work in such a method. Which leads to the next Smalltalk OO principle: put off the work as long as possible — make another method do it. The ease of writing Smalltalk code makes it possible to put off real work until later, so a lot of methods will do nothing but divide up the work. Eventually someone has to do the work, but if you consciously put off the work as long as you can you will end up with a more object-oriented system.

Smalltalk might be considered the procrastination language — procrastinate as long as possible and maybe you won't need to do anything. When in doubt, put it off. Here's an example of poor code that we will try to refine using the principles just described.

```
MyClass>>myDoLoop
    [object := self mySharedQueue next.
    object isHeartbeat
        ifTrue: [self myHeartbeat: object].
    object isSuccessResponse
        ifTrue: [self mySuccessResponse: object].
    object isFailureResponse
        ifTrue: [self myFailureResponse: object]
    ] repeat.
```

If we strip this down to the bare bones, we get something from a SharedQueue and process it, then repeat these actions. So we might write:

```
MyClass>>myDoLoop
    [object := self mySharedQueue next.
    self myProcessObject: object ] repeat.
```

If we put off the decision on where to get the object, we might end up with:

```
MyClass>>myDoLoop
    [self myProcessObject: self myGetObject] repeat
```

We now have a very generic loop, one that could be put in a superclass and inherited. It doesn't care where the input comes from or how we plan to process the object. In our case, myGetInput is very simple. It just does:

```
MyClass>>myGetInput
    ^self mySharedQueue next.
```

In another problem domain it might be a lot more complex, getting input from the user, a socket, a file, a serial line, a UNIX pipe, etc.

(A side benefit of doing the processing in other methods is that you can't modify a running loop and have the changes take effect. Because the code is already running, the changes will be ignored until next time you run the loop. By putting the processing code in other methods, you can put debugging changes in them and have the changes take effect the next time the method is executed.)

Tell, Don't Ask

What about myProcessObject: in the above section? We could certainly put our conditional code there — we would have moved it away from the main processing — but the code would still be very procedural. We need to rethink our objects so that we can simply ask the objects to process themselves. Procedural code gets information then makes decisions. Object-oriented code tells objects to do things.

```
MyClass>>myProcessObject: anObject
    anObject processYourself
```

Another example might be displaying graphical objects in a window. If we were thinking procedurally, our Window object might have code that looks like

```
MyWindow>>displayObject: aGraphicalObject
    aGraphicalObject isSquare ifTrue: [self myDisplaySquare: aGraphicalObject].
    aGraphicalObject isCircle ifTrue: [self myDisplayCircle: aGraphicalObject].
    aGraphicalObject isTriangle ifTrue: [self myDisplayTriangle: aGraphicalObject].
```

We are asking questions, getting back information, and executing code based on the information. If we were thinking more in OO terms, we would be trying to avoid getting information and making decisions. Instead, we'd be *telling* the object to do something. Our example might be transformed into:

```
MyWindow>>displayObject: aGraphicalObject
    aGraphicalObject displayYourselfOn: self
```

One benefit we get out of this transformation is that it becomes a lot easier to handle different types of graphical objects. Rather than having to modify the window code every time we come across a new type of graphical object, we just need to make sure that each class of graphical object we write knows how to display itself. So if we add a Hexagon class, we just need to write displayYourselfOn: for the Hexagon (unless it can inherit from a superclass).

Don't Check the Results of Doing Things

In a procedural system we typically make a function call, get back some status information about the results of the call, check the status information, and perhaps do some error-handling. In a Smalltalk OO system it's much more appropriate to just tell an object to do something, then forget about it. It's as if we are sending messages out into space, never to return.

Obviously we need to handle error situations in production quality code, but Smalltalk provides a special mechanism for that. Chapter 20 provides more information, but briefly, we can wrap a whole hierarchy of message sends in an exception handler. If an exception is raised because of some error, the exception bubbles up the stack until it finds an exception handler that can handle it. The exception handler then takes the necessary actions. The beauty of this scheme is that, once we wrap our code in an exception handler, we can write it as though every message send is successful.

There will be some situations in which it might be appropriate to get back a status object from a method, such as if we are requesting information from an external source. However, the majority of error handling can be done with exceptions rather than by checking status returns.

Signs of Object-Oriented Thinking

Short methods

The average Smalltalk method length is seven lines. I've always made it a rule that methods should fit into my browser window, and I very seldom break that rule. If a method is too long, I'll try to find two or three conceptual things that the method is doing and create separate methods for each of them. If you consistently have methods that don't fit in a browser window, you are probably thinking procedurally. (The other value in having all methods fit within the window is that, if you can see the whole thing, you can better grasp what is going on.)

No dense black methods

Another indication that your methods are doing too much is when they look too black. This is an aesthetic judgment, but can be a useful heuristic to determine whether you are trying to do too much in a method. Try to make methods "stupid." A stupid method is one that is so simple it's obvious what it's doing; it doesn't need to be documented. Black methods are usually the opposite of stupid methods, too much black being an indication that a lot is going on in the method.

No super-intelligent objects

There is no rule for how many methods an object can have, but there are some aesthetic judgments you can make. If you find that one object has many more methods than other objects, it might be that you are not distributing the workload well. In a good object-oriented system, you don't have super-intelligent objects. Instead, you have many peer-type objects cooperating. Super-intelligent objects often indicate that there is too much procedural thinking (in a sense, a procedural system is one with a single super-intelligent object). It might be time to rethink your objects if you have classes with an uneven distribution of methods between them.

No manager objects

It's very easy to write systems with manager objects telling other objects what to do. A good object-oriented system tends to have a lot of peers cooperating, with a reasonably equal distribution of responsibilities and workload. Managers tend to make a lot of decisions that other objects could be making. If you have a classes whose name ends in Manager, you might give some thought to how you could distribute the manager's workload to the objects it is managing.

Objects with clear responsibilities

Each class should have a clear responsibility. If you can't state the purpose of a class in a single, clear sentence, then perhaps your class structure needs some thought.

Not too many instance variables

If a class has a lot of instance variables, this can mean that it's trying to do too much; that you are not distributing the workload well. It might be possible to create other objects that can act in a supporting role or can collaborate with this objects of this class.

Getting Started with Object-Oriented Thinking

It can be difficult to start thinking in terms of objects if you've been programming in a procedural language for some time. One approach I've found very useful in learning Smalltalk and object-oriented techniques is to work in pairs at a workstation. One keyboard, one screen, two people. One person types while the other person makes suggestions, asks questions, and points out errors. After a while they change roles and the other person types. In this approach, you get the best of two people rather than the best of one person. Designs are better thought through because there's another person asking why and suggesting alternatives. Code has fewer bugs because there's someone else looking at the code. The code usually ends up being more efficient, maintainable, and consistent. Because there is a second person looking at all the code, there's much less need to review low-level designs and code.

Because two people work on all features, you now have two people who understand the code rather than just one. And both people learn from each other. Programmers have their own styles, techniques, and toolboxes of solutions. By working in pairs, they learn these things from each other and grow as programmers. By periodically changing partners, they pass these techniques and solutions from person to person, with each person, in effect, learning from everyone his or her partner has previously worked with.

When I started programming in Smalltalk I worked with another developer as a pair. It was great fun and we both learned a lot from each other. Since then I've always favored the pair approach, and so I read with interest two pieces that I later came across, both praising the concept of programming in pairs. In an article in the July/August 1995 issue of *The Smalltalk Report*, Kent Beck says "The most productive form of programming I know (functionality/person/hour) is to have two people working with one keyboard, mouse, and monitor." The second piece was a section called "Dynamic Duos" on page 118 of Larry Constantine's book, *Constantine on Peopleware*. Constantine praises the two-person concept, remarking that "The operating principle here is very broad: Increasing work visibility leads to increased quality!"

Part

2

Basic System Classes

10

Object

Smalltalk is a *rooted* system, which means that there is a root super-class from which all other classes are descended. That root superclass is Object. (Actually, there other root classes, and you can see them by inspecting Class rootsOfTheWorld. However, for most application development you can consider Object to be the single root class.)

Object provides a lot of behavior that is inherited by all its subclasses, although sometimes they will override that behavior. It's worth looking through all the protocols and methods of Object to become familiar with the general behavior that is inherited by all classes. Let's take a look at some of the instance side protocols of Object. We won't look at all protocols, or even all methods in the protocols we do look at, but we'll cover enough to give you a feel for what your classes will be inheriting from Object.

Accessing

The message at: will give the object at the specified index, while at:put: puts an object at that index. The size message returns the number of indexable fields in the object. These messages work only with index-able objects; that is, collection-type objects. Similar methods, basicAt:, basicAt:put:, and basicSize, do the same things, but should never be overridden by subclasses. The intent is that you can always rely on the *basic* methods to provide the functionality without worrying that some intermediate superclass might have overridden them. Finally, yourself returns the receiver of the message. It is often used in cascades to make sure that the correct object is returned. For example, in list := List new add: 1; yourself, the yourself makes sure that the variable contains the list rather than the number one.

Changing

The messages changed, changed:, and changed:with: are all used to set off dependency notification. The typical use is that an object sends one of these messages to itself when it has changed, and all dependents of the object are informed. We'll see more about the dependency mechanism in Chapter 19.

The changeRequest message is sent when an application wants to change and is asking its dependents if they agree to the change. Your application can override changeRequest to put in any application-specific checking.

Class Membership

The message isMemberOf: tells if the receiver is an instance of the specified class; isKindOf: tells if the receiver is an instance of the specified class or one of its subclasses; and respondsTo: tells if the receiver understands the specified message. The use of all three methods often indicates that you are thinking in procedural terms, that you are not using polymorphism well. These three methods should generally be avoided. The message class gives you the class, of which the receiver is an instance.

Comparing

The message == tells you if the receiver and parameter are the *same* object, if they are identically equal. The message = tells you if the receiver and parameter are equal. For example, two strings with the same characters are not the same object, but they are equal, so == returns false and = returns true. Because different classes have different criteria for judging their instances to be equal (for example, two Employee objects might be equal when the social security numbers are the same), the default implementation of = is simply to invoke ==, leaving subclasses to override = with more appropriate behavior. (You should never override ==.) Corresponding to = and == are ~= and ~~, which are not equal and identically not equal. The message hash returns a hash value for an object and should be overridden whenever you override =, because two objects that are equal should have the same hash value. For more information on all this, see Chapter 6.

Converting

The message -> returns an Association with the receiver as the key and the parameter as the value. Associations are useful when you want a pair of objects, and they are used in Dictionaries, which hold all the key-value pairs in Associations. The message asValue puts the receiver in a ValueHolder and returns this. ValueHolders are widely used by the user interface dependency mechanism, which wants a level of indirection when referring to an object.

Copying

The copy message copies the receiver. It is implemented by sending shallowCopy then postCopy. The shallowCopy method makes a shallow copy of the receiver; that is, it doesn't make copies of any of the instance variables, leaving both the original object and its copy sharing instance variables. The message postCopy is a hook that gives you an opportunity to copy instance variables by overriding postCopy. For more information, see Chapters 22 and 25.

Dependents Access

The messages addDependent: and removeDependent: provide the basic mechanism for setting up and closing down a dependency relationship on another object. The messages expressInterestIn:for:sendBack: and retractInterestIn:for: provide a more sophisticated mechanism. There is more information on these messages in Chapter 19.

Error Handling

The message subclassResponsibility is sent in methods that should be overridden by subclasses. The typical use is for the superclass method to do self subclassResponsibility. If a subclass fails to override the method, an exception is raised. The opposite message, shouldNotImplement is sent in a subclass method to show that, although the subclass has inherited the method, it is not appropriate behavior for this subclass. The messages halt, halt:, error:, and notify: are all used to generate exceptions and raise a Notifier/Debugger window (for example, self halt). The messages errorSignal and messageNotUnderstoodSignal return signals that can be used in signal handlers to trap exceptions. The message doesNotUnderstand: is sent when a message is not understood by the receiver, and its default behavior is to raise a Notifier/Debugger window. Override this method if you want to trap messages that were not understood so you can pass them to another object. We use this mechanism in Chapter 21.

File In/Out

The messages binaryRepresentationVersion and representBinaryOn: provide specialized behavior for use with the BOSS facility when storing and retrieving binary objects. In particular, by overriding representBinaryOn:, you can specify how you want an object to be stored. Returning nil, which is the default implementation, says to store the default representation of the receiver. Returning 0 says to not store the object at all. The other common return is a MessageSend, which provides a way to store the object in one form and reconstitute it in a different form when it is read back.

Initialize—Release

The release message breaks any dependencies that might have been established on this object. It is sent when the object is no longer needed and allows the object to be garbage-collected.

Message Handling

The perform: family of messages allow you to create a method name at run time, then to invoke the method. It is widely used when you don't know the name of the method at compile time and have to wait until run time. For example, the user interface uses it heavily because the names of the accessor methods for variables and menus are specified by the user when building the user interface, but the underlying user interface code is part of the system classes. We'll talk more about the perform: messages in Chapter 28, and we'll use it in Chapter 30.

Printing

The most commonly used methods in the printing protocol are printString, printOn:, and displayString. You send printString to an object to get a printable representation — one that can be shown on the Transcript. The printString message invokes printOn:, so to override what printString returns you override printOn:. The displayString message returns a more suitable representation of the receiver for use in labels and list boxes (SequenceViews). It defaults to printString, but is overridden by classes such as String.

System Primitives

The messages allOwners and allOwnersWeakly: return collections of objects that reference the receiver. The messages firstOwner and ownerAfter: return individual objects from those collections. The become: message swaps the references of two objects. One use of become: is when collections grow in size. A new collection is created, the elements are copied across, and the new collection becomes the old collection. The messages instVarAt: and instVarAt:put: allow you direct access to instance variables without having to name them. However, because

use of these two methods violates encapsulation, they should be used sparingly, if at all.

Testing

This protocol contains methods that return true or false. Most of the methods return false, allowing them to be overridden when appropriate. For example, isInteger returns false, but is overridden in Integer to return true. The isBehavior message tells if the receiver can be the class of another object. The isImmediate message tells if the receiver is an immediate object, such as a SmallInteger or a Character that can be represented in thirty-two bits, or whether the receiver is being represented by an object pointer. The messages isNil and notNil tell whether the object is nil and are overridden by UndefinedObject . The message isSequenceable tells if the object is a sequenceable collection — that is, a subclass of SequenceableCollection. The message isString tells if the object is a String, and isSymbol tells if it is a Symbol. The respondsToArithmetic message tells if the object belongs to a subclass of ArithmeticValue.

Use of testing messages allows you to avoid messages such as isKindOf: and isMemberOf:. In your own classes, use isXxx types of messages if you need to determine if an object is of a particular type. For example, suppose you have a Response class with subclasses of SuccessResponse and FailureResponse. In Response, implement the methods isResponse, isSuccessResponse and isFailureReponse, with the first returning true and the next two returning false. SuccessResponse should override isSuccessReponse to return true, and FailureResponse should override isFailureResponse to return true. If you have many different types of domain objects for which you want to implement isXxx-type messages, consider creating an ApplicationObject that is subclassed off Object, where you write a series of isXxx methods, each returning false. Then, in each domain class you override the corresponding testing method, returning true.

Updating

The methods in this protocol that you are most likely to be interested in are the update: family — update:, update:with:, and update:with:from:. These are all used in the dependency mechanism to inform dependents about changes. An object that changes sends itself a message from the changed: family, and eventually these messages send a message from the update: family to each dependent. Dependents therefore need to override one of the update: messages if they want to take action based on the notification. We talk more about the dependency mechanism in Chapter 19.

User Interface

The browse message opens a class Browser on the class of the receiver. The inspect message opens an Inspector on the receiver. This message is overridden by some classes to provide an Inspector more suitable for the class. For example, OrderedCollection overrides inspect to hide the internal implementation details of the collection. To see the internal details you can send the message basicInspect, which shows all the instance variables of an object. Figure 10-1 shows an instance of OrderedCollection, inspected by sending first inspect and then basicInspect.

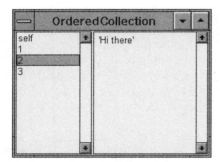 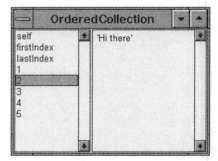

Figure 10-1. Inspecting using inspect and basicInspect.

Collections

Collections are objects that each contain a group of other objects. Collections are among the most useful classes in Smalltalk, and you'll find yourself using them constantly—even a string is nothing more than a collection of characters. The top-level collection class is Collection, which is an abstract superclass that provides the generic behavior common to all collections. For example, Collection implements the methods size and capacity; the testing methods isEmpty, contains:, and includes:; the converting methods such as asArray, asOrderedCollection; the powerful enumeration methods such as do: and collect:; and the basic adding and removing methods add:, remove:, and remove:ifAbsent:. (Many of these methods are inherited by subclasses of Collection, but some act as placeholders to tell subclasses they should implement the method appropriately.)

The main subclasses of Collection that you will use are Bag, Set, and SequenceableCollection. SequenceableCollection is an abstract superclass for all the collections that understand sequencing, such as Array, OrderedCollection, and String. Because it expects all its subclasses to understand the concept of sequencing, SequenceableCollection adds behavior such as first and last, which is not generic enough to be placed in Collection. As we go further down the hierarchy, each subclass provides increasingly specific functionality, sometimes by adding new methods and sometimes by overriding methods defined in one of its superclasses. The hierarchy of basic collection classes that you will use is shown in Fig. 11-1.

Not described here, but worth looking at so you know of their existence are: IdentitySet, WeakDictionary, Symbol, IntegerArray, ByteArray, WordArray, RunArray, WeakArray, and KeyedCollection.

Unfortunately, the hierarchy doesn't tell us as much as we'd like about the operations that can be performed. For example, if we look at removing items from a collection, Bags and Sets allow removal. In the

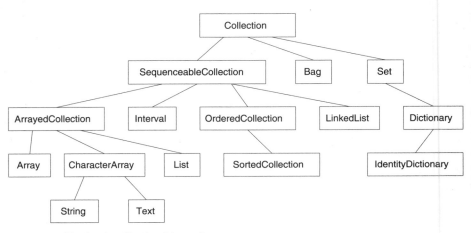

Figure 11-1. The basic collection hierarchy.

SequenceableCollection hierarchy, Intervals don't allow removal, but LinkedLists and OrderedCollections do. Most ArrayedCollections don't allow removal, but Lists do allow it. So we'll try to generalize where possible, but will largely have to consider each class on its own.

Because there is so much specific functionality associated with collections, we will look at mainly the basic functionality. We'll start by looking at the main types of collection, with a brief explanation of *how* to use them and *when* you might use them. Then we'll take a look at the general mechanism for creating a collection, at the general aspects of adding objects and removing objects, at the powerful enumeration methods that are used to loop through collections, and at the general messages that collections understand. However, I've left out a vast amount of behavior so it's well worth spending some time looking through the Collection hierarchy. If you use a Full Browser (from the VisualWorks Advanced Tools) and switch on supers, you will get a better feel for what behavior is inherited and what is implemented by each collection you look at.

Collection Types

In what follows, note that collection indexing schemes are 1-based, rather 0-based as in C or C++. If the collection allows indexing, such as an Array or an OrderedCollection, the first element has index 1.

OrderedCollection

OrderedCollection is the workhorse of collection; I use OrderedCollections and Dictionaries more than any other types of collection. OrderedCollection stores objects in the order they were added, and will grow and shrink as you add and remove objects. Because the size is dynamic, OrderedCollections are generally more useful than Arrays, which are not dynamic. Because OrderedCollections are sequenced, you can use them as queues (FIFO) or stacks (LIFO). Here's an example that shows the chronological sequencing of OrderedCollection. You will see the string 'xyz' if you do the following.

```
orderedCollection := OrderedCollection new.
orderedCollection add: 'xyz'; add: 'abc'.
orderedCollection first inspect
```

The basic operations to add and remove items in an OrderedCollection are add:, remove:, and remove:ifAbsent:. This last message is useful because remove: raises an exception if the object is not present. For example:

```
orderedCollection := OrderedCollection new.
orderedCollection add: #here.
orderedCollection remove: #here.
orderedCollection remove: #there ifAbsent: [nil].
```

OrderedCollections also understand a lot of messages related to order of objects in the collection, such as first, last, after: and before:.

SortedCollection

If you want the objects sorted according to some collating sequence, use a SortedCollection. SortedCollection is subclassed off OrderedCollection and inherits most of its behavior. The main difference between a SortedCollection and an OrderedCollection is the order in which they keep their elements. SortedCollection keeps its elements in sorted order by comparing pairs of elements. Its default mechanism is to send the <= message to one element, passing the second element as a parameter. The alternative way is for the programmer to specify a block of code that will compare two objects, in which case the SortedCollection executes the block for pairs of elements.

If you let the SortedCollection send the <= message, the only requirement is that each object you add to the collection should respond to the <= message and should return true if it is less than or equal to the parameter object, and false otherwise. This generally means that SortedCollections will contain homogeneous objects, objects of the same type. Numbers and strings both know how to respond to <=, but if you are storing your own objects you will need to implement <=. Your implementation might compare the values of instance variables, or might do something as simple as:

```
MyClass>> <= anObject
    ^self printString <= anObject printString
```

If you choose to specify the sort algorithm, you can create an instance of SortedCollection by sending the sortBlock: message to the SortedCollection class. The parameter is the block of code that does the comparison. For example:

```
sortedCollection := SortedCollection sortBlock: [ :x :y | x name < y name
```

Alternatively, you can specify a new sort algorithm by sending the sortBlock: aSortBlock message to the instance of SortedCollection. This causes the collection to be resorted, and any additions are put in the correct place. You can create a new instance of SortedCollection, with a different sort sequence, by sending a collection the message asSortedCollection: aSortBlock.

Keeping elements in sorted order makes it expensive to add objects. If you spend a lot more time adding elements than reporting on elements, three options are more efficient. The first is to use a List, which is described below. The second is to use an OrderedCollection, then to ask a SequenceableCollectionSorter to sort it in place when required. The easiest way to do this is to send the messages sort: or sort:using: to the SequenceableCollectionSorter class. For example, the following code sorts the array in place, giving #(1 2 3 4 5).

```
array := #(5 4 3 2 1).
SequenceableCollectionSorter sort: array.
array inspect.
```

The third option is to send the collection asSortedCollection or asSortedCollection: if you don't mind getting back a new collection.

List

List is a collection that provides the chronological ordering (and indexing) of OrderedCollection, the sorting of SortedCollection, and the dependency notification of Model. Because of their dependency notification, Lists are used by both SelectionInList and MultiSelectionInList in user interface applications.

Because of the versatility of Lists, there is a school of thought that says Lists should be used instead of OrderedCollections and SortedCollections. (For a time I did just this, but have now gone back to using the OrderedCollection as my workhorse. I liked having to type in only four characters for the class name, but disliked the seeming lack of elegance of a List. In particular, I like my classes to do one thing well, but a List tries to be all things to all people. Also, I never really liked inspecting a List.)

To sort a List in place, simply send it the sort message, or the sortWith: message to specify a sort algorithm. Internally, Lists use a SequenceableCollectionSorter to sort themselves.

Array

Arrays are fixed-size collections in which objects are stored in fixed locations, referenced by integer indexes. Because Arrays are fixed size, you can't add to the end of an array or delete elements from an array. However, Arrays provide faster accessing than other collections and are most useful when there will be lots of accessing. Unlike C and C++, where all elements of an array must be of the same type, in Smalltalk, array elements can be of arbitrary type. The disadvantage of Arrays are that you need to know the size of the array when you create it, and they are of fixed size.[1]

If you send the new message to Array, you get an instance of Array with a size of 0, so the usual way to create an instance of Array is to send the new: message and specify the size. For example:

```
array := Array new: 10.
```

The usual way to access an array is to send at:put: to put an object in the array and at: to retrieve the object at an index. The parameter to at: must be an integer. For example:

```
array at: 3 put: anObject.
anObject := array at: 3.
```

Dictionary

Dictionary is one of my favorite classes. A Dictionary is a collection in which you look up values based on a key, and the key can be any object (except nil). A Dictionary is like an Array in that you access it using at: and at:put:. However, whereas Arrays are fixed size and you need an integer index to access elements, a Dictionary can automatically grow and you can access elements using *any* object as a key. For example:

```
dictionary := Dictionary new.
dictionary at: 'abc' put: 'def'.
```

Dictionaries store Associations, so besides at:put:, you can add Associations directly to a Dictionary. The example above could also be written as one of:

```
dictionary := Dictionary new.
dictionary add: 'abc' -> 'def'.
```

```
dictionary := Dictionary new.
dictionary add: (Association key: 'abc' value: 'def').
```

---

[1]Actually, you can grow an array in one of two ways, by sending changeSizeTo: or grow to it or by creating a Stream on the Array, the latter being the preferred technique. We'll talk more about Streams in Chapter 13.

To remove an object from a Dictionary, send either the removeKey: or removeKey:ifAbsent: message.

In the section on centralized error messages in Chapter 20, we'll see the use of Dictionaries with symbols as their keys. If you choose to use objects of your own creation as keys, you will need to implement = and hash for your object (whenever you implement =, you need to implement hash because two objects that are equal should also generate the same hash value).

IdentityDictionary uses == rather than = to compare keys, so it is a little faster than Dictionary if you have symbols for keys. Because many Dictionaries use symbols for their keys, you'll often find IdentityDictionaries used in preference to Dictionary. However, where Dictionaries keep a collection of Associations, IdentityDictionaries keep two parallel collections for keys and values. Because of the way PoolDictionaries are implemented, you can't use an IdentityDictionary as a PoolDictionary.

Set

A Set is an unordered collection of unique objects, so if you want a collection that guarantees no duplicates, use a Set. There is no structured accessing of a Set because there is no order to the elements. Instead, the way to access the elements of a Set is through the enumeration messages described below. If you try to add an object that already exists, the Set silently ignores it. If you try the following, you'll see a size of 2 because nothing was added when we tried to add the duplicate 7.

```
set := Set new add: 7; add: 8; add: 7; yourself.
set size inspect
```

When adding an object, a Set uses both the hash and = messages to determine if it is a duplicate of any other object in the collection. Sets are fairly expensive if you are doing a lot of adding, so use them only when you specifically want the property of uniqueness. One use of Set is to test for duplicates in a collection; for example, the following gives a Boolean that says whether the collection includes duplicate items:

```
includesDuplicates := collection size ~~ collection asSet size.
```

Bag

A Bag is another unordered collection that contains objects of arbitrary type. It is very similar to a Set except that a Bag keeps track of the number of occurrences of each object. Like a Set, it sends both hash and = to determine if an object already exists in the collection. One use of a Bag would be to collect duplicate items from another type of collection by doing something like the following. However, I've never seen a Bag used in an application.

```
duplicateList := List new.
collection asBag valuesAndCountsDo:
    [:each :count | count > 1 ifTrue: [duplicateList add: each]].
```

LinkedList

A LinkedList is a collection in which each element points to the next element. OrderedCollections can do everything LinkedLists can do, the only difference being that LinkedLists are more efficient at doing large numbers of inserts and deletes. Elements of a LinkedList must be instances of Link or one of its subclasses (or at least should be polymorphic with Link; i.e., should respond to the same messages), which means that you will usually create a new subclass of Link in order to use a LinkedList. VisualWorks uses LinkedLists to manage processes, so Process is defined as a subclass of Link. This is the only example of LinkedList I've seen used.

Creating New Collections

There are three usual ways to create a collection. One is to send the new message to the collection class. The second is to send new: aCapacity. The third is to use a message from the with: family and pass in the initial elements of the collection.

new:

The underlying instance creation mechanism is to use new:, which is implemented as a primitive by the class Behavior. Some of the collection classes override new:, usually invoking super new: then adding class-specific code. new: creates an instance of a collection with indexed variables, in which the parameter to new: specifies the number of indexed variables. (You can tell if a class is indexed because the top line of the class definition will say variableSubclass: rather than subclass:. The other type of variable is the named variable, which is an instance variable with a name.)

For fixed-size collections such as Array, the parameter to new: is both the capacity and the size of the collection. For collections that can grow, such as OrderedCollection, the collection has an initial size of 0 and the parameter specifies the capacity — the number of elements the collection can hold before it has to grow.

Because new: is used to specify a capacity, it's poor style to use new: to pass in parameters other than the capacity. When writing your own classes, it's better style to use with:, or to specify the parameter type in the instance creation message, such as newLabel:.

new

The new message is also implemented by Behavior but is overridden by the collection classes, and is usually implemented by sending new: someInitialSize. For example:

```
OrderedCollection class>>new
    ^self new: 5
```

Many collections will grow automatically as you add to them, so you don't need to specify an initial size and can simply send new. However, growing a collection is expensive, so if you know how large the collection will be it's more efficient to send the new: message, specifying the size. In a timing test, it took over three times as long to add a hundred items to an OrderedCollection when the OrderedCollection was created using new, as when it was created using new:. The first example took 1253 microseconds while the second example took 372 microseconds.

```
orderedCollection := OrderedCollection new.
    1to: 100 do: [:index | orderedCollection add: index]

orderedCollection:= OrderedCollection new: 100.
    1to: 100 do: [:index | orderedCollection add: index]
```

The with: family

You can create a collection and populate it with some initial elements by sending the class a message from the with: family of messages. There are five messages, each specifying a different number of objects to add. If you want to add more than four objects, they must already be in a collection of some type (in which case you could have sent the original collection the asSomeTypeOfCollection message; for example, asOrderedCollection).

```
with: objectOne
with: objectOne with: objectTwo
with: objectOne with: objectTwo with: objectThree
with: objectOne with: objectTwo with: objectThree with: objectFour
withAll: aCollectionOfObjects
```

For example:

```
collection := OrderedCollection with: 'how' with: 'are' with: 'you'.
collection := List withAll: #('how' 'are' 'you' 'today' 'Alec?').
```

Adding to and Removing from Collections

The standard messages to add elements to a collection are at:put: for keyed collections such as Array and Dictionary, and add: for collections such as Bag, Set, and OrderedCollection. The general behavior when adding to or removing from a collection is to return the object being added or removed. Thus, both add: and at:put: return the object being stored. When you add to a collection, the collection might have to grow to fit in the new object. OrderedCollections will grow in size automatically when necessary. For more information, see the section on growing collections, below.

An alternative, and efficient approach to adding objects to collections is to create a Stream on the collection. We'll talk more about Streams in Chapter 13.

A common bug when using add: is forgetting that add: returns the object added rather than self. So, if you are creating a collection and adding to it, the following will *not* give you what you expect.

```
collection := OrderedCollection new
    add: objectOne;
    add: objectTwo.
```

Instead, use one of the following techniques.

```
collection := OrderedCollection new.
collection
    add: objectOne;
    add: objectTwo.

(collection := OrderedCollection new)
    add: objectOne;
    add: objectTwo.

collection := OrderedCollection new
    add: objectOne;
    add: objectTwo;
    yourself.
```

The standard messages to remove elements from a collection are remove: and remove:ifAbsent:. For keyed collections such as Dictionary, use removeKey: and removeKey:ifAbsent:. Note that you can't remove elements from an Array. When you send remove:, the object that was removed will be returned. If the object can't be found in the collection, an exception is raised. The alternative message, remove:ifAbsent:, will return the object if it is successfully removed. If the object can't be found it will execute the block of code passed as the parameter to ifAbsent:, returning the value of the block.

A subtle remove: bug is to iterate over a collection and remove from the same collection. This will cause problems, because the collection might be reorganized underneath you when you remove elements. Instead, you should iterate over a copy of the collection and remove from the original collection. For example:

```
collection:= OrderedCollection withAll: #(1 2 3 4 5 6).
collection copy do: [ :each | each even ifTrue: [collection remove: each]].
```

Sometimes you don't even need to remove objects explicitly. Instead, you can use select: or reject: to create a new collection. We'll talk more about these messages below, in the section on enumerating, but here are examples of doing the above operation using these two messages:

```
collection:= OrderedCollection withAll: #(1 2 3 4 5 6).
collection select: [:each | each odd].
```

```
collection:= OrderedCollection withAll: #(1 2 3 4 5 6).
collection reject: [:each | each even].
```

Enumerating

One reason it is difficult to have off-by-one errors or array size errors in Smalltalk is that collections provide some very powerful ways of iterating through their elements without having to specify sizes or bounds. Collections *know* how big they are. Methods that do things over all the elements of a collection live in the enumerating protocol.

The enumeration messages go through each element in the collection, executing a block of code for each element. The block of code always takes the element as a parameter. In the examples below you'll see that, instead of getting fancy with the parameter name, I use each (I also use index for objects that are guaranteed to be index numbers). This has the benefit that, if you see each or index, you know it refers to the collection element being processed. You can usually tell what the item is from the collection name or from where it was built.

do:

The do: message is the basic enumeration message. It goes through all the items in the collection (in order, if the collection is sequenceable) and performs a programmer-specified block of code for each item in the collection. For example:

```
#(1 2 3 4 5) do: [ :each | Transcript cr; show: each printString].
```

The block is executed for each item in the collection and is passed to that item as a parameter. Use do: when you want to perform some action for all or some of the elements in the collection. If you just want to create a new collection, use one of the messages below. The method reverseDo: iterates over the collection in reverse.

If you send do: to a Dictionary, it iterates through the values in the Dictionary. Three other methods, keysDo:, associationsDo:, and keysAndValuesDo: iterate over the keys, the associations, and the key and value pairs.

Another message, with:do:, allows you to iterate over two parallel collections, passing corresponding elements from the two collections to the do: block.

collect:

The collect: message allows you to do something for each item in the collection, and puts the result of your action in a new collection. For example, if you wanted to create a new collection of the squares of a collection of numbers, you could do either of the following. However, collect: is both better style and is more efficient, because it doesn't use any variables declared outside the block. A timing test showed the first technique taking 103 microseconds while the second technique took 31 microseconds.

```
squareCollection := List new.
#(1 2 3 4 5) do: [ :each | squareCollection add: each * each].

squareCollection:= #(1 2 3 4 5) collect: [ :each | each * each].
```

It's useful to remember collect: because it's easy to find yourself writing code similar to the first example when you should be using collect:. Any time you iterate over a collection and add objects to another collection, consider using collect: or select:.

select:

The select: message allows you to create a subcollection where items from the original collection are selected based on some condition being true for them. For example, we get the result #(1 3 5) from the following example.

```
#(1 2 3 4 5) select: [ :each | each odd].
```

reject:

The reject: message is similar to select: but works the opposite way — items are rejected from the new subcollection if the condition is true. Using the same example as for select:, we get the array #(2 4).

```
#(1 2 3 4 5) reject: [ :each | each odd].
```

detect:

The detect: message returns the first item in a collection that satisfies a condition. For example, we get the value 4 from the following example.

```
(1 to: 5) detect: [ :each | each > 3].
```

If no item satisfies the condition, an exception is raised. You can avoid this by using detect:ifNone: and providing another block, which is executed if no item satisfies the condition. For example, we get the value 99 from this example:

```
(1 to: 5) detect: [ :each | each > 30] ifNone: [99].
```

inject:into:

The inject:into: message is a strange message. Some people never use it, while others love it and use it whenever possible. The classic example is subtotaling.

```
(1 to: 5) inject: 0 into: [ :subtotal :each | subtotal + each].
```

When the block is executed for the first item in the collection, the parameter to the inject: keyword is passed in as the first parameter. The block returns subtotal + each, which for the first item is 0 + 1. This returned value is then used as the first parameter for the next invocation of the block. Each invocation, the block returns a value that is passed in as the first parameter for the next invocation. In fact, it might be easier to understand if we wrote the above example as:

```
(1 to: 5) inject: 0 into: [ :injectedValue :each | injectedValue + each].
```

It takes a while to get used to inject:into: and to figure out situations where it is useful. To make this process a little shorter, here are some examples of its use. Inspect the results and understand what each example is doing.

```
(1 to: 5) inject: 0 into: [ :max :each | max max: each].
```

```
(1 to: 5) inject: 1 into: [ :factorial :each | factorial * each ].
```

```
#('Now' 'is' 'the' 'time' 'for' 'all' 'good' 'men')
    inject: String new
    into: [ :string :each | string, each, ' '].
```

```
(#(3 $x 'hello' #mySymbol)
    inject: String new writeStream
    into: [ :stream :each |
        stream
            print: each class;
            nextPutAll: ' value ';
            print: each;
            cr; yourself]) contents.
```

Note that, in this last example, we send yourself as the last message to make sure that the stream is returned from the block. A common error is to not return the object that will be injected in the next iteration. In this case we didn't actually need yourself, but it's good practice to send it just to make sure the correct object is returned.

Enumeration Wrap-up

The abstract superclass Collection implements all the enumeration methods in terms of do:. By requiring the subclasses of Collection to implement do: in a way that is appropriate for the subclass, the other enumeration methods can then be defined by Collection and inherited by all its subclasses. This is shown in Fig. 11-2. It illustrates the useful object-oriented technique of having an abstract superclasses implement behavior in terms of a few undefined methods that are implemented by its subclasses.

General Messages for Collections

Below are some of the messages that collections respond to. I've listed them here to give you a feel for the types of things you can do. However, not all collections respond to all the messages. For example, some of them make sense only with collections that have a concept of sequence, while others make sense only in collections where you can remove items.

Adding objects

You can add an object with at:put: and add:, you can add to the front of the collection (addFirst:), to the end (addLast: [which is the same as add:]), after another object (add:after:) or before another object (add:before:). You can add all the objects in another collection to this collection (addAll:, addAll:after:, addAll:before:).

Removing objects

Not all collections allow you to remove things. For example, what does it mean to remove the second element of an array, or to remove the third character in the string 'abcde'? Collections that don't allow you to use add: also don't allow you to use remove:.

To remove an object from a collection that allows removing, you again have many options. You can remove an object (remove:), which raises an exception if the object is not found, or you can remove an

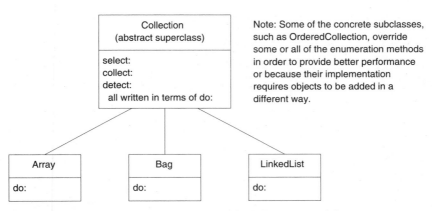

Figure 11-2. Implementing behavior in terms of subclass responsibilities.

object without raising an exception (remove:ifAbsent:). You can remove the first object in the collection (removeFirst), or the last (removeLast), or the first or last so-many objects (removeFirst: and removeLast:). You can remove all the objects that satisfy a condition (removeAllSuchThat:), or all the objects that are contained in another collection (removeAll:). To remove objects from Dictionaries send the removeKey: or removeKey:ifAbsent: messages.

Accessing and locating objects

To access objects in a collection, you again have a rich set of options. If the collection understands indexing or keyed access, you can send at: to get the object at that index or key. For collections that understand sequencing, you can get the first object (first) or the last object (last), and you can find the object before or after another object (before: and after:). You can find the first position of an object (indexOf: or indexOf:ifAbsent:), or the last position of an object (lastIndexOf: or lastIndexOf:ifAbsent:). From there you can find the position of the next or the previous object (nextIndexOf:from:to: and prevIndexOf:from:to:). You can also find the position of a subcollection of the original collection (indexOfSubCollection:startingAt: or indexOfSubCollection:startingAt:ifAbsent:).

Replacing objects

You can replace all occurrences of a particular object with another object (replaceAll:with:), or do the replacement within a range (replaceAll:with:from:to:). Or you can replace all the elements in a range with elements from another collection (replaceFrom:to:with: or replaceFrom:to:with:startingAt:). Finally, you can copy a collection, adding another object to it as you copy it (copyWith:), or copy it and lose all the elements that are equal to a specified object (copyWithout:).

Sizes and counts

Collections will tell you how many elements they contain (size), and how many objects they are capable of holding (capacity). Note that for Arrays, these give the same answer. A collection will also tell you how many times an object occurs in it (occurrencesOf: anObject).

Testing

Collections respond with Boolean values (true or false) to the following messages. You can tell if a collection is empty (isEmpty) and you can see if an object is contained in a collection (includes: anObject). A similar method, contains: [some code], returns true if the code block evaluates to true for *any* item in the collection. For example, lines three and four both evaluate to true.

```
collection := OrderedCollection new.
collection add: 'abc'; add: 'def'; add: 'xyz'.
collection includes: 'def'.
collection contains: [:each | each includes: $y]
```

Creating other collections from a collection

Collection provides several methods for creating a collection of one type from a collection of another type. They are located in the converting protocol. For example, you can send the following messages to create a new collection of the specified type: asArray, asBag, asList, asOrderedCollection, asSet, asSortedCollection, asSortedCollection: aSortBlock. If you do the following you will see an instance of SortedCollection with elements 'abc', 'mno', and 'xyz'.

```
list := List new.
list add: 'xyz'; add: 'abc'; add: 'mno'.
list asSortedCollection inspect.
```

You can also send reverse to a sequenceable collection to create a new collection in reverse order.

Growing collections

Many collections can grow in size simply by sending the add: message. If the collection is not large enough to add another object, it expands the collection. (It does this by creating a new collection of larger capacity, copying over the collection elements, then *becoming* the new collection.) However, expanding the collection is fairly expensive, so if you know the eventual size of the collection it's more efficient to create it with the new: message, passing a value that is your best guess of the eventual size.

If you create a subclass of a collection that can grow and add instance variables to your subclass, they won't be automatically copied when the collection grows. To make sure that the values of your instance variables are retained when the collection grows, you should override the copyEmpty: method that is defined for Collection. The best way to do this is something like the following. For more information on copyEmpty:, see Chapter 25.

```
MyClass>>copyEmpty: size
    |new |
    (new := super copyEmpty: size)
        instVar1: self instVar1;
        instVar2: self instVar2.
    ^new
```

12

Strings

A string is just another type of collection, one that consists of a sequence of characters. However, we tend to use strings enough to warrant a chapter of their own. String is subclassed off CharacterArray, which is subclassed off ArrayedCollection, which is subclassed off SequenceableCollection, which is subclassed off Collection, which means that strings inherit a lot of behavior. We will cover a lot of the most useful behavior, but there is still a great deal more. To learn about the other behaviors, you'll have to browse the methods that String implements and inherits.

Creating a String

The easiest way to create a string is to enclose a sequence of characters in single quotes. To create a string with a single character, send with: to the class String. You can specify the size of a string and initialize it to be filled with a specified character by sending new:withAll:. For example:

```
string := 'here is a string'.                          'here is a string'
string := String with: $X.                             'X'
string := String new: 5 withAll: Character space.      '     '
```

Once you have a string, you can tell how big it is by sending the size message. For example:

```
'here is a string' size.      16
```

Adding to a String

When you add something to a string you are creating a new string that contains both the old string and the added characters. The most common way of adding to a string is to concatenate another string by sending the , (comma) message.

'now ', 'is ', 'the'   'now is the'

Unfortunately, the , message doesn't allow you to concatenate a single character. To append a character to a string you can send copyWith:, or you can create a string from the character and concatenate this. The former technique is more than twice as fast as the latter. For example:

'Why' copyWith: $?.   'Why?'
'Why' , (String with: $?). 'Why?'

I dislike the semantics of both approaches and prefer to write and use nonstandard methods that are more intuitive. In the examples below, the performance is about the same as for the techniques shown above. The examples are shown first, and the method definitions afterwards.

'Why' + $?.   'Why?'
'Why' , $? asString.   'Why?'

SequenceableCollection>> + anObject
    ^self copyWith: anObject

Character>>asString
    ^String with: self

Depending on how many strings you are concatenating, it might be more efficient to create a Stream and write the strings to the stream. See Chapter 13 for more information on how to use Streams with Strings.

Comparing Strings

To compare two strings for equality, you can use the = message. This checks to ensure that the two strings are exactly the same — that is, it is case-sensitive. To compare two strings for equality when you *don't* care about differences in case, use sameAs:.

'abcde' = 'ABCDE'.   false
'abcde' sameAs: 'ABCDE'.   true

To compare two strings for the various *less* and *greater than* combinations, you can use the standard <, <=, >, and >= messages. These four messages all ignore case. (These four messages use the private message compare:. Another private message, trueCompare:, uses a primitive and is about eight times faster than compare:. Unfortunately, they return different results so you can't just substitute one for the other.)

'abcde' < 'ABCDF'.   true
'ABCDE' < 'abcdf'.   true

The sameCharacters: message will tell you how many characters are the same before the strings start differing. For example:

'abcdef' sameCharacters: 'abcxyz'.   3

Changing Case and Converting to a Number

To change the case of a String, you can send it the messages asLowercase and asUppercase. (You can also send these messages to instances of Character.)

```
'HELLO' asLowercase.      'hello'
'there' asUppercase.      'THERE'
```

You can convert numbers in string format (e.g., '54' or '3.14') to number objects by sending the asNumber message. It will figure out what type of number the string represents and create the correct type of number. A string that does not represent a valid number will be converted to 0. So, for example:

```
'54' asNumber.        54
'3.14' asNumber.      3.14
'abcd' asNumber.      0
'a12c' asNumber.      0
```

Pattern Matching

To see if a string matches a pattern, send the message match: to the pattern, passing the string as a parameter. (I find this counter-intuitive: I expect to send the message to the string passing the pattern as the parameter. However, it is easy to remember by thinking of the term *pattern matching*—pattern match: string.) Wildcard characters are *, which means any sequence of characters, and #, which means any single character. match: does case-insensitive matching. For example:

```
'Hello *' match: 'Hello Alec'.        true
'Hello #ave' match: 'HELLO Dave'.     true
'Hello #ave' match: 'Hello Alec'.     false
```

You can specify whether to be case-sensitive or case-insensitive by sending match:ignoreCase: instead, passing a boolean parameter (match: simply invokes match:ignoreCase: passing true as the parameter). For example:

```
'HELLO' match: 'hello' ignoreCase: true.      true
'HELLO' match: 'hello' ignoreCase: false.     false
```

Looking for Characters or Words in a String

If you have a string, you can tell whether it is empty by sending the isEmpty message. If you want to know if a character appears somewhere in a string, send includes:. An alternative message, contains:, allows you to be a bit more sophisticated and execute a block of code for each character until it finds a character for which the block evaluates to true.

(Note that the testing protocol of Character contains many useful messages.) You can find the number of times a specified character appears in the string by sending occurrencesOf:.

'Now is the time for all' isEmpty.	false
'Now is the time for all' includes: $f	true
'Now is the time for all' contains: [:each | each asUppercase == $F].	true
'Now is the time for all' occurrencesOf: $t	2

To find *where* things are in a string, you have various options. To find the position of the first occurrence of a character, send indexOf:. For the position of the last occurrence, send lastIndexOf:. Both of these methods return 0 if the character is not found. Both also have an alternative message in which you can specify a block of code to be executed if the character is not found. Alternatively, send findFirst: or findLast: to find the first or last character that satisfies a condition specified in a block of code. Both methods return 0 if no character satisfies the condition. If you are at a known position in the string and want to find the next or previous occurrence of a character, send nextIndexOf:from:to: or prevIndexOf:from:to:.

'Now is the time for all' indexOf: $t	8
'Now is the time for all' lastIndexOf: $t	12
'Now is the time for all' findFirst: [:char | char isLowercase].	2
'Now is the time for all' findLast: [:char | char isSeparator].	20

To find the position of a substring, you can send findString:startingAt:. Again, this returns 0 if the substring is not found, and a similar message will execute a block of code if the substring is not found. If you want to do a case-insensitive search or want to use wildcards, you can send findString:startingAt:ignoreCase:useWildcards: (this message returns an interval rather than an integer).

'Now is the time for all' findString: 'time' startingAt: 4.	12
'Now is the time for all'	
findString: 'T#ME'	
startingAt: 1	
ignoreCase: true	
useWildcards: true	(12 to: 15)

Replacing Characters

There are two standard ways of changing the characters in a string. One creates a new string while the other modifies the string in place.

Creating a new string

Because we are creating a new string, we have the flexibility to insert additional characters or to remove characters from the string, as well as changing characters. The standard method is changeFrom:to:with:, which takes a start position, a stop position, and a replacement string as parameters, and returns a new string. For example:

'now is the time' changeFrom: 12 to: 15 with: 'tune'.   'now is the tune'

If stop is greater than or equal to start, both stop and start must be within the string bounds. Otherwise, an exception is raised. If the replacement string contains the same number of characters as specified by the range from start to stop, we are doing a straight replacement. If the replacement string size is less than the range, we are replacing and deleting characters. If the replacement string size is greater than the range, we replace and insert. If we are strictly inserting characters, we insert before the start position and the stop position should be exactly one less than the start position — that is, stop := (start - 1). So, to insert before the string, start is 1 and stop is 0. To append to the end of the string, start is the string size + 1 and stop is the string size. Let's look at some examples to clarify this:

'now is the time' changeFrom: 12 to: 15 with: 'tune'.   'now is the tune'
'now is the time' changeFrom: 12 to: 11 with: 'right '.   'now is the right time'
'now is the time' changeFrom: 1 to: 0 with: 'right '.   'right now is the time'
'now is the time' changeFrom: 16 to: 15 with: ' for'.   'now is the time for'
'now is the time' changeFrom: 8 to: 11 with: ''.   'now is time'
'now is the time' changeFrom: 8 to: 10 with: 'a'.   'now is a time'
'now is the time' changeFrom: 8 to: 10 with: 'a great'.   'now is a great time'

If you want to go through an entire string, replacing all occurrences of one substring with another substring, use copyReplaceAll:with:. This method does all the replacements regardless of whether the substrings are the same length, returning the converted string.

'now is not the time' copyReplaceAll: 'no' with: 'yes'.   'yesw is yest the time'

Modifying the string in place

To change characters of a string in place, we use a method from the replace family. Obviously, if we are modifying the string in place we can specify ony a range of characters that exists in the string. Also, the number of characters we want to replace must be the same as the length of the replacement string.

To replace a single character, use at:put: (remember that this method returns the parameter to put: rather than the receiver). To replace every occurrence of a specified character with another character, use replaceAll:with:. To do the same thing within a specified range of positions, use replaceAll:with:from:to:. To replace a substring with another string of the same length, use replaceFrom:to:with:, specifying the start and end positions of the substring. For example:

```
string := 'now is the time'.
string at: 1 put: $N.
string.                                              'Now is the time'
```

```
'now is the time' replaceAll: $t with: $T.           'now is The Time'
'now is the time' replaceAll: $t with: $T from: 1 to: 10.   'now is The time'
'now is the time' replaceFrom: 12 to: 15 with: 'tune'.     'now is the tune'
```

Getting a Substring

There are two standard ways to get a substring from a string. If you want to start at the beginning and copy up to a particular character, use copyUpTo:. Note that the character you specify is *not* included in the new string. For example:

```
'now is the time' copyUpTo: $m.      'now is the ti'
```

If you know the starting and ending position, you can use copyFrom:to:. For example:

```
'now is the time' copyFrom: 5 to: 10.   'is the'
```

One useful message that does not come standard with VisualWorks is asArrayOfSubstrings, which breaks a string into its component substrings and returns an array of those substrings. Here is an implementation. You'll need to also add a method to SequenceableCollection: findFirst:startingAt:, an easy extension to findFirst:. By adding asArrayOfSubstrings to CharacterArray rather than to String, it will also work with a Text object, creating an array of Text objects, each holding one of the space separated substrings.

```
CharacterArray>>asArrayOfSubstrings
    |first last collection |
    collection := OrderedCollection new.
    last := 0.
    [first := self findFirst: [ :char | char isSeparator not] startingAt: last + 1.
    first ~= 0]
        whileTrue:
            [last := (self findFirst: [ :char | char isSeparator] startingAt: first) - 1.
            last < 0 ifTrue: [last := self size].
            collection add: (self copyFrom: first to: last)].
    ^collection asArray
```

Here's an example of using asArrayOfSubstrings. We've gone further and sorted the array, then recombined it so that we are creating a string of sorted words. This shows another example of inject:into:. The result is 'all come for good is men now the time to '. (We end up with an extra space at the end of the string, which we could strip off easily.)

```
'now is the time for all good men to come' asArrayOfSubstrings asSortedCollection
    inject: String new
    into: [ :string :word | string , word , (String with: Character space)].
```

Expanding a Format String

VisualWorks 2.5 provides a family of messages (expandMacros) that are implemented by CharacterArray, and which allow you to expand strings by doing parameter substitution. The message is sent directly to the format string, which uses a new class, StringParameterSubstitution, to do the work. Note that you are returned an instance of Text. The basic formatting capabilities are:

<n>	Insert a CR in the string.
<t>	Insert a tab in the string.
<1p>	Replace with the first argument's printString.
<2s>	Replace with the second argument, which must be a CharacterArray.
<3?now:then>	Replace with 'now' if the third argument evalues to true or 'then' if it evaluates to false.
<4#now:then>	Replace with 'now' if the fourth argument == 1, and with 'then' otherwise. The fourth argument must be a Number.

For more information on the parameter substitution, look at the class comments for StringParameterSubstitution. Here's an example of using these parameter substitution capabilities. If you try this with count set to 1 then 2, you get back instances of Text with the strings 'There is 1 apple in the box' and 'There are 2 apples in the box'.

```
count := 1.
'There <1#is:are> <1p> apple<1#:s> in the box' expandMacrosWith: count.
```

Here is another example using carriage returns and tabs. Notice that you can combine these two. The result is an instance of Text containing the string shown.

```
'Variables are:<nt>Var1=<1p><nt>Var2=<2p>'
    expandMacrosWithArguments: #(11 22).

'Variables are:
    Var1=11
    Var2=22'
```

Additional Useful Methods

Trimming white space from a string

VisualWorks doesn't come with a method to trim leading and trailing white space from a string. I find this a very useful method and so added it to CharacterArray. For a String, the method returns a new string with white space removed from both ends. For a Text object, it returns a Text object with white space removed from the string.

```
CharacterArray>>trimWhiteSpace
    "Remove leading and trailing white space"
    |first |
```

```
first := self findFirst: [:ch | ch isSeparator not].
^first = 0
    ifTrue: [String new]
    ifFalse: [self copyFrom: first to: (self findLast: [:ch | ch isSeparator not])]
```

Capitalizing a string

I find it useful to add a method that will capitalize a String or a Text object. We'll use this method in Chapter 29.

```
CharacterArray>>capitalize
    |newString |
    newString := self copy.
    newString size > 0 ifTrue: [newString at: 1 put: (newString at: 1) asUppercase].
    ^newString
```

13

Streams

Streams and Their Uses

It's not immediately obvious what a Stream is and why you should use one, so let's approach this chapter the opposite way and show how certain things are done. We'll look at streams being used for printing objects, for reading and writing files, and for speeding up string manipulation. Then we'll take a look at how to create streams and the messages you can send them. In what follows, to save space I've put more cascaded messages on a line than I would in a real method.

Streams in printOn:

If you have ever modified the information returned from an object when it's sent the printString message, you've had to write or modify the printOn: method, which writes to a stream. For example:

```
printOn: aStream
    super printOn: aStream.
    aStream
        crtab; nextPutAll: 'instVar';
        space; print: instVar.
```

You'll notice from this example that streams know the current location in the stream. We haven't had to specify where to put anything. Instead, the stream keeps track of its current location and writes the next information starting at that point. There is a lot of built-in sequencing with streams.

You'll also notice that you can send some useful messages to a Stream (you can send a lot of the same messages to the Transcript, a global instance of TextCollector). For example, crtab writes a carriage return and a tab character, nextPutAll: writes a string (actually a collection), space writes a space character, and print: sends printOn: to its parameter.

Streams in file access

We'll talk a lot more about files in Chapter 14, but here we'll look at the stream aspects of reading and writing files. The usual way to access a file is by using the buffered IO mechanism, which is the Stream mechanism. For example, if we want to create a file, write to it, then read from it, we can do something as simple as:

```
writeStream := 'myfile' asFilename writeStream.
writeStream nextPutAll: 'Here I am, writing to my file'.
writeStream cr; nextPutAll: 'Here is line two'.
writeStream close.
```

```
readStream := 'myfile' asFilename readStream.
Transcript cr; show: (readStream upTo: Character cr).
Transcript cr; show: readStream upToEnd.
readStream close.
```

Note that this code is not very robust, and in Chapter 14 we'll talk more about robustness and the different options available to you when reading and writing files. Here we are simply showing the power of streams for dealing with file access.

Streams on strings

The most common use of a stream with a string is to create a large string out of smaller strings. In the following example, the stream technique is more than three times as fast as string concatenation. If you were simply concatenating two strings, it would be more efficient to use the comma message. However, as the number of concatenations increases, so does the performance benefit of using a stream. The main reason for the efficiency is that concatenation creates a new string each time.

On the other hand, in the stream technique, we created a large enough string up front so all we have to do is fill the string using the stream messages. If we had created the string using String new, the string would have been created with a size of zero, and would have had to grow several times as it was filled up. This is very expensive; if you change the stream example to say stream := String new writeStream, the performance is about fifty percent *slower* than using string concatenation.

```
string := 'There are ' , 4 printString, ' apples in ', 1 printString, ' basket.',
          (String with: Character cr), 4 printString, ' of you can have ', 1 printString.
```

```
stream := (String new: 100) writeStream.
stream
    nextPutAll: 'There are '; print: 4;
```

```
    nextPutAll: ' apples in '; print: 1;
    nextPutAll: ' basket.';
    cr; print: 4;
    nextPutAll: ' of you can have '; print: 1.
string := stream contents.
```

Streams can be created on any sequenceable collection, and you will also find them used with Arrays. However, Streams are used with Strings more than with other types of sequenceable collection.

The Benefits of a Stream

Why bother using a stream? As we saw in the examples above, you don't have a choice if you want to write your own printOn: methods or if you want to use buffered I/O with files. Leaving these aside, why are streams useful? Streams provide several benefits.

1. First, they often provide better performance when adding to collections.

2. Second, a stream can automatically grow a collection to which it is adding, even if the collection is a fixed-size collection such as an Array.

3. Third, streams provide many more messages for manipulating collections.

4. Fourth, you don't have to keep track of the position in a stream. For example, If you want to move about a string, you have to do operations to discover a position in the string, then do some operation at that position. With a stream, you can move around and do operations without needing to know precise positions in the collection.

Creating Streams

There are two fundamental subclasses of Stream: InternalStream, which streams over a collection, and ExternalStream, which streams over a file and provides buffered access to the file. In Chapter 14 we will look at how to create streams on files; here we will just look at creating streams on collections. InternalStream has three subclasses: WriteStream, ReadStream, and ReadWriteStream, which allow write access, read access, and read/write access to the collection.

There are two basic ways of opening a Stream on a collection. You can send the on: or with: message to the stream class, passing the collection as a parameter, or you can send a message such as readStream to the collection. The difference between on: and with: is that writing to a stream created with on: will start writing at the beginning of the collection, overwriting the collection, while writing to a stream created with with: will append to the end of the collection. Here are some examples of creating streams of different types. Interestingly, there is no readWriteStream message for collections, perhaps because most collection streaming is either reading or writing, but not both.

```
readStream := ReadStream on: aString.
readStream := aCollection readStream.

writeStream := WriteStream on: (Array new: 100).
writeStream := (String new: 100) writeStream.

readWriteStream := ReadWriteStream on: (Array new: 100).
```

In the VisualWorks image there are a few streams on arrays, but the great majority of collection based streams are on strings.

Reading, Writing, and Positioning Streams

Writing

Typically, we write to streams more than we read from them, so we'll look at writing first. There are relatively few writing operations; the ones that are used most of the time are nextPut:, nextPutAll:, and print:, plus some character writing methods. There are a few other messages, which you can find by browsing the methods for WriteStream and its superclasses. As we mentioned above, you can create a writeStream on an arbitrary collection, although it is more usual to see a writeStream on a String. Note that, when you write to a collection, the collection will grow automatically if it needs to.

The nextPut: message puts a single object on the stream. You can put a whole collection on the stream as a single collection object using nextPut:. The whole collection will be read back as a single object. However, when using a writeStream on a String, nextPut: only writes characters. If you try to use nextPut: to write a string (a collection), you will get an error.

The nextPutAll: message puts collections on the stream as individual objects. They will be read back as separate objects. When using a writeStream on a String, use nextPutAll: to write a string.

The print: message puts onto the stream the printString representation of an object by sending printOn: to its parameter. If you are using a writeStream on a String, print: anObject is a convenient way to do the same as nextPutAll: anObject printString. The following two lines achieve the same result.

```
writeStream nextPutAll: anObject printString.
writeStream print: anObject.
```

There are a few special characters that are difficult to represent using the $ prefix. It's easy to represent the letter X by writing $X, but representing a space or a carriage return is less obvious. Streams provide some messages to make it easier to write these types of character to the stream.

space	Write a space
tab	Write a tab character
tab: anInteger	Write the specified number of tabs
cr	Write a carriage return
crtab	Write a carriage return followed by a tab
crtab: anInteger	Write a carriage return followed by the specified number of tabs
lf	Write a line feed.

Reading

There are a lot of messages for reading a collection, and we won't go over all of them here. To learn more about the other messages, browse the methods defined by ReadStream and its superclasses. Some of the more useful messages are:

next	Return the next object on the stream (the next character if this is a string based stream). If we are at the end of the stream, nil is returned.
next:	Return the next specified number of objects. If this takes us past the end of the stream, an exception is raised.
nextAvailable:	Return the next specified number of objects, or the stream up to the end of the stream, whichever is less.
contents	Return the entire contents of the stream.
upToEnd	Return the contents from the current position to the end of the stream.
through:	Return the objects up to and including the first occurrence of the specified object or the end of the stream, whichever comes first.
throughAll:	Return the objects up to and including the first occurrence of the specified collection or the end of the stream, whichever comes first.
upTo:	Return the objects up to but not including the first occurrence of the specified object or the end of the stream, whichever comes first. The stream will be positioned after the specified object.
upToAll:	Return the objects up to but not including the first occurrence of the specified collection or the end of the stream, whichever comes first. The stream will be positioned before the specified collection.

Positioning

The basic positioning messages are:

atEnd	Are we at the end of the stream?
position	The current position in the stream.
position:	Set the current position.
readPosition	The current reading position in the stream.
writePosition	The current writing position in the stream.
reset	Set the position to the start of the stream.
setToEnd	Set the position to the end of the stream.
skip:	Skip forward the specified number of elements.
skipSeparators	Skip foward over separator characters: space, tab, carrriage return, etc.

| skipUpTo: | Position the stream just before the object. |
| skipThrough: | Position the stream just after the object. |

You can move to different positions in the stream using the position: message or one of the skip messages. For convenience, reset and setToEnd set the position to the start and the end of the stream. You can determine if you are at the end of the stream by sending atEnd, which returns a Boolean. In fact, when reading a stream we often stay in a loop that looks something like one of the following:

```
[readStream atEnd]
    whileFalse: [self myProcessObject: stream next].

[readStream atEnd]
    whileFalse:
        [doneWithStream := self myProcessObject: readStream next.
        doneWithStream ifTrue: [readStream setToEnd]]
```

Example

Here's an example of writing to a stream on an array, then reading it back. Notice that we can write out collections either as a collection object using nextPut: or as a sequence of individual objects using nextPutAll:. When we read back what we wrote, it comes back just as we wrote it. Following the code of the example is the output to the Transcript. (Note that the Transcript, an instance of TextCollector, also responds to many of the same writing messages as a Stream. You can therefore use messages such as cr, nextPutAll:, print:, and flush with the Transcript.)

```
stream := ReadWriteStream on: (Array new).
stream nextPut: 2.
stream nextPut: 'How are you'.
stream nextPutAll: 'Alec'.
stream nextPutAll: #('Fine' 'thanks').
stream nextPut: OrderedCollection new.
stream reset.
[stream atEnd]
    whileFalse:
        [Transcript cr; show: stream next displayString]
```

```
2
How are you
$A "16r0041"
$l "16r006C"
$e "16r0065"
$c "16r0063"
Fine
thanks
OrderedCollection ()
```

14

Files

In this chapter we will be looking at buffered reading and writing of files, which is all you will need for most file access. Non-buffered I/O is beyond the scope of this book. However, if your application needs to use non-buffered I/O, take a look at the subclasses of IOAccessor.

Filename

The class Filename is associated with files. Filename provides various utilities for finding out about files, and is also used to open files. There is a lot of behavior associated with Filename, both on the class side and the instance side. We'll show some of it here, but it's worth browsing the class to see what else is available.

To create an instance of Filename there are two basic approaches. You can send a message to the Filename class, or you can send a message to a string. For example:

```
fileName := Filename named: 'c:\baseDir\file.ext'.
fileName := 'c:\baseDir\file.ext' asFilename.
```

If you have a directory, and want to create a Filename from the directory and the name of a file, there are two ways to do it. If the directory is already a Filename, you construct another Filename from the directory and the name of the file. If the directory is a string, you concatenate the directory, a separator, and the name of the file to create the full name of the file, then send the asFilename to the new string. (By convention, the name of a directory does not end in the separator character.) So, you would do one of the following.

```
fileName := directoryFilename construct: 'myFile.ext'.
fileName := (directoryPathString, (String with: Filename separator), 'myFile.ext')
            asFilename.
```

To ensure portability across platforms, you might want to add a new class side method to Filename that creates a Filename from a list of directories and a file. Here's an example of what it might look like:

```
Filename class>>construct: aFileString directories: anArrayOfDirectoryStrings
    |stream|
    stream := (String new: 30) writeStream.
    anArrayOfDirectoryStrings do:
        [:each | stream nextPutAll: each; nextPut: Filename separator].
    aFileString == nil ifFalse: [stream nextPutAll: aFileString].
    ^self named: stream contents
```

Because you can open a Filename but not a String, there's a difference between a Filename and a string containing the name of a file. It can get confusing to talk about file names because it's hard to know whether we are talking about a string or an instance of Filename. A convention often adopted is to refer to strings containing names as *paths,* so you might see something like the following in code:

```
filePath := '/baseDir/subDir1/subDir2/file'.
fileName := filePath asFilename.
directoryPath := 'c:\baseDir\subDir1\subDir2'.
directoryName := directoryPath asFilename.
```

If you have an instance of Filename, you can find the various component parts by sending messages to it. Similarly, if you have a string that contains the name of a file, you can find the various components by sending messages to the class side of Filename.

```
fileName := 'c:\baseDir\subDir\myFile.ext' asFilename.
fileName directory.                         a FATFilename('c:\basedir\subdir')
fileName head.                              'c:\basedir\subdir'
fileName tail.                              'myfile.ext'

filePath := 'c:\baseDir\subDir1\fileName.ext'.
Filename components: filePath.              OrderedCollection ('c:' 'baseDir' 'subDir1'
                                               'fileName.ext')
Filename breakup: filePath.                 OrderedCollection (#('c' ':\') #('baseDir' '\')
                                               #('subDir1' '\') #('fileName' '.')
                                               #('ext' ''))
Filename splitExtension: filePath.          #('c:\baseDir\subDir1\fileName' 'ext')
Filename splitPath: filePath.               #('c:\baseDir\subDir1\' 'fileName.ext')
```

Opening Files

The stream classes associated with file access are ExternalReadStream, ExternalWriteStream, ExternalReadWriteStream, and ExternalReadAppendStream. However, it's not usual to send messages directly to these classes to create a stream, because they expect to be passed an already open file connection. Instead, the usual way to open a file and create a stream on the file is to send the appropriate message to a Filename. So, for example, if you send the readStream message to a Filename, it will open the file in the correct mode, then create an ExternalReadStream on the opened file. The following messages sent to a Filename open the underlying disk file in different modes and give back a stream of the appropriate class. Table 14-1 summarizes the information.

- The message readStream opens an existing file for reading.

- The message appendStream opens a file for appending. If the file already exists, its contents are left untouched. If the file doesn't exist, it will be created. Reading is not allowed, and writing will always append to the end.

- The message readAppendStream opens a file for reading and appending. If the file already exists, its contents will be left untouched. If the file doesn't exist, it will be created. The stream can be positioned anywhere for reading, but writing will always append to the end.

- The message newReadAppendStream opens a file for reading and appending. If the file already exists, its contents will be deleted. If the file doesn't exist, it will be created. The stream can be positioned anywhere for reading, but writing will always append to the end.

- The message writeStream opens a file for writing. If the file already exists, its contents will be deleted. If the file doesn't exist, it will be created. This stream cannot be positioned because it always writes to the end of the stream.

- The message readWriteStream opens a file for reading and writing. If the file already exists, its contents are left untouched. If the file doesn't exist, it will be created. This stream can be positioned anywhere for reading and writing.

- The message newReadWriteStream opens a file for reading and writing. If the file already exists, its contents will be deleted. If the file doesn't exist, it will be created. This stream can be positioned anywhere for reading and writing.

TABLE 14-1 Summary of File Opening Messages

Message	Delete contents	Create file	Read	Write
readStream	n	n	a	n
writeStream	y	y	n	e
appendStream	n	y	n	e
readAppendStream	n	y	a	e
newReadAppendStream	y	y	a	e
readWriteStream	n	y	a	a
newReadWriteStream	y	y	a	a

Key: y = Yes, n = No, a = Anywhere, e = at End

Closing Files

When you have finished reading a file it's important to close it. It's easy to do — you simply send the close message to the stream. However, if you rely on the garbage collector to dispose of the stream and don't explicitly close the file, the file remains open to the operating system. Because operating systems allow only a limited number of open files, you'll eventually run out of file descriptors and won't be able to open any more files. The simplest way to make sure that you close a file is to do something like the following.

```
writeStream := 'c:\temp\myfile' asFilename writeStream.
[writeStream
    nextPutAll: 'Some data';
    cr; nextPutAll: 'More data']
        valueNowOrOnUnwindDo: [writeStream close]
```

The valueNowOrOnUnwindDo: message makes sure that the code in the parameter block is always executed, whether the receiver block terminates naturally or an exception is raised. (If you wanted to execute a block of code only if the block is terminated by an exception, you would send valueOnUnwindDo:.) The unwind aspect of the message refers to the fact that the exception unwinds the stack. In the event of an exception, the exception handler is invoked before the block parameter is executed.

Sometimes, however, you can't wrap the reading or writing code with a valueNowOrOnUnwindDo: because you want to leave the file open. For example, if you create a log file, you might decide for performance reasons to leave it open rather than to open and close it every time you want to log something. In situations like this you need a different mechanism to close the file. For more information on how you might do this, see Chapter 18.

What files are open?

If you forget to close a file by sending close to the stream, you might find yourself out of files descriptors and unable to file out your changes. Fortunately, there is a way to find out what files are open, and then to close them. To find out what files are open, you can inspect the following. OpenStreams is a class variable of ExternalStream that contains all the open files (assuming they were opened using the normal mechanisms related to a subclass of ExternalStream).

```
(ExternalStream classPool at: #OpenStreams) copy inspect.
```

The reason for the copy message is that, if you close a file, the collection held by OpenStreams will shift under you, while a copy of the collection will continue to point to the files correctly. To close a file, open an inspector on the element of the collection corresponding to the file, then in the righthand pane, evaluate self close. If you want a more automatic way to close the files, you can do the following. (In Chapter 31, we show a way to put this in the VisualLauncher menu.)

```
(ExternalStream classPool at: #OpenStreams) copy do:
    [:each | each name = 'someFilePath' ifTrue: [each close]].
```

Reading From and Writing to Files

Reading text files

Many applications read files containing data that is used to set parameters and direct behavior. These files often use the pound (#) symbol to denote a comment. Here is some code that reads a line from a file, and strips off the comments. We've added the method nextUncommentedLine to the Stream class to make it available to anyone who needs it. It requires the trimWhiteSpace method that we showed in Chapter 12. There are three things to note in this example.

1. We've wrapped the opening of the file in a signal handler to trap errors associated with the file not existing or not being readable.
2. We keep reading the file until we are at the end, which we discover by sending the atEnd message.
3. We are wrapping all the read operations with valueNowOrOnUnwindDo: to make sure that the file gets closed.

```
Stream>>nextUncommentedLine
    "Read a line, remove any comment, then trim the white space"
    ^((self upTo: Character cr)
        copyUpTo: $#) trimWhiteSpace

MyClass>readFile: aFilename
    |readStream |
    OSErrorHolder errorSignal
        handle: [:ex | ex restartDo: [^self myHandleError: ex]]
        do: [readStream := aFilename readStream].
    [[readStream atEnd]
        whileFalse: [self myProcessLine: readStream nextUncommentedLine]]
        valueNowOrOnUnwindDo: [readStream close]
```

Reading and writing binary data

Besides reading and writing text data, ExternalStream provides the ability to read and write binary data. If you want to store binary data, first send the stream the binary message to tell it to expect binary rather than text data. To tell if a stream is a binary stream you can send isBinary, which returns a Boolean.

To write a 32-bit integer to the next four bytes of the stream, send nextLongPut:. To read the next four bytes as a 32-bit integer, use nextLong. To write and read the next two bytes as an integer, use nextWordPut:

and nextWord. To get the next two bytes as a signed integer, use nextSignedInteger. You can specify the number of bytes to treat as an integer when writing or reading by sending nextNumber:put: or nextNumber:. You can write out a string, where the string's length will be written in the first one or two bytes (depending on the number of bytes in the string, then read the same string, with the messages nextStringPut: and nextString. Here's an example:

```
stream := 'c:\temp\binfile' asFilename readWriteStream.
stream binary.
[stream nextStringPut: 'Hi Alec'.
stream nextLongPut: 999999.
stream nextWordPut: 33.
stream reset.
Transcript cr; show: 'String = ', stream nextString.
Transcript cr; show: 'Long = ', stream nextLong printString.
Transcript cr; show: 'Word = ', stream nextWord printString]
    valueNowOrOnUnwindDo: [stream close].
```

Positioning

Besides the normal stream positioning messages, file-based streams support some additional positioning and padding messages. Without going into much detail, they include the ability to skip to the end of the next chunk of data, assuming that the stream consists of a series of chunks of the specified size (padTo:), to skip to the end of the next chunk writing the specified character in the skipped positions (padTo:put:), to skip to the end of the current word, assuming that the stream consists of two-byte words (padToNextWord), to skip to the end of the current word and replace the skipped characters with the specified character (padToNextWordPut:), to skip the specified number of two-byte words (skipWords:), and to get and set the current position in the stream, assuming the stream consists of two-byte words (wordPosition and wordPosition:).

End of line character

You can discover what convention the file uses to indicate end-of-line characters by sending the lineEndConvention message to the stream. The line end conventions for the different platforms are:

Macintosh	LineEndCR
PC	LineEndCRLF
Unix	LineEndLF

When you are simply in the Smalltalk image, you can send the cr message to a stream or a TextCollector and it will do the correct thing (from my experience, you can substitute the lf message for cr within Smalltalk and get the same results). However, if you are sending text to another process or writing text to a file, you need to make sure that the end-of-line character is appropriate for the reader of the text, which you can do by setting the line end convention for the stream by sending it the lineEndConvention: message.

Flushing buffers to disk

The flush message makes sure that the stream contents are flushed to the disk file buffers. Some operating systems, such as Unix, manage the synchronization of disk buffers and files on disk, so flushing Smalltalk streams to disk buffers doesn't necessarily guarantee that the data will get to the disk, only that the disk file buffers contain the data. To get the data to disk, send commit, which goes to the operating system and asks it to sync the buffers with the disk, assuming the operating system provides this capability.

Utilities

Class side utilities

Some of the more useful utilities on the class side of Filename are shown below. The isCaseSensitive message tells you whether file names are case-sensitive. For example, on Windows, there is no distinction between 'fileName.ext' and 'FILENAME.EXT'. However, on Unix, these are very different files. The defaultDirectory message tells you the default directory you are in. The confusingly named currentDirectory tells you the relative directory name for constructing relative paths. The volumes message tells you what volumes are reachable. Finally, you can find all the files that match a specified pattern.

```
Filename isCaseSensitive.          false
Filename currentDirectory.         a FATFilename('.')
Filename defaultDirectory.         a FATFilename('c:\visual\image')
Filename volumes.                  #('A:\' 'B:\' 'C:\' 'D:\')
Filename filesMatching: '*.im'.    OrderedCollection ('visual.im' 'alec.im' 'math.im' 'mkim.im')
```

Instance Side Utilities

Directories

If the instance of Filename is a directory, you can find its contents or get all the files that match a certain wildcard pattern. For example:

```
dirName := Filename defaultDirectory.
dirName directoryContents.         #('VISUAL.IM' 'VISUAL.SOU' 'VISUAL.CHA' 'ST'
                                     'ALEC.IM' 'ALEC.CHA' 'SYSCHANG' 'MATH.IM'
                                     'MKIM.IM' 'MYFILE' 'MKIM.CHA' 'GOODIES')
dirName filesMatching: '*.im'      OrderedCollection ('c:\visual\image\visual.im'
                                     'c:\visual\image\alec.im' 'c:\visual\image\math.im'
                                     'c:\visual\image\mkim.im')
```

You can also create a directory by sending the makeDirectory message. Of course, this might fail if there is already a file with that name or the parent directory is unwritable. You can check for these conditions in advance, or wrap the directory creation code with a signal handler.

Contents of files

You can read the contents of a file into a string by sending contentsOfEntireFile (which closes the file after reading it). You can even bring up an editor on a file by sending edit.

Information about files

You can find the various access and modification dates associated with a file by sending the dates message. You can check to see if a file exists by sending either exists, or definitelyExists, which handles inacessible network files differently. The size of the file in bytes can be found by sending fileSize. You can determine if a file is readable or writable by sending isReadable and isWritable (for a directory to be writable, it must be possible to create and rename files in it). To find if the file is a true writable file (i.e., not a directory), send canBeWritten. If you want to know if a file is a directory, send isDirectory. You can tell if the file has an absolute or relative path by sending isAbsolute or isRelative. Let's look at some examples of these on a Windows machine.

```
dirName := 'c:\baseDir' asFilename.
fileName := dirName construct: 'myfile'.
fileName exists.                    true
dirName definitelyExists.           true
fileName fileSize.                  20
dirName fileSize.                   0
fileName isReadable.                true
dirName isWritable.                 true
fileName canBeWritten.              true
dirName canBeWritten.               false
fileName isDirectory.               false
dirName isDirectory.                true
fileName isAbsolute.                true
dirName isRelative.                 false
```

Manipulating files

Among other utilities, you can delete a file (delete), you can copy a file to another file (copyTo:), and you can rename a file by moving it (moveTo:, which copies the file then deletes the original). If your platform supports it and it is a meaningful operation — for example, you are not trying to rename across disks — you can rename a file using the much more efficient renameTo: message.

Skills and Techniques

15

Printing Objects

If you want to print information about an object, you send it the message printString and get back a string containing some information about the object. For example, 3 printString returns '3'. OrderedCollection new printString returns 'OrderedCollection ()', which shows that you have an empty collection.

Why is this useful? The printString message is used to display information for debugging. In particular, it is sent by inspectors; whenever you open an inspector on an object, the inspector sends the printString message to the object and displays the result.

The default printString is implemented by Object. It first creates a stream, then does self printOn: stream. Object also implements a default printOn: method that writes to the stream a string containing the class name preceded by 'a' or 'an'. If you create a new object, by default it will inherit printOn: from Object. Try the following. Define a new class MyClass and then evaluate MyClass new printString.

If you want to change what printString returns, it's a simple matter of implementing printOn: (in the printing protocol). Take a look at the printOn: method for Array, Association, and ValueHolder.

Here's an example of a very general printOn:. It makes heavy use of meta-programming, which involves writing code that manipulates the information about such things as classes and instance variables. Not for the faint of heart, but it can be a lot of fun to look around classes such as Behavior and ClassDescription. (For more on meta-programming, see Chapter 29.)

```
printOn: aStream
    super printOn: aStream.
    self class allInstVarNames
        do:
            [:each | | index |
            index := self class instVarIndexFor: each.
            aStream
```

```
crtab;
nextPutAll: each;
nextPut: $:;
space;
print: (self instVarAt: index)]
```

I use this scheme in a slightly modified way. I write this method as Object>>printAllOn:, replacing the super printOn: aStream line with the code from Object>>printOn:. Then, in my new classes I write the printOn: method to simply invoke printAllOn:. Sometimes this doesn't give me the formatting I want so I'll write a specific printOn:, but often this will suffice.

```
MyClass>>printOn: aStream
    super printAllOn: aStream
```

Display Strings

There is another message, displayString, which returns a value suitable for displaying. Where printString provides a representation of the object that is useful for debugging, displayString provides a representation that can be presented to the user. The default displayString, implemented by Object, just does ^self printString but is overridden, for example, by CharacterArray (the superclass of String) so that strings do not have surrounding quotes. For example:

```
Transcript cr; show: 'Hello' printString.      'Hello'
Transcript cr; show: 'Hello' displayString.    Hello
```

The displayString message is used when displaying objects in a List box. A List box has a SequenceView as its view, or widget. Its model is a SelectionInList containing the collection of objects. The widget displays what the objects return when sent displayString, although you can change this. To have a message different from displayString sent to the objects, send displayStringSelector: aSymbol to the List box widget (the SequenceView), passing as the parameter the message selector you want sent.

Printing Formatted Numbers, Dates, and Times

Sending the printString message to a number returns the obvious representation of the number as a string. Sent to dates and times it returns a good representation, but in a predefined format. For example:

```
234 printString.                '234'
Date today printString.         '28 September 1995'
Time now printString.           '9:59:04 am'
Timestamp now printString.      '09/28/1995 09:59:29.000'
```

There are times when you want more. For example, when printing a number you might want commas to separate the thousands, parentheses to show a negative number, or zero-fill to a specified length. When specifying a date or a time you might have international formatting concerns. The Date class has an additional method, called printFormat:, that allows some, but not enough, flexibility. In the example below, we ask to print the month number, the day number and the two-digit year number, with the slash character as separator.

```
(Date newDay: 34 year: 1996) printFormat: #(2 1 3 $/ 1 2)      '2/3/96'
```

The class PrintConverter lets you do some reasonably sophisticated formatting. You create a PrintConverter of the right type, specifying the format string you want, then you can ask the instance to format your numbers or dates when needed. Note that the PrintConverter returns an instance of Text so you'll need to send this the string message to get a string. Let's look at some examples of formatting numbers, dates, and times. The string returned will be shown on the following lines.

```
pc := PrintConverter for: #number withFormatString: '00000'.
(pc formatStringFor: 234) string.
'00234'

pc := PrintConverter for: #date withFormatString: 'dddd, mmmm d, yyyy'.
(pc formatStringFor: Date today) string.
'Thursday, September 28, 1995'

pc := PrintConverter for: #timestamp withFormatString: 'mmm d, hh:mm:ss.ffff'.
(pc formatStringFor: Timestamp now) string.
'Sep 28, 09:55:48.0000'
```

The PrintConverter actually uses the classes NumberPrintPolicy and TimestampPrintPolicy to do the formatting. To understand all the formatting options, look at the class comments for these classes. You can also use these classes directly if you wish, and here are some examples of this. Again, the policy returns an instance of Text, which we convert to a string.

```
(NumberPrintPolicy print: 1234 using: '#,###') string.               '1,234'
(NumberPrintPolicy print: -1234 using: '#,###;(#,###)') string.      '(1,234)'
(TimestampPrintPolicy print: Date today using: 'yymmdd') string.     '950928'
(TimestampPrintPolicy print: Time now using: 'mm:ss.ff') string.     '01:12.00'
```

There are more ways of using these classes than I've shown here. For example, you can write the formatted data to a stream, and you can create instances of the policy classes. The PrintConverter class also gives you an easier but less powerful interface for numbers. You can specify digit positions using #, so, for example, the following gives a string with two leading spaces.

```
PrintConverter print: 234 formattedBy: '#####.###'.     '  234.000'
```

VisualWorks 2.5

VisualWorks 2.5 provides some extra formatting capabilities. In particular, dates and times now respond to the new messages longPrintString
and shortPrintString. For example:

Date today printString.   'December 2, 1995'
Date today longPrintString.   'December 2, 1995'
Date today shortPrintString.   '12/2/95'

You can also create a string from a format string and arguments
using a message from the expandMacros family in the class
CharacterArray. For information on the parameter substitution, look at
the class comments for StringParameterSubstitution. Here's an example,
with the output following the example message. Note that the
expandMacrosWithArguments: message returns an instance of Text, which
we convert to a string.

('Hello <2s>.<n>There are <1p> <3?apples:oranges> in the basket'
    expandMacrosWithArguments: #(4 'Alec' true)) asString.

'Hello Alec.
There are 4 apples in the basket'

printf-scanf

In the Smalltalk archives there is a fileIn called printf-scanf which gives
you the capability of doing formatted printing as if you were using C's
printf function. Its location in the MANCHESTER archive is
usenet/st80-r4.X/printf-scanf. For more information on retrieving code
from the Smalltalk archives, see Chapter 35.

16

Processes

Smalltalk allows you to create separate processes so that your application can do several things in parallel. For example, you might have a process for handling communication with sockets, another process for handling communication with an external device, and separate processes for each request that comes over a socket. Note, however, that processes are *not* operating system processes — they are internal to the Smalltalk image. There is a process scheduler that schedules the Smalltalk processes, allocating time based on their priority and when they last ran. The scheduler is stored in the global variable Processor, and is the single instance of the class ProcessorScheduler. The most common way to fork a new process is to send a block of code the fork message. For example:

```
[Transcript cr; show: 'Hello World'] fork.
```

When this process runs, it prints 'Hello World' to the Transcript. Once the righthand bracket of the block is reached, the process terminates. Let's took at the interactions of two processes.

```
[10 timesRepeat: [Transcript show: '1']] fork.
[10 timesRepeat: [Transcript show: '2']] fork.
```

```
11111111112222222222
```

You will see ten 1s printed on the Transcript, then ten 2s. This is because processes are *partially preemptive*. A running process will not be interrupted by another process of equal or lesser priority. A process will keep running until it does a time-consuming operation, such as waiting on a socket read or on an instance of Delay, or the process explicitly gives up control, or a higher priority process is ready to run. If we add a delay to both loops we see that the numbers alternate.

```
[10 timesRepeat: [Transcript show: '1'. (Delay forMilliseconds: 1) wait]] fork.
[10 timesRepeat: [Transcript show: '2'. (Delay forMilliseconds: 1) wait]] fork.
```

```
12121212121212121212
```

Alternatively, we can give up control by sending a yield message to Processor. The scheduler will then figure out the next process to run.

```
[10 timesRepeat: [Transcript show: '1'. Processor yield]] fork.
[10 timesRepeat: [Transcript show: '2'. Processor yield]] fork.
```

```
12121212121212121212
```

Priority

When the process scheduler is looking for the next process to run, it looks first at the priority of the processes that are waiting to run. When you create a new process using fork, it inherits the priority of the process that forked it. However, you can specify the priority of the processes you create by sending the forkAt: message to the BlockClosure, with the priority as the parameter.

For example, if your application communicates with other applications via sockets, you might have one process sitting in an input loop, another process sitting in an output loop, and other processes doing the application work. You might run the application processes at one priority, the input process at a higher priority, and the output process at a still higher priority.

Let's look at how a higher priority process can preempt a lower priority process. We'll use absolute numbers rather than names for our priorities, to make the examples clearer. VisualWorks supports priorities from 1 to 100, where the default priority is 50.

In the first example, we fork a process with priority 50. Because the user interface is also running at priority 50, the forked process is not interrupted and therefore completes. The user interface then forks the second process, which also runs to completion. (The delay exists to make sure that the first process gets a chance to run. If we didn't have the delay, the user interface process would keep running and would fork the second process. At that point it would have nothing to do so the scheduler would look for another process to run, and would run the second process because it has higher priority.)

```
[10 timesRepeat: [Transcript show: '1']] forkAt: 50.
(Delay forMilliseconds: 1) wait.
[10 timesRepeat: [Transcript show: '2']] forkAt: 51.
```

```
11111111112222222222
```

In the second example, the first process is forked with a priority of 49, which is lower than the priority of the user interface process. The forked process just gets started and is then interrupted by the user interface process, which forks the second process. The second process is running at a higher priority than the first process, so it runs to completion. Then the first process gets the scheduler and completes.

```
[10 timesRepeat: [Transcript show: '1']] forkAt: 49.
(Delay forMilliseconds: 1) wait.
[10 timesRepeat: [Transcript show: '2']] forkAt: 51.
```

1122222222222111111111

In the third example, the first process gives up control after printing the first number. The user interface then forks the second process, which gets to run because it has a higher priority. Even though the second process gives up control after printing its first number, it is immediately run again because it is the highest priority process with something to do.

```
[10 timesRepeat: [Transcript show: '1'. Processor yield]] forkAt: 50.
(Delay forMilliseconds: 1) wait.
[10 timesRepeat: [Transcript show: '2'. Processor yield]] forkAt: 51.
```

12222222222111111111

Smalltalk processes are *partially preemptive*. They can be interrupted by higher priority processes, but will *not* be interrupted by lower or equal priority processes. This is different for a multitasking system such as Unix, which gives timeslices to the different processes, interrupting them when they have consumed their timeslice. Because a Smalltalk process will not be interrupted by another process of equal or lower priority, it is easy to get into loops that you can't break out of. We'll look more at this in the section titled *Working with processes* later in this chapter.

We used numbers in these examples, but a much better policy is to use the names defined in the priority names protocol of ProcessorScheduler, sending these messages to Processor. For example, at the time of writing, VisualWorks defines the following priorities.

systemRockBottomPriority	1
systemBackgroundPriority	10
userBackgroundPriority	30
userSchedulingPriority	50
userInterruptPriority	70
lowIOPriority	90
highIOPriority	98
timingPriority	100

Using names allows the values to be changed in future releases of the image, without affecting your application. In fact, I'd go further and define my own names, then fork the processes using my names.

MyGlobals class>>appProcessPriority
  ^Processor userSchedulingPriority

[some code] forkAt: MyGlobals appProcessPriority

Unless you have good reason, application process priorities should be kept in the range from userBackgroundPriority to userInterruptPriority.

Communicating Between Processes

In a production application, you will often find two types of process. One type of process is started, runs to completion, then automatically terminates. The other type of process stays in a loop waiting for an object to appear, then sends a message to the object. This requires an ability to communicate between processes, and Smalltalk provides such a mechanism, the SharedQueue.

The SharedQueue

To set up communication between processes, you create an instance of SharedQueue and tell both processes about it. One process will put objects on the shared queue using nextPut:, and the other process will send next to get an object from the queue. When a process sends the next message, it blocks until there is something on the queue. (It blocks by waiting on a semaphore, which is set when an object is put on the SharedQueue. We'll talk more about semaphores in Chapter 17.) Figure 16-1 illustrates two processes communicating via a SharedQueue.

In the following example, the second process prints a number, then puts it on a shared queue, while the first process reads the queue, then prints the number. If you try this example, the Transcript will show: W1 R1 W2 R2 W3 R3 W4 R4 W5 R5.

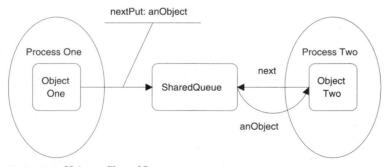

Figure 16-1. Using a SharedQueue.

```
sharedQueue := SharedQueue new.
readProcess := [[Transcript show: ' R', sharedQueue next printString] repeat] fork.
[1 to: 5 do: [:index |
    Transcript show: ' W', index printString.
    sharedQueue nextPut: index.
    Processor yield]] fork.
(Delay forSeconds: 5) wait.
readProcess terminate.
```

Notice that the read process will stay in a loop forever unless we terminate it. This we do with the terminate message (there is more on terminating processes in the next section). If you try this example again after removing the Processor yield in the second process, you will see: W1 W2 W3 W4 W5 R1 R2 R3 R4 R5. This is because Smalltalk is only partially preemptive, and the first process doesn't get a chance to run until the second process is completed. I generally add Processor yield after putting an object on the SharedQueue, which ensures that the process waiting on the queue has a chance to run. For example:

```
sharedQueue nextPut: anObject.
Processor yield.
```

If the reading process doesn't want to block it can send isEmpty to find out if there is anything on the SharedQueue, or peek to get the next object from the SharedQueue without removing it.

The PrioritySharedQueue

SharedQueues are FIFO queues — objects are read from the queue in the order they were put on it. However, sometimes a simple FIFO queue is not sufficient because you might need a prioritization scheme. SharedQueues don't provide a mechanism for prioritizing objects on the queue, but you can subclass off SharedQueue to create a PrioritySharedQueue. Here is a simple example of a PrioritySharedQueue, with an instance variable, defaultPriority. You can find the code for this example in the file psq.st.

```
PrioritySharedQueue>>defaultPriority: aPriority
    defaultPriority := aPriority

PrioritySharedQueue>>defaultPriority
    ^defaultPriority isNil
        ifTrue: [defaultPriority := 0]
        ifFalse: [defaultPriority]
```

A simple implementation puts all objects on the shared queue in an Association of the priority and the object. You will need to override next, peek, and nextPut: to handle the Association. Additionally, nextPut: will simply invoke nextPut:priority: as follows.

```
PrioritySharedQueue>>nextPut: anObject
    ^self nextPut: anObject priority: self defaultPriority
```

The heart of the PrioritySharedQueue is in the nextPut:priority: method, which places objects in the queue according to their priority first, and their chronology second. Higher numbers indicate higher priority.

```
PrioritySharedQueue>>nextPut: anObject priority: aPriority
    [accessProtect critical:
        [| foundElement |
        foundElement := contents
                reverseDetect: [:element | aPriority <= element key]
                ifNone: [nil].
        foundElement isNil
            ifTrue: [contents addFirst: (aPriority -> anObject)]
            ifFalse: [contents add: (aPriority -> anObject) after: foundElement]]
    ] valueUninterruptably.
    readSynch signal.
    ^anObject
```

A general SharedQueue reading mechanism

A general mechanism for taking objects off a SharedQueue and processing the objects is to sit in a loop like the following. This is very generic code and can easily be inherited. It has two specific virtues. First, it makes no assumptions about where the object is coming from and how it will be processed, so myProcessObject: and myGetObject can be overridden by subclasses to do things differently. Second, it allows you to put breakpoints in these two methods when you are debugging. Because myDoLoop is in a repeat loop, you can't add a breakpoint to this method while it is executing and have the breakpoint take effect.

```
MyClass>>myDoLoop
    [self myProcessObject: self myGetObject.
    Processor yield] repeat

MyClass>>myGetObject
    ^self mySharedQueue next.
```

We can extend this further for situations in which we process the object in its own forked process. There are operations in which it might be necessary to cancel the processing, such as time-consuming operations or operations wherein a needed resource does not become available. If we need to cancel the processing, we can set an instance variable in the object (protected by a mutual exclusion semaphore). At appropriate times during its processing, the object can look to see if it has been cancelled and take the appropriate action. In the code below, we store the object; then, after the the object has executed the processYourself method, we remove the object from our collection. The valueNowOrOnUnwindDo: message ensures that the object is removed whether the processYourself method completes or is interrupted by a raised exception.

```
MyClass>>myProcessObject: anObject
    self myAdd: anObject.
    [[anObject processYourself]
        valueNowOrOnUnwindDo:
            [self myRemove: anObject]] fork
```

Terminating Processes

Processes terminate when they reach the right square bracket of the block that was forked. However, some processes are set up to stay in a loop, never reaching the right square bracket. We therefore need another way to terminate processes, which we get by sending the terminate message to the process. For example:

```
process := [[Transcript cr; show: 'Hi there'. (Delay forSeconds: 1) wait] repeat] fork.
(Delay forSeconds: 5) wait.
process terminate.
Transcript cr; show: 'All Done'.
```

You can send terminate to an already terminated process with no ill effects, so terminate is a benign message. If you are concerned about terminating a process that is in the middle of doing something, you might want a way to shut down the process gracefully, allowing it to complete what it is working on. One option is to allow the process to terminate itself by sending Processor terminateActive or Processor activeProcess terminate. If the process reads from a SharedQueue, you can put a special termination object on the SharedQueue. If the SharedQueue reader does something like sharedQueue next processYourself, this special object would have the following code.

```
TerminationObject>>processYourself
    Processor terminateActive
```

Making Shared Data Threadsafe

Objects running in different processes often require access to shared data. To make sure that only one process is reading or modifying the data, you need a mechanism to *serialize* access to the data. Smalltalk provides the mutual exclusion semaphore for just this situation. To create a mutual exclusion semaphore, you send the forMutualExclusion message to Semaphore. To serialize access to shared data, you ask the semaphore to run the access code. For example:

```
mutexSemaphore := Semaphore forMutualExclusion.
mutexSemaphore cricital: [code to access shared data]
```

We talk more about mutual exclusion semaphores in Chapter 17.

Controlling the Running of the Process

In most applications you won't suspend and resume processes, but the ability is there should you need it. When you want to suspend a process, send it the suspend message. To resume the process, send it the resume message. You can start a process in suspended state by sending newProcess to a BlockClosure. In fact, fork is implemented by sending newProcess followed by resume. Here's an example of creating a process that does not immediately run:

```
process := [Transcript cr; show: 'Done'] newProcess.
(Delay forSeconds: 3) wait.
process resume
```

If you decide to control the running of processes using suspend and resume, be very careful about when you suspend the process. It might be in the middle of doing something that should be completed before the process is suspended. One option is to have the process suspend itself when it is safe to do so. If you try the following code, you'll see that the process prints out the time five times, suspends itself, then is resumed five seconds later.

```
process :=
    [1 to: 10 do: [:index |
        Transcript cr; show: Time now printString.
        index = 5 ifTrue: [Processor activeProcess suspend]]] fork.
(Delay forSeconds: 5) wait.
process resume.
```

Interrupting Processes

Smalltalk allows you to interrupt a process to have it do something else. You might never need to do this, but we'll mention the mechanism briefly. To interrupt another process and have it run some code, send interruptWith: aBlockOfCode to the process. The process saves its context, executes the passed-in block, restores its context, then resumes its business.

There is a way to prevent interruptions, in case the process is doing something it really doesn't want interrupted. You can protect the uninterruptable code by putting it in a block and sending the block the message valueUninterruptably. SharedQueues make use of this capability. All access to a SharedQueue is protected by a mutual exclusion semaphore. This access is wrapped in another block, which is executed by sending valueUninterruptably. For example, SharedQueue>>size is implemented as ^[accessProtect critical: [contents size]] valueUninterruptably. Will you ever use the interrupt capability? Probably not, but it's worth knowing about.

Working with Processes

When you first work with processes, it's easy to write processes that stay in a tight loop so that you can't do anything. You can't even interrupt them with Ctrl-C if they are running at userSchedulingPriority or above — that is, at or above the priority of the user interface process. For this reason, it's always a good idea to file out (or save in some way) your changes before trying out new process code. It's also a good idea to run processes at a priority lower than userSchedulingPriority.

If you do get locked up, you can kill the virtual machine process or you can use the Emergency Evaluator. Unless you have remapped the interrupt key, pressing Shift-Ctrl-C will bring up the Emergency Evaluator. From here you can type ObjectMemory quit followed by pressing the Escape key, which will cause Smalltalk to quit.

Another thing that can happen when working with forked processes is that you can lose them. Suppose you have a process running in a loop, possibly even yielding control. If you don't have a way to reference the process you can never terminate it. Here are some mechanisms for tracking processes.

Tracking processes with a global variable

One way to track your processes is to keep each process in a global variable. Let's say you choose to keep track of global variables in class MyGlobals. If you have a class variable called Processes that you initialize to an OrderedCollection (using class initialization or lazy initialization), you can have two methods:

```
MyGlobals class>>addProcess: aProcess
    ^Processes add: aProcess

MyGlobals class>>removeProcess: aProcess
    ^Processes remove: aProcess ifAbsent: [nil]
```

At any time you can inspect MyGlobals to see a collection of all the processes you have forked. You can terminate them individually or create a method to terminate all of them. To better know what process you are looking at, you could add an Association of the process and a name.

```
MyGlobals class>>addProcess: aProcess name: aName
    ^Processes add: aProcess -> aName

MyGlobals class>>removeProcess: aProcess
    ^Processes removeAllSuchThat: [:each | each key == aProcess]
```

This scheme assumes that the forked processes you add can also be removed. Many processes are simply short-lived process that terminate naturally, and there will be no easy way to remove them from the collection (unless they remove themselves before expiring). This scheme works best with long-lived processes that the application can both start and terminate.

Tracking processes by subclassing

Another approach is to create your own process class, say MyProcess, as a subclass of Process (you can find the code in the file process.st). We'll give it an instance variable to store the process name.

```
Process subclass: #MyProcess
    instanceVariableNames: 'processName '
    classVariableNames: ''
    poolDictionaries: ''
    category: 'MyStuff'
```

Add processName and processName: accessors, and write a printOn: method.

```
MyProcess>>printOn: aStream
    super printOn: aStream.
    aStream nextPutAll: ' ('.
    aStream nextPutAll: self processName.
    aStream nextPut: $)
```

Without going into all the details, this involves writing three new methods for BlockClosure. The first method is newProcessWithName:, which creates an instance of MyProcess rather than Process, and sets the process name. The other two methods are forkWithName: and forkAt:withName:, which send newProcessWithName: rather than newProcess. You will then need to add an allInstancesAndSubInstances method to Behavior (we show this method in Chapter 29). Once you have this, the final change is to modify Process>>anyProcessesAbove: to send allInstancesAndSubInstances rather than allInstances. You can now fork all your processes by doing:

```
[some code] forkWithName: 'some name'.
```

If you then inspect MyProcess allInstances, you can take a look at all your processes that are running (or which have terminated but have not been garbage collected). To terminate a lost process, you can open an inspector on the appropriate element of the array then evaluate self terminate in the inspector window.

To handle the problem of a process locking up the image, you can write a class side method to terminate all instances of MyProcess. From the Emergency Evaluator (Shift-Ctrl-C), you can now type MyProcess terminateAll followed by Esc, and you should get back your cursor.

```
MyProcess class>>terminateAll
    self allInstances do:
        [:each |
            Transcript cr; show: each printString.
            each terminate]
```

It might be easier to modify Process rather than subclass off it. If you choose this approach, you would add a processName instance variable. You will still need to add fork-type methods to BlockClosure to set the process name before sending resume to the process. Finally, instead of MyProcess class>>terminateAll, you might write something like the following.

```
Process class>>terminateNamed
    self allInstances do:
        [:each | each processName notNil ifTrue:
            [Transcript cr; show: each printString.
            each terminate]]
```

17

Coordinating and Sequencing Events

When you program an application in which many things happen at the same time in different threads or processes, you have to concern yourself with access to shared resources. You have to program some amount of event coordination.

Regular Semaphores

Semaphores allow you to wait for a resource to become available or to change state before you continue processing. One example might be an object that needs to have a certain event happen, such as the opening of a door or the pressing of a button. One solution would be to wait on a semaphore that gets signaled by a process monitoring the door or the button. Another example might be a tape drive that is shared among several processes that want to mount and dismount tapes. We could use a semaphore to coordinate and serialize the events.

To use a semaphore, you first create an instance of Semaphore by sending it the new message. A process waits on the semaphore by sending it the wait message. This suspends the process until another process signals the semaphore by sending it the signal message. The semaphore will then resume the suspended process that is waiting on it. Figure 17-1 illustrates this. Here's a simple example of waiting on a Semaphore:

```
semaphore := Semaphore new.

[Transcript cr; show: 'About to wait'.
semaphore wait.
Transcript cr; show: 'Semaphore signaled'] fork.

[(Delay forSeconds: 5) wait.
semaphore signal] fork.
```

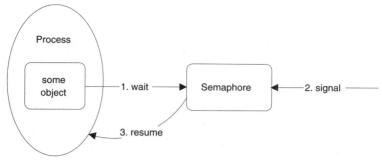

Figure 17-1. The semaphore mechanism.

In our tape example, the tape drive object has a semaphore. When a tape wants to be mounted in a drive, the tape waits on the drive's semaphore. When the drive becomes available it signals its semaphore, which allows the tape to continue mounting itself. Semaphores have the additional virtue of queuing wait requests in the order they were received, so that we could have many tapes waiting for the drive. As the drive becomes available and signals its semaphore, the first tape in the queue will mount itself, while the other tape processes remain suspended until the drive becomes available and it is their turn.

```
Tape>>mountYourselfOn: aDrive
    self doSomeMountStuff.
    aDrive reserve.
    self doMoreMountStuff

Tape>>dismountYourselfFrom: aDrive
    self doSomeDismountStuff.
    aDrive release.
    self doSomeMoreDismountStuff

Drive>>reserve
    semaphore wait

Drive>>release
    semaphore signal
```

Besides queueing up wait requests by sending multiple wait messages to a semaphore, you can also prime a semaphore by sending multiple signal messages. This could be useful if you are using a semaphore to control access to a resource that allows several accesses at once. By sending several signal messages to the semaphore when it is created, you allow the first few objects access to the resource. As they release the resource they signal the semaphore, allowing the next object to gain access.

Mutual Exclusion Semaphores

Sometimes you want to serialize access to shared data. A good example is tracking the state of a resource that is being modified by different processes. The state data needs to be read and written, but you need to make sure you don't have different processes trying to access it at the same time. (In fact, because Smalltalk is only partially preemptive, this will probably not be a problem, but it's better to be defensive in our programming.) Another example is reserving a resource, where you want to first check the state of the resource and then reserve it if it is available. You want the checking and reserving to be an atomic operation, without the possibility of interruption.

We use a special type of semaphore called a mutual exclusion semaphore, which runs a block of code when sent the critical: message. A mutual exclusion semaphore will only run one block of code at a time. This is illustrated in Fig. 17-2. As long as all our data access routines are run by the mutual exclusion semaphore, we are guaranteed that the data will be only be accessed by one routine at a time. Here's an example of how we might use a mutual exclusion semaphore to protect a shared resource:

```
MyClass class>>initialize
    AccessProtect := Semaphore forMutualExclusion.

MyClass>>stateData
    ^AccessProtect critical: [code to get the value]

MyClass>>stateData: aValue
    AccessProtect critical: [code to set the value]
```

We ask the mutual exclusion semaphore to run the code critically. The semaphore will run only one block of code at a time, queuing up the other blocks in the order it was asked to run them.

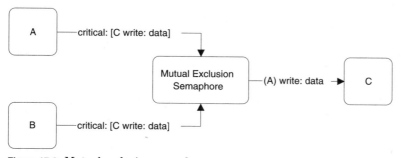

Figure 17-2. Mutual exclusion semaphore.

A mutual exclusion semaphore works by immediately signaling itself when it is created. This allows the first block of code to run without waiting (it tries to wait, but because the semaphore has already been signalled, no waiting is needed). Once the block has been executed in the critical: method, the method signals the semaphore again. If there is another block of code waiting, it will now run. If there is no code waiting to be run, the semaphore is primed so that the next block to come along will run without waiting. (The code block is run by sending valueNowOrOnUnwindDo: [self signal] to the BlockClosure. This causes the code block to be run, and then self signal to be executed no matter whether the block runs to completion, returns, or is interrupted by an exception.)

Here's an example of a mutual exclusion semaphore that you can run in a Workspace. It protects access to the Transcript, which in fact is a reasonable thing to do because the Transcript is not threadsafe.

```
accessProtect := Semaphore forMutualExclusion.

[accessProtect critical:
    [Transcript cr; show: 'Process1 ', Time now printString.
    (Delay forSeconds: 5) wait]] fork.

[accessProtect critical:
    [Transcript cr; show: 'Process2 ', Time now printString]] fork.
```

An important point to note is that, to protect access to shared data, the processes must cooperate. If one process asks a mutual exclusion semaphore to control its access to the data, but another process goes directly to the data, that data is no longer threadsafe. Ideally, your shared data will only be accessible through access routines, which all cooperate and use a mutual exclusion semaphore.

RecursionLock

Sometimes we might find ourselves in a situation in which a mutual exclusion semaphore is executing code in a critical block, and the code needs access to another resource that is protected by the same semaphore.

If we use a mutual exclusion semaphore our code will hang, because the semaphore is already running code. To solve the problem we use a RecursionLock rather than a mutual exclusion semaphore. A RecursionLock knows which process is running, and allows additional access by that process to resources it is protecting.

Summary

To summarize, use a regular semaphore (Semaphore new) to coordinate events such as waiting for a button to be pressed. Use a mutual exclusion semaphore (Semaphore forMutualExclusion) to serialize access to resources such as data stores. Use a RecursionLock (RecursionLock new) instead of a mutual exclusion semaphore when the code that accesses the resource might need to access another resource protected by the same semaphore.

18

Cleaning Up at Termination

Having a garbage collector to take care of memory management for you is wonderful. Not having to worry about allocating and freeing memory makes life a lot easier and code a lot more bug-free. However, there are some things that the garbage collector does not take care of, and which you need to explicitly handle in the code.

In particular, external resources will stay open even if the objects that reference them are garbage collected. For example, if you open a file or a socket, it will stay open until you close it (or your Smalltalk image exits). Internally, if you have a Smalltalk process that stays in an infinite loop waiting for input to process, that process will never terminate even if you no longer reference the process in your code.

Often you will open files, read or write them, then close them. Similarly, often you will fork Smalltalk processes that do some work, then simply terminate. However, on other occasions you might open a file that you plan on keeping open for a while, such as a log file. You might have a Smalltalk process that sits in an infinite loop waiting for input from a socket or waiting for input from another Smalltalk process.

Exiting your image will close external files and sockets and terminate Smalltalk processes. However, when you are developing and debugging an application, bugs in your code will often raise an exception, which you try to debug, then eventually terminate. This leaves processes running and files open. This chapter talks a little about how you might close files and terminate processes when you terminate the application in situations like this. For more information, see the article, "Cleaning up after yourself," by Alec Sharp and Dave Farmer, in the March-April, 1995 issue of *The Smalltalk Report*.

The CleanUp Object

We define a new class called CleanUp, which tracks, for example, the sockets, files, and Smalltalk processes that are permanently open. We don't add files that are opened, read, and then closed in a valueNowOrOnUnwindDo: block. Here's the definition of CleanUp, followed by the class initialization and instance creation code. This code can also be found in the file cleanup.st.

```
Object subclass: #CleanUp
    instanceVariableNames: 'processes files sockets '
    classVariableNames: 'AccessProtect '
    poolDictionaries: ''
    category: 'CleanUp'

CleanUp class>>initialize
    "self initialize"
    AccessProtect := Semaphore forMutualExclusion

CleanUp class>>new
    ^super new initialize
```

We create the mutual exclusion semaphore because our application might be running in many forked processes. To make sure that only one process is trying to add to the CleanUp object at a time, we use the semaphore to protect access to the various collections. On the instance side, we initialize the variables that hold on to the files, sockets, and processes, and we provide methods to add files, processes, and sockets to the CleanUp object. We also need methods to remove them from the object should the application code close them itself. We'll just show the code that adds files, because the code for processes and sockets is very similar.

```
CleanUp>>initialize
    processes := OrderedCollection new.
    files := OrderedCollection new.
    sockets := OrderedCollection new

CleanUp>>addFile: aFile
    ^AccessProtect critical: [files add: aFile]

CleanUp>>removeFile: aFile
    ^AccessProtect critical: [files remove: aFile]
```

When the application terminates, we want to close all the open files and sockets, and terminate all the processes. We nil the instance variables at the end so the garbage collector can recover the objects that were contained in the collections (we assume that a new CleanUp object will be created next time the application is run).

```
CleanUp>>doCleanUp
    AccessProtect
        critical:
```

```
[processes do: [:each | each terminate].
files do: [:each | each close].
sockets do: [:each | each close].
processes := files := sockets := nil]
```

Using the CleanUp Object

Now that we have a CleanUp class defined, how do we use it in our application? The first decision is where to store it so that it is globally accessible. There's a lot more information on that topic in Chapter 7. For now, we'll just assume that it's stored in the class MyGlobals and is accessible through the cleanUp accessor. The next section of code shows (in a non-robust way) how we might add files, sockets, and processes to the CleanUp object in our code.

```
MyClass>>myStartInputOutput
    MyGlobals cleanUp addSocket: self myCreateInputSocket.
    MyGlobals cleanUp addSocket: self myCreateOutputSocket.
    MyGlobals cleanUp addProcess: [self myDoInputLoop] fork.
    MyGlobals cleanUp addProcess: [self myDoOutputLoop] fork.

MyClass>>myOpenLogFile
    logFile := self logFileName writeStream.
    MyGlobals cleanUp addFile: logFile
```

Finally, we need code to invoke the docleanUp message to the CleanUp object so that all files and sockets are closed and all processes are terminated. We do this by wrapping our main application start code in a valueNowOrOnUnwindDo: block. This makes sure that clean up is done whether the application terminated normally, we interrupted the application with Ctrl-C, or we got an exception.

```
MyApplication>> start
    [self myStartInputOutput.
    [self myProcessObject: self myGetObject] repeat]
        valueNowOrOnUnwindDo: [MyGlobals cleanUp doCleanUp]
```

Other Approaches

There are, of course, other approaches to the problem of making sure that you close and terminate everything that is open and running. The technique described in this chapter is a fairly easy and expedient technique. As you move toward a production system, a better and more object-oriented approach is to spread the responsibility to each subsystem or component. Each subsystem tracks what it has open or running. When the main application is shut down, it sends a shutDown message to each subsystem. The subsystem then shuts itself down gracefully, closing files, terminating processes, and doing any other appropriate operations.

19

The Dependency
Mechanism

Perhaps the most magical thing about Smalltalk is the way it can automatically inform objects when other objects change their state. It does this by allowing one object to register an interest in getting change messages — by registering as a dependent of another object. The terminology is that the object registering an interest, in being informed of changes, is called the *dependent*. The object that it is dependent on is called the *parent*.

Being able to use the dependency mechanism allows you to write code where an object registers as a dependent then forgets about the parent completely. When the parent changes, the object will be informed and can do whatever it needs to do, but until that time it can forget the parent even exists. From the perspective of the parent, there is no need to programatically keep track of all the objects it needs to inform of changes. Instead, all you have to do is have the parent tell itself that it has changed, and all the dependents will be automatically notified. The dependency mechanism allows you to think of an application as a group of objects with wiring between them. A major part of the application now boils down to determining the wiring between the objects.

How is this useful? There are many applications in which one object is interested in the state of another object, but the second object really doesn't care about the first object. It doesn't care whether there are many objects interested in it, or no objects interested in it. One example would be a stock object that holds onto its current trading price. There might be many applications interested in the price of the stock as it changes, but the stock really doesn't care about those applications. Another example would be a factory floor. There might be many monitors interested in the temperature and quantity of a liquid in a container, but the container has no interest in the monitors. However, in the examples, the stock and the container have to let other objects know about changes in their state.

There are two mechanisms for doing this. The interested objects could *poll* the stock and container objects, asking for their state every few seconds. However, this has disadvantages. It takes computer resources to constantly ask for information, and this can add up if there are lots of objects polling. It also means that objects aren't informed of changes in real time. If an object polls every five seconds, it could be five seconds before it discovers a state change, which could be disastrous on a factory floor. If it polls every hundredth of a second, huge amounts of computing bandwidth will be used if you have many objects polling.

The other approach is to use the dependency mechanism. The interested objects register an interest in some aspect of the stock or container's state, then wait until they are informed of changes. The stock or container doesn't know or care how many interested objects there are. Let's go through an example and see how the dependency mechanism works.

We'll look at a simple example of a stock object and a watcher object that is monitoring the stock price. As a stock is traded, the stock object gets updated with the latest price and the number of shares in the trade. Because we don't know how many stock watchers will be monitoring any particular stock, and we don't know what they will do with the values, we don't want the stock to be responsible for who to tell and what to tell them.

Instead, we use the dependency mechanism. When the stock receives information about a new trade, it updates its instance variables. When it updates an instance variable, it tells itself that it has done so. This act of telling itself that it has changed triggers the whole dependency notification mechanism.

We'll be showing several mechanisms, and each example will be suffixed with a number. To execute the example, type the following into a workspace, highlight it, and evaluate it (don't do it yet because we haven't yet defined any classes and methods). Make sure that the number is appropriate for the example. The code for all these examples can be found in the file depend.st.

```
|stock |
stock := MyStock1 new.
MyStockWatcher1 watchStock: stock.
stock traded: 200 price: 20.
stock traded: 100 price: 30
```

Basic Dependency

Here are the class definition and the instance methods for the stock class. Notice that instance variables are changed through their accessors; their accessors are responsible for telling the stock object what has changed, and the old value. This is the key part of the parent's role in the dependency mechanism. By sending changed:with:, a whole set of dependency code is invoked. The normal convention is to send the *old* value because the dependent can send a message to get the new value, and might otherwise not know the old value. Sometimes, however, you will see the new value sent. Whichever approach you take, be consistent.

Most of the methods of the stocks are defined in the superclass, MyStock. Where necessary we will override this behavior. The accessor methods look very similar for each variable, so we'll write them just for price. The other accessors will simply have different names for the variables.

```
Model subclass: #MyStock
    instanceVariableNames: 'price trade totalTraded '
    classVariableNames: ''
    poolDictionaries: ''
    category: 'DependencyTests'

MyStock>>traded: aCount price: aPrice
    self price: aPrice.
    self trade: aCount.
    self totalTraded: self totalTraded + aCount

MyStock>>price
    ^price isNil
        ifTrue: [price := 0]
        ifFalse: [price]

MyStock>>price: aPrice
    |oldPrice |
    oldPrice := self price.
    price := aPrice.
    self changed: #price with: oldPrice
```

The stock watcher adds itself as a dependent of the stock (the parent) when it is created. To do this it simply sends the stock an addDependent: message with itself as the parameter. Note that all the examples have the same watchStock: method, so we will define it in the superclass, MyStockWatcher. The stock watcher has no instance variables so we are not showing the class definition.

```
MyStockWatcher class>>watchStock: aStock
   ^super new initialize: aStock
```

```
MyStockWatcher1>>initialize: aStock
   aStock addDependent: self
```

```
MyStockWatcher1>> update: aSymbol with: oldPrice from: aStock
   Transcript cr; print: thisContext; tab; print: aSymbol; tab.
   aSymbol == #price ifTrue:
      [Transcript
         nextPutAll: 'Price changed from: '; print: oldPrice;
         nextPutAll: ' to '; print: aStock price].
   Transcript flush.
```

We'll see the details of how this works in the next section, but briefly, the stock watcher is informed of all the changes and has to decide if the change is one that it is interested in. Because our stock watcher is only monitoring the price, it ignores all the other changes. If you run this code, you'll see that it is informed of several different changes but only reports on the price change.

Underlying Mechanisms

There are some very sophisticated mechanisms that allow dependency to work but they all rely on the very basic mechanism of the parent sending itself a message from the changed family and the dependent being sent a message from the update family.

The dependency mechanism is implemented by Object, which means that any object can register itself as a dependent of any other object. When the parent changes, the most primitive mechanism for letting others know is to send itself self changed. This method is implemented by Object, so let's see what it does.

```
Object>>changed
   self changed: nil
```

```
Object>>changed: anAspectSymbol
   self changed: anAspectSymbol with: nil
```

```
Object>>changed: anAspectSymbol with: aParameter
   self myDependents
      update: anAspectSymbol
      with: aParameter
      from: self
```

As you see, if your object simply sends the changed message, this becomes transformed into a changed:with: message with both parameters being nil. Usually you will provide more information by sending either the changed: or the changed:with: message. If you want to inform your dependents what changed, send changed: and pass a symbol as the parameter. When the dependent gets an update message, it will be able to look at the symbol and decide if it is interested in the change. If you want to go further, send the changed:with: message, passing the symbol and either the old or new value as parameters. This is what we did in our stock watcher example, sending the old value.

(There are two conventions worth knowing about. First, it's possible to send anything as the argument to changed:. However, by convention, most people send a symbol, the symbol being the selector that is used to retrieve the new value. Second, the usual convention is to send the old value in changed:with:, on the assumption that the dependents might no longer know the old value, but they can always get the new value by asking the parent. However, some people prefer to send the new value because there is less message sending involved. They take the approach that, if any dependent cares about the old value, they can store it, Whichever approach you take — sending the old value or the new value — make sure you do the same thing everywhere so that other programmers can rely on getting what they expect.)

Eventually the parent sends all its dependents the update:with:from: message, so the dependents must implement one of the update family of messages. What if you don't care about all the parameters of update:with:from:? Just as Object expanded changed up to changed:with:, it contracts update:with:from: down to update:.

```
Object>>update: anAspectSymbol with: aParameter from: Sender
    ^self update: anAspectSymbol with: aParameter

Object>>update: anAspectSymbol with: aParameter
    ^self update: anAspectSymbol

Object>>update: anAspectSymbol
    ^self
```

Your dependent object thus has a choice of which of the three messages in the update family to override. Once you've implemented it, your method will be invoked rather than Object's method, because you are overriding Object's implementation. If you don't implement any update method, the results will be benign and you won't even notice that anything happened. In our example, we implemented update:with:from:. Figure 19-1 illustrates our example.

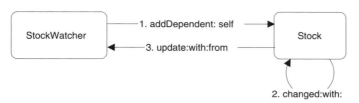

Figure 19-1. The addDependent: mechanism.

Model

In the changed:with: method, Object sends the myDependents message to get a collection of dependents. Object has a class variable, DependentsFields, which is a Dictionary indexed by objects that have dependents. The general access mechanism is DependentsFields at: objectWithDependents put: collectionOfDependents.

The main problem with this scheme is that, if an object doesn't remove itself as a dependent by sending its parent removeDependent: self, the dependents collection will never disappear from Object's class variable. (You can see if you are cluttering up this collection by inspecting Object's DependentsFields class variable.) Because the dependent objects continue to be referenced, they will not be garbage collected even though they are no longer needed. What we'd like is a mechanism that automatically gets rid of the dependency relationship when the parent is garbage collected, allowing the dependents to also be garbage collected when they are no longer needed.

This is where the class Model comes in. It is a subclass of Object, and has a single instance variable called dependents. An instance of Model keeps its dependents in a collection held by the dependents instance variable. This means that, if the instance is garbage collected, the dependents collection will disappear even though dependents never send the removeDependent: message (however, it's good practice to always send removeDependent:). If you look back to example one, you'll notice that our stock class is subclassed off Model.

If you don't fully understand this, it doesn't matter. Just remember the basic rule: If you are going to use dependencies a lot, subclass your parent class off Model rather than off Object.

expressInterestIn:for:sendBack:

Notice that the update:with:from: method in the example above has to compare the symbol it receives with all the possible symbols it cares about (in effect, doing a switch statement). The basic dependency mechanism suffers from the disadvantage that *all* dependents are sent *all* changed messages, even if they are not interested in most of them. Dependents must implement one of the update family of messages and must check to see if they are interested in the particular symbol that was sent.

We can eliminate the conditional checking that we saw in the update method by sending expressInterestIn:for:sendBack: instead of addDependent: to the parent object. In this approach, we tell the parent to express an interest in a particular change for us and send us a specified message when it sees the symbol associated with the change (i.e., the symbol sent by the parent when that particular thing changes). The syntax is confusing because you would expect the dependent to express interest in the parent. However, the syntax is such that the dependent tells the parent to express an interest in the dependent. Let's look at an example using this approach:

```
MyStockWatcher2>>initialize: aStock
    aStock
        expressInterestIn: #price
        for: self
        sendBack: #priceChanged:by:

MyStockWatcher2>>priceChanged: oldPrice by: aStock
    Transcript
        cr; print: thisContext; tab;
        nextPutAll: 'Price changed from: '; print: oldPrice;
        nextPutAll: ' to '; print: aStock price; flush
```

So how does this work? Rather than asking the parent to send us all changed messages and then filtering them out, we ask the parent to do the filtering, sending us a different message for each change we are interested in. If the message we asked to be sent has no parameters, we will just be sent the message. If the message has one parameter (binary message or keyword message with one colon), we will be sent the old value as the parameter. If the message has two colons, as does our example, we will be sent the old value and the object that changed.

If you are interested in how this is done, the parent creates a DependencyTransformer and adds the DependencyTransformer as a dependent. The DependencyTransformer gets all the update messages and looks for the one we have expressed interest in. When it sees the change we care about, it sends us the message that we registered as the parameter to the sendBack: keyword. The DependencyTransformer is very clever when it comes to sending us the message. When we expressed interest in changes, the DependencyTransformer figured out how many parameters our message expected based on whether it was a binary message or how many colons were in the message. It implements update:with:from: so that it knows what changed, the old value, and the object that sent itself the changed message, and it sends us the appropriate number of parameters. Of course, if the parent didn't send changed:with:, one or more of the arguments will be nil. Figure 19-2 illustrates this mechanism.

Finally, to stop being told about changes, the dependent has to retract interest in that particular change of the parent. It does so by sending the retractInterestIn:for: message, which should always be done. For example,

```
parent retractInterestIn: #number for: self
```

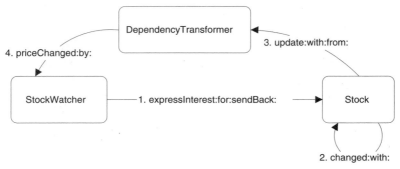

Figure 19-2. The expressInterestIn:for:sendBack: mechanism.

onChangeSend:to:

Hiding the complexity further is the onChangeSend:to: message, which is implemented by the abstract class ValueModel. It takes two parameters, the message that should be sent and the object to send it to. Notice that we don't specify what change we are interested in. This is because a ValueModel handles both the expression of interest in changes and the notification of changes, so it can make certain decisions for us. All that onChangeSend:to: does is express an interest in the symbol #value.

```
ValueModel>>onChangeSend: aSymbol to: anObject
    self
        expressInterestIn: #value
        for: anObject
        sendBack: aSymbol
```

So what is a ValueModel? It is basically a wrapper around a value — it holds the value. We can't change the value directly and can change it only through the ValueModel. Because the ValueModel has control of the change, it can notify dependents of the change. To set a new value, you send the ValueModel the value: message with the new value as a parameter, and value: simply sets the value and notifies any dependents by doing self changed: #value.

```
ValueModel>>value: newValue
    self setValue: newValue.
    self changed: #value
```

Because onChangeSend:to: translates into expressInterestIn:for:sendBack: and this latter message creates a DependencyTransformer, we now have a DependencyTransformer waiting for its parent to send self changed: #value. Once it receives this, it will send back the message we registered. ValueModel and its subclasses are widely used in the user interface widgets.

Let's look at our third example, which uses instances of ValueHolder, the simplest subclass of ValueModel. In this example the get accessors return a ValueHolder (sending the asValue message to an object returns a ValueHolder holding the object). The set accessors go through a level of indirection because they can't set the value directly; they have to ask the ValueHolder to set it. So they send the value: message to the ValueHolder, which updates the value it is holding and informs itself about the change. Unlike the previous two examples, which inform their dependents of the old value, the ValueHolder mechanism provides no ability to do this. Figure 19-3 illustrates this mechanism.

In the example we'll show just the accessors for price, because the other accessors have the same structure, just different variable names. Additionally, the traded:price: message knows that we are dealing with a ValueHolder, so it sends the value message to get the current value of totalTraded.

```
MyStock3>>traded: aCount price: aPrice
    self totalTraded: self totalTraded value + aCount.
    self price: aPrice

MyStock3>>price
    ^price isNil
        ifTrue: [price := 0 asValue]
        ifFalse: [price]

MyStock3>>price: aValue
    self price value: aValue
```

If you look at the following stock watcher methods, you'll notice that we have an instance variable, stock, which we need to add to the class

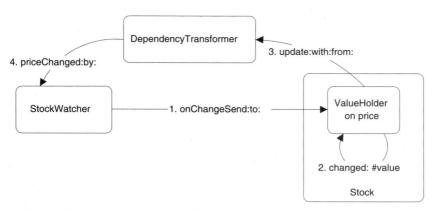

Figure 19-3. The onChangeSend:to: mechanism.

definition for MyStockWatcher3. Because ValueHolders do self changed: #value rather than sending the changed:with: message, they don't pass back a value. When our StockWatcher discovers that the price has changed, it needs to send the stock a message to find out the new price. To do this, it needs to keep hold of the stock in an instance variable. Also, because no value is passed, we don't have a way to track the old value unless we were to keep it in an instance variable.

```
MyStockWatcher3>>initialize: aStock
    stock := aStock.
    stock price onChangeSend: #priceChanged to: self

MyStockWatcher3>>priceChanged
    Transcript
        cr; print: thisContext; tab;
        nextPutAll: 'New price='; print: stock price value;
        flush
```

We can dispense with the instance variable if we are prepared to specify a two keyword message where we know the parameter to the first keyword will be nil. So we might write the above two methods as follows:

```
MyStockWatcher3>>initialize: aStock
    aStock price onChangeSend: #priceChanged:by: to: self

MyStockWatcher3>>priceChanged: aPlaceHolder by: aStock
    Transcript
        cr; print: thisContext; tab;
        nextPutAll: 'New price='; print: aStock value;
        flush
```

To cancel the dependency we set up with onChangeSend:to:, we send the retractInterestIn:for: message. For example:

```
parent retractInterestIn: #priceChanged for: self
```

Which Mechanism Should You Use?

Some people use onChangeSend:to: for basic dependencies, because it is an elegant message. However, for general dependencies the ValueHolder mechanism suffers from some disadvantages. To register as a dependent, an object must send onChangeSend:to: to a ValueHolder. This means that the parent object, which might be an instance variable, must hold a wrapper rather than real data, which is conceptually inelegant. A more serious disadvantage is that for an object to register an interest in a variable, you have to open up the details of the object. The data is no longer fully encapsulated in the sense that other objects now know how the data is stored.

With either the expressInterestIn:for:sendBack: or the addDependent: mechanism, the parents are free to change the way they store and manipulate their data, as long as they still notify themselves of changes with the same symbol.

ValueHolders and other subclasses of ValueModel are widely used in the User Interface widgets, and you'll see a lot more of them in Chapters 23 and 24. However, for basic dependencies, I prefer the other mechanisms: expressInterestIn:for:sendBack: and addDependent:. Of the two, my preference is for the former. With the addDependent: mechanism you have a single method that receives notification of all changes to all parents. It's now up to your method to make sense of all the notifications, which can result in a very procedural-looking set of booleanCondition ifTrue: statements. On the other hand, expressInterestIn:for:sendBack: allows you a narrower focus on the specific problem. When a particular aspect of the parent changes, send me a particular message. When another aspect in a different parent changes, send me a different message. It's a nice object-oriented approach.

Broadcasting

VisualWorks provides the ability for a parent to broadcast a message to all its dependents. In our stock example, there might be cause for concern if a stock price changes more than thirty percent in a single trade. Who's responsibility is it to care about this? A good argument can be made that the stock itself doesn't care, and that it's the responsibility of the stock watchers to handle the situation. For the sake of this discussion, however, let's make the case that the stock cares that its price has risen more than twenty percent, and that it needs to inform its dependents.

The broadcast mechanism lets it do that. There are two messages, broadcast: aMessage and broadcast: aMessage with: aParameter. Because the stock watchers need to know which stock is sending the message, it makes more sense to use the second message. So, we might see code in the traded:price: method in Stock to do something like the following:

```
MyStock traded: aCount price: aPrice
    ... code to set values ...
    price notNil ifTrue:
        [(aPrice - price / price) abs > 0.3
            ifTrue: [self broadcast: #bigChange: with: self]].
```

This unilaterally sends the bigChange: message to all dependents passing the stock object as the parameter. If the dependents haven't implemented bigChange:, an exception will be raised. So there's a responsibility on the dependents to implement this message, even if they don't care about large changes in price. There's also an argument against specifically broadcasting a large change in price, because one might argue that the responsibility of stock is simply to inform its dependents about changes in price. It's the responsibility of the dependents to decide if a given change is too high.

In the dependency scheme, the general philosophy is that dependents know about and care about the parent, but the parent doesn't know or care about the dependents. This philosophy breaks down with broadcasting, because if the parent decides to send a new message, some programmer has to figure out all the objects that register as dependents, then add the new message to each of them. An alternative and better approach would be to modify the broadcast messages to do safe performs (look for implementors of safelyPerform: to see how this is done).

If you modify traded:price: to include the broadcast code without adding the bigChange: method to the stock watchers, then run the three examples, you will see some interesting results. In the first example, an exception will be raised saying that StockWatcher1 doesn't understand the message. In the second example, it will be a DependencyTransformer that doesn't understand the message. In the third example, no exception will be raised because the Stock3 object has no dependencies — it's the instance variable ValueHolders that have the dependencies.

So, to use broadcasting, you'll have to use the addDependent: mechanism. Note that none of the system classes send either broadcast: or broadcast:with:, and personally, I'd recommend against using them for the above reasons.

Dependency Considerations

There are two things to be aware of when using the dependency mechanism. First, parents should not send explicit messages to their dependents. Second, and most important, it's worth getting into the habit of always breaking dependencies when they are no longer needed.

Dependency violation

The dependency mechanism is supposed to be a one-way mechanism. The parent or model doesn't know anything about its dependents. It doesn't even know if it has any dependents. However, sometimes people write code so that the parent, in Jim Dutton's phrase, "gropes" its dependents. Here's an example:

```
self myDependents do:
    [:each | (each isKindOf: SomeClass)
        ifTrue: [ each grope ] ]
```

This code violates the basic rule of dependencies — that a parent should have no knowledge of its dependents.

Breaking dependencies

When the product is almost complete, most organizations try to run it as they think customers will use it. Usually they notice that the product has memory leaks, and that it slowly consumes the available memory. Memory leaks occur because objects are not being garbage collected, and objects are not garbage collected if one or more other objects reference them. When dependencies are not broken, dependent objects are referenced by their parents. If the parent object is held in a class variable or a global, or is refererenced by another object in a class variable or a global, or is referenced by an object that is referenced by an object in a class variable or a global, etc., the dependents will never be garbage collected.

Sometimes it is extremely difficult to track down exactly why an object is not being garbage collected, because the reference path can be very long. In fact it's more difficult to track down memory leaks when the parent is a subclass of Model, because the dependencies of non-Models are tracked in one place, in Object's class variable DependentsFields.

To reduce the chances of memory leak, you should get into the habit of *always* breaking dependencies when the dependent is no longer needed, or the dependent no longer needs the dependency. If the dependency was set up using addDependent:, break it with removeDependent:. If it was set up with expressInterestIn:for:sendBack: or onChangeSend:to:, break it with retractInterestIn:for:. The breaking of dependencies is usually done in a release method such as shown below. In the example, the MyClass object removes itself as a dependent of another object, then tells one if its instance variables to break any dependencies it might have. Finally, it gives its superclass a chance to do any releasing.

```
MyClass>>release
    someObject removeDependent: self.
    self someVariable release.
    super release.
```

Error Handling

The usual way of handling errors in a procedural language, such as C, is to return a status from a function call, then check the status in the calling function. If there is a problem you might take some action in the caller, or more usually, you return from the caller, passing back the status code and possibly logging an error message. Typically, you end up with a lot of code whose sole purpose is to handle errors. It's not uncommon for the majority of the code in a robust application to be associated with error handling.

Smalltalk makes it much easier to focus on the domain problem you are trying to solve by eliminating much of the error-handling code. It does this by providing a wonderful mechanism, called *exception handling*. We'll start by taking a look at basic exception handling, then, because there are a lot of additional capabilities, we'll look at these finer points later in the chapter.

The general idea behind exception handling is that you assume everything works, and so you don't check return values. Of course, sometimes things will go wrong. Perhaps you try to divide by zero, or perhaps you try to write to a read-only file. These events will raise an exception, which makes its way up the stack, looking for a signal that can handle it. Rather than checking a status at every level in the call stack (i.e., in every method), you simply need to have an exception handler at the appropriate level in the code where you can take some action. This is illustrated in Fig. 20-1.

To trap, or handle, an exception, you send the handle:do: message to an instance of Signal. This message takes two blocks as parameters. The parameter to do: is the block that you want to execute, usually consisting of several lines of code. The parameter to handle: is the block that will be executed if an exception is trapped as a result of a signal's being raised while executing the do: block. This block takes one parameter, the exception that was raised. The exception contains information

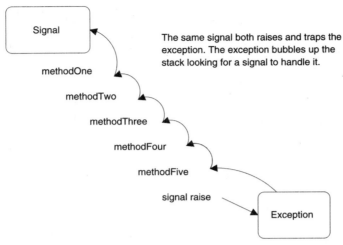

The same signal both raises and traps the exception. The exception bubbles up the stack looking for a signal to handle it.

Figure 20-1. The exception-handling mechanism.

about the error, which you can use in the handler block. You'll usually see the exception parameter called :ex. Let's take a look at how code might look when using an exception handler.

```
MyRequest>>processYourself
    |tape drive |
    MySignals appSignal
        handle: [:ex | self myHandleFailure: ex]
        do:
            [self myCheckRequest.
            tape := self myReserveTape.
            drive := self myReserveDrive.
            tape mountYourselfOn: drive.
            self myRespondSuccess].
    self myReleaseTape: tape.
    self myReleaseDrive: drive

MyRequest>>myReserveTape
    self tapeName isReserved ifTrue:
        [MySignals appSignal raiseWith: #tapeBusy].
    ...code to reserve the tape...
```

In myReserveTape, we raise an exception if the tape is already reserved. In processYourself we have a signal to trap these raised exceptions. You'll see that we don't explicitly test the results of any of the message sends in processYourself, relying on the signal to trap the errors. This makes the code much more compact and easy to read. It allows us to focus on the problem we are trying to solve, rather than on the possibilities that things will go wrong.

Let's now look at an example of how you would trap an exception raised by the system classes. The classic example is division by zero. You can find the signals in the Signal constants protocol on the class side of ArithmeticValue. (In Chapter 29, we see how to find all the classes with a specified protocol.) If you evaluate the following code, you will get a message displayed on the Transcript.

```
ArithmeticValue divisionByZeroSignal
    handle: [:ex | Transcript cr; show: ex errorString]
    do: [ 4 / 0 ].
```

Signals and Exceptions

Two classes play a role in exception handling, Signal and Exception. The basic idea is that a signal both raises and traps an exception. When a signal raises an exception in a method, the exception code works its way up (unwinds) the message stack, looking for a signal to handle it. Signals that can handle the exception are the signal that raised the exception, and any signal in the raising signal's parent hierarchy (more on this later). If the exception can't find a signal to handle it, it asks Object noHandlerSignal to raise an unhandled signal exception. If this new exception can't find a handler it invokes the EmergencyHandler. The default EmergencyHandler puts up a Notifier window that displays information about the original exception and gives you the option to bring up a Debugger.

The beauty of this scheme of raised exceptions and exception handlers is that you don't have to have lots of error-handling code. Instead, at the level that knows what action to take in response to an error, you create the exception-handling code. Then, if a lower level method comes across an error, it simply raises an exception.

Creating Your Own Signal

Exceptions can be raised by the system classes, and your code must be able to handle these. However, for your application you should raise application-defined signals and trap them with application-defined signals. When you write your application, you might be several methods deep and realize that you can't continue because of some error. Perhaps you have bad data, perhaps some resource you need is already in use, perhaps some condition has not been satisfied. In any of these cases, you will need to raise an exception that you will trap at a higher level. So you must first create a signal to use.

The easiest way to create a signal is to do Signal new, which creates a new signal with Object errorSignal as its parent. An alternative way to do the same thing (and, in fact, Signal new does this) is Object errorSignal newSignal, which we could also do with self errorSignal newSignal if our class is subclassed from Object. We'll talk more about the details of signal creation later. Now let's create a signal that we can use in our application. We have a couple of choices: we might create several signals, each appropriate for a specific situation, or we might create a more general signal that the whole application can use.

A single application signal

One approach is to create a single signal for the whole application. This works well in applications in which the response to an error is the same, no matter what the error. I've used this approach in applications in which we were processing requests from other computers, with no user interaction. If we detected an error we simply rejected the request, passing back an error number and error message in the response. Here's an example of how we might create and access such as signal.

```
MySignals class>>setValues
    (AppSignal := Object errorSignal newSignal)
        notifierString: 'Application Error:';
        nameClass: self message: #appSignal

MySignals class>>appSignal
    ^AppSignal
```

Multiple application signals

Applications that are more user-interface-intensive usually have a need for multiple application signals. For example, you might have one or more signals for file errors, one for validation errors, and so on. Then, for example, any time you try to validate something you assume that the validation works unless a validation signal is raised. To create and access these signals you might have something like:

```
MySignals class>>initialize
    AppSignal := Object errorSignal newSignal notifierString: 'Application Error:'.
    ValidationSignal := AppSignal newSignal notifierString: 'Validation Error:'.
    FileSignal := AppSignal newSignal notifierString: 'File Error:'.
    FileNotFoundSignal := FileSignal newSignal notifierString: 'File Not Found:'.

MySignals class>>fileNotFoundSignal
    ^FileNotFoundSignal

MySignals class>>validationSignal
    ^ValidationSignal
```

Note the signal hierarchy we set up in the initialize method. AppSignal is our top-level signal, with ValidationSignal and FileSignal as children. FileNotFoundSignal is a child of FileSignal. Thus we can trap file not-found errors with any of FileNotFoundSignal, FileSignal, AppSignal, or Object errorSignal.

Overriding errorSignal

Sometimes you might decide to override errorSignal to provide different catchall error-handling behavior, for a class or for a hierarchy of classes. If you override errorSignal, you'd like your new behavior to be invoked rather than the default behavior. For example, suppose you have overridden errorSignal for MyClass and you are sending a message to an instance of MyClass that might generate any number of exceptions. You would ask your class rather than Object to handle the error. Your handling code would now look like the following:

```
anInstanceOfMyClass class errorSignal
    handle: [ :ex | ex return ]
    do: [ anInstanceOfMyClass processYourself ].
```

There are two points to note with this technique. First, you can use it as a standard technique because, if a particular class hasn't overridden errorSignal, it will inherit the default errorSignal from Object. Second, the behavior you write in your errorSignal method must be able to handle signals that are generated by any object, because you can't guarantee that the instance of MyClass is the only object that will raise an exception.

Another approach is always to use self errorSignal as the catchall signal handler, rather than Object errorSignal. This gives you the opportunity to override the catchall behavior in the class sending the message, rather than using the behavior inherited from Object. If you don't override errorSignal, then it is simply inherited.

```
MyClass>>doSomething
    self errorSignal
        handle: [ :ex | ex return ]
        do: [ self myDoSomethingElse ].
```

Central Error Messages

Let's take a look at what we might do in the myHandleFailure: method in the example at the beginning of the chapter. We have the exception because it was passed in. Now we need to report or log the error condition. How we do this is very application-specific, but let's look at one way of transforming the exception into something a human would understand.

We do this with a central error message facility that contains the error number and error text. The text will directly tell what is wrong, and the number will allow the user to consult an error codes manual for more information about what this error means. In the class side initialization of MyErrorMessages we create an IdentityDictionary containing instances of Association, each association being a message number and the corresponding message text. The dictionary keys are the symbols that are passed as parameters when raising the signal. To retrieve the message number and the message text, we send numberFor: and textFor: respectively. (You can find code for this example in the file errormsg.st.)

```
MyErrorMessages class>>initialize
    "self initialize"
    (Messages := IdentityDictionary new)
        at: #tapeNotFound      put: 1 -> 'The specified tape could not be found';
        at: #tapeBusy          put: 2 -> 'The tape is in use'.

MyErrorMessages class>>numberFor: aSymbol
    ^(Messages at: aSymbol ifAbsent: [0 -> nil]) key.

MyErrorMessages class>>textFor: aSymbol
    ^(Messages
        at: aSymbol
        ifAbsent: [nil -> 'Code ', aSymbol printString, ' not found']) value.
```

Now we just need to see how we would use this message facility when handling the failure. In myHandleFailure: we extract the error number and the error text from the centralized error message facility. Next, we append any additional text that was given when the signal was raised. Then we take some domain-specific action to report the error.

```
MyRequestClass>> myHandleFailure: anException
    number := MyErrorMessages numberFor: anException parameter.
    text := MyErrorMessages textFor: anException parameter.
    anException localErrorString notNil ifTrue:
        [text := text, ' - ', anException localErrorString].
    .... now do something domain specific with the number and text ....
```

In this example, we generate the message text when we trap the exception. This is acceptable in situations in which we don't need to add information about the values of the objects at the time of the error. In other situations we might need to also log or display the values of objects. To pass back information, we could create an ExceptionParameter class that contained the error symbol, a collection of parameters, and possibly an additional error string. We would then raise the exception with raiseWith:, passing our ExceptionParameter as the parameter, and have the exception-handling code construct an error message from the ExceptionParameter. (An alternative approach is to use the mechanisms described below in the section on Parameter Substitution, and have the exception create a fully formed string.)

The scheme described above is fairly simple because we only have error numbers and error text. In a production system we would probably have a MyMessages superclass that defined most of the behavior, then MyErrorMessages and MyInformationMessages as subclasses. We would also store more information with each message, such as the message severity and message categorization to help route error responses and error reporting. One approach would be to code this information into the message string, but this would not be very object-oriented. A more powerful and more object-oriented approach would be to create MyMessage objects to put in the dictionary, rather than instances of Association. We might have something like the following. It would be straightforward to write methods to extract the message text and categorize and sort it for easier viewing.

```
MyErrorMessages class>>initialize
    "self initialize"
    (Messages := IdentityDictionary new)
        at: #tapeNotFound
        put: (MyMessage
            number: 1
            severity: #warning    '
            routing: 'TN'
            text: 'The specified tape could not be found');
        at: #tapeBusy
        put: (MyMessage
            number: 2
            severity: #warning
            routing: 'TN'
            text: 'The tape is in use').
```

The severity codes might include #information, #warning, #error, and #fatal, while the routing information tells what type of message it is. In this example, T refers to tapes and N refers to the non-existence of things. We might further encapsulate information and create a specific routing object rather than code routing information into a string. We might also create subclasses of MyMessage for errors and warnings (for example, MyErrorMessage and MyWarningMessage). By having subclasses that encapsulate the information, we could later decide to encapsulate behavior specific to the message type.

The severity and routing information allows clients of the messaging system, such as other computers, the error log, and the system console, to register for the types of messages they want to receive. If an error message is created in response to a request, the message would be sent to the originator of the request. It would also be sent to a central message router that would distribute it to all message clients whose registration criteria matched the information in the message.

If you are using ENVY, you might consider using the provided error reporting mechanism, which uses the ErrorReporter class. There is more about ENVY in Chapter 34, ENVY.

More on Signal Creation

We've seen the basics of creating a signal, so now let's take a look at some of the details. Signals can be proceedable or non-proceedable, you can specify the string to be displayed in a Notifier window, and you can specify the message that will return the signal. Additionally, we'll take a look at parents of signals, and how signal trapping works within the parent hierarchy.

Specifying the proceedability of the signal

Signals can be proceedable or non-proceedable. A proceedable signal allows the exception handler to proceed from the point at which the exception was raised. In general you won't do this, and thus won't care about this feature, but it's useful to know. When you send newSignal, you inherit the proceedability of the parent signal. Object errorSignal is proceedable, so Object errorSignal newSignal gives you a new proceedable signal with Object errorSignal as its parent. If you care about the proceedability, you can use the newSignalMayProceed: message with a Boolean parameter that specifies whether the signal is to be proceedable. For example, Object errorSignal newSignalMayProceed: true gives you a proceedable signal. If you want to be able to proceed from an exception, you must raise exceptions by sending your signal a message from the raiseRequest family rather than the raise family.

Notifier strings and inspector information

There are two other aspects to consider when creating a new signal. If you send notifierString: aString to an instance of Signal, you set the default string that is returned by the errorString message — the string that will be displayed at the top of any Notifier window raised by this signal. If you send nameClass: aClass message: aSymbol to the signal, you are by convention specifying that you can get this signal by sending the message specified by aSymbol to the class specified by aClass (this is really just a documentation aid; you'll still have to write the method that returns the signal). Additionally, aClass and aSymbol are stored in instance variables in the signal, and give inspectors more information to display. For example, you might create a signal by doing the following, also remembering to write the appErrorSignal method:

```
(AppErrorSignal := self errorSignal newSignal)
    notifierString: 'Application Error: ';
    nameClass: self message: #appErrorSignal
```

Parents handling signals

Earlier, we trapped a division-by-zero error using ArithmeticValue divisionByZeroSignal. Now let's trap the same error with the parent signal, ArithmenticValue domainErrorSignal. Then we'll trap the signal with its parent, ArithmeticValue errorSignal, then with its parent, Object errorSignal. You can see how the signals are created from their parents in the class initialization of ArithmeticValue.

```
ArithmeticValue domainErrorSignal
    handle: [:ex | Transcript cr; show: ex errorString]
    do: [ 4 / 0 ].
```

```
ArithmeticValue errorSignal
    handle: [:ex | Transcript cr; show: ex errorString]
    do: [ 4 / 0 ].
```

```
Object errorSignal
    handle: [:ex | Transcript cr; show: ex errorString]
    do: [ 4 / 0 ].
```

Because we also know how to create new signals of our own, let's see another example of how the parent of a signal can trap exceptions raised by the signal, but other signals derived from the same parent (i.e., siblings of the signal) can't trap the exception. In our example, parent1 and parent2 are two signals with the same parent, Object errorSignal. child2 has parent2 as its parent. If we ask parent1 to trap an exception raised by child2, it doesn't. If we ask parent2 to trap the exception, it does. Try the code below twice, once with parent1 handling the exception and once with parent2 handling it. Moral of the story: an exception can be trapped by the signal that raised it, or by its parent or grandparent, ..., up to Object errorSignal.

```
parent1 := Object errorSignal newSignal notifierString: 'Error1:'.
parent2 := Object errorSignal newSignal notifierString: 'Error2:'.
child2 := parent2 newSignal.
parent1
    handle: [:ex | Transcript cr; show: 'in handler']
    do: [child2 raise].
```

Signal Collections

If your application can raise several different signals but the way of dealing with the exception is the same for all the signals, you have two alternatives. You can use a generic signal, such as Object errorSignal, or a common parent signal to handle all the possible exceptions. Or, if you know exactly which signals can be raised, you can use a SignalCollection.

To do this, add the signals you want to trap to the SignalCollection, then send handle:do: to the SignalCollection. When a signal is raised, it looks at each signal in the collection until it recognizes one. You can build the SignalCollection in one place then reuse it in different places.

Try the following example twice, reversing the order of the statements in the do: block. You'll get a different exception reported on the Transcript.

```
sigCollection := SignalCollection
    with: Dictionary keyNotFoundSignal
    with: Dictionary valueNotFoundSignal.
sigCollection
    handle: [ :ex | Transcript cr; show: ex errorString]
    do:
```

```
[Dictionary new at: 3.
Dictionary new keyAtValue: 4].
```

How useful are SignalCollections? I've worked on applications in which they were not very useful, because it was easier to have the top-level application signal or Object errorSignal do the trapping. I've also worked on applications in which we used SignalCollections because we needed to be specific about the errors we were trapping. The VisualWorks system classes use a SignalCollection only two times, and one of those is an empty collection!

HandlerLists/Collections

If you have a set of signals you want to trap but you want to take different actions for each exception, you can use a set of nested handlers. For example:

```
signalOne
    handle: [:ex | some code]
    do: [signalTwo
        handle: [:ex | some code]
        do: [signalThree
            handle: [:ex | some code]
            do: [some application code]]
```

If there are a lot of signals you want to look for, the code will get pretty messy. The HandlerList (VisualWorks 2.5) or HandlerCollection (VisualWorks 2.0) class provides a shorthand way of doing the same thing. The handlers will still be nested when the code is executed, but the code is a lot tidier and is therefore easier to understand and maintain. Here's the above example coded using a HandlerList. Note that because the handlers are really nested, the last signal added is the first signal that will get a chance to trap the exception. So, put the most general signals first and the most specific last. Again, you can build the HandlerList in one place and reuse it in different places.

```
(handlerList := HandlerList new)
    on: signalOne handle: [:ex | some code];
    on: signalTwo handle: [:ex | some code];
    on: signalThree handle: [:ex | some code].
handlerList handleDo: [some application code].
```

How useful are HandlerLists? Again, I've worked on applications in which we never used them. I've also worked on applications in which we wanted to trap errors generated by the file system, and give the user a different message for each type of error. In my experience, HandlerLists are most useful when handling errors generated by the interaction of the Smalltalk image with the operating system, where the action you take depends on the exact problem detected. The

VisualWorks system classes use a HandlerList or HandlerCollection only once.

(In VisualWorks 2.5, HandlerCollection was replaced with HandlerList. Unless you have been subclassing from HandlerCollection, the behavior is identical.)

Passing Information with an Exception

Let's now look at the various ways of passing information with the exception. We'll examine only non-proceedable signals; for proceedable signals you substitute raiseRequest for raise in all the examples.

To get a string describing the exception, you send the errorString message to the exception. The signal's notifier string and the parameters to the raise message are all used when creating the error string, and in the following examples, we will show how they affect the error string. Notifier windows display the value returned by errorString.

raise

The raise message simply raises an exception, passing back no information.

raiseWith: aParameter

The raiseWith: aParameter message passes back information in the parameter. To retrieve the parameter, send parameter to the exception. In our example above, we passed the symbol #tapeBusy as the parameter and then used it to look up the error message.

raiseErrorString: aString

The raiseErrorString: aString message passes back a string. You can access the string by sending localErrorString to the exception. The value returned by errorString depends on spaces in aString. The rule is:

aString has no space in front — replace notifier string

aString has a space in front — append aString to notifier string

raiseWith: aParameter errorString: aString

The raiseWith: aParameter errorString: aString message passes back both a parameter and a string. You can access the parameter by sending parameter to the exception and the string by sending localErrorString to the exception. The value returned by errorString depends on spaces in aString. The rule is:

aString has no space in front — replace notifier string

aString has a space in front — append aString to notifier string

aString has a space at the end — append parameter to aString

Parameter substitution

At the time you raise an exception you have access to all the information that is relevant to the error. VisualWorks provides a parameter substitution mechanism where you can raise an exception, passing a template string and a collection of parameters to be substituted. (If you are using a centralized messaging facility, you could get the message template from it, using a symbol as the lookup key.) The exception substitutes the parameters, generating a fully formed message. However, my preference would be to create the ExceptionParameter object that we discussed above, because this provides more power and flexibility.

The parameter substitution mechanism is different in VisualWorks 2.0 and 2.5, so we'll look at both. In both messages below, the template is a string with embedded formatting information. The parameter is expected to be a collection, where each element of the collection corresponds to a formal parameter in the template string. Sending parameter to the exception will return the parameter collection, and sending localErrorString will return the expanded string. The errorString message conforms to the space rules shown in raise:ErrorString: above.

raiseWith:errorTemplate:

The raiseWith: aParameterCollection errorTemplate: aString message is the parameter substitution message used in VisualWorks 2.0. The template string contains embedded percent signs (%). The string will be expanded before the handler gets to trap the exception, with the % being replaced by the printString representation of the appropriate collection element. For example, the following brings up a Notifier window with the message:

Unhandled exception: Received bad value 3 and bad value 'm:\temp'.

```
Object errorSignal
    raiseWith: #(3 'm:\temp')
    errorTemplate: 'Received bad value % and bad value %.'
```

raiseWith:errorPattern:

The raiseWith: aParameterCollection errorPattern: aString message is the parameter substitution message used in VisualWorks 2.5. It provides a new, more powerful parameter substitution mechanism using a new family of messages (expandMacros). For more information on the parameter substitution options, see Chapter 12. For example, the following brings up a Notifier window with the message:

```
Unhandled exception: Received bad value 3 and bad value m:\temp.
```

```
Object errorSignal
    raiseWith: #(3 'm:\temp')
    errorPattern: 'Received bad value <1p> and bad value <2s>.'
```

Handling the Exception

There are several ways to handle the exception in the handle: block of the handle:do: message. Remember that the block will look something like [:exception | some code], where the exception is passed in as the parameter. If you hit the right bracket of the handle block, the return value of the block (i.e., the value of the last statement executed) will be the value returned from handle:do:. If there is no code in the block, the exception will be returned.

Alternatively, you can send a message to the exception as the last thing in the block. This is the preferred approach, because it gives the exception a chance to gracefully unwind the stack. The messages you can send are return, returnWith:, reject, restart, restartDo:, proceed, proceedWith:, and proceedDoing:. We will look at some of these messages. For the others, you'll have to examine the system code and read the manuals.

return

The return message returns nil from the handle block. It's the same as doing returnWith: nil. Note that return leaves you in the method containing the exception handler. If you don't want to do anything in the handler block, it's good practice to do ex return. The following code prints nil to the Transcript.

```
Transcript cr; show:
    (self errorSignal
        handle: [:ex | ex return]
        do: [self errorSignal raise]) printString.
```

returnWith:

The returnWith: message allows you to set a value as the return value from handle:do:. The parameter to returnWith: will be the return value. Note that returnWith: leaves you in the method. The following code prints 3 to the Transcript.

```
Transcript cr; show:
    (self errorSignal
        handle: [:ex | ex returnWith: 3]
        do: [self errorSignal raise]) printString.
```

reject

The reject message allows you to take some action then reject the exception, or reject the exception based on some criteria. In the following example, in the handle block we print to the Transcript then reject the exception. Because the exception is rejected, it continues to look for a handler but doesn't find another one, so it raises a Notifier window.

```
self errorSignal
    handle: [:ex |
        Transcript cr; show: ex errorString.
        ex reject]
    do: [self errorSignal raiseWith: 3 errorString: 'Error '].
```

restart

The restart message allows you to figure out what caused the exception to be raised, fix the condition, then restart the handle:do: expression. The following code gives you a chance to correct the error that you get if you divide by zero.

```
self errorSignal
    handle: [:ex |
        Dialog warn: 'You divided by zero'.
        ex restart]
    do: [| answer |
        answer := Dialog request: 'Divide 4 by what?' initialAnswer: '0'.
        Transcript cr; show: (4 / answer asNumber) printString].
```

restartDo:

The restartDo: message allows you to figure out what caused the exception to be raised, possibly to fix the condition, then to restart execution with a different code block. While you can use ^ in a handle: block to return from the method, restartDo: is the recommended way of doing this. For example, ex restartDo: [^nil] exits the method, returning nil.

```
MyClass>>myMethod
    someSignal
        handle: [:ex | ex restartDo: [^nil] ]
        do: [some code that raises an exception]
```

self error:

Another way to raise an exception is to send the error: message, passing a string as a parameter. By default, this raises a Notifier window and allows you to bring up a Debugger. To change the default behavior, you can override error:. If you are using the application signal mechanism described above and you have a single centralized message file in your image, you could write, for example, Object>>error:args:string: to take a symbol, an array of arguments, and an additional string as arguments. It would handle raising the exception in the appropriate way. To invoke it you would do something like:

```
self error: #tapeNotFound args: (Array with: tapeName with: driveName) string: nil.
```

A more elegant approach would be to have your own subclass of Object, say MyObject, and to defined error:args:string: on MyObject. All application objects that used to be subclassed from Object would now be subclassed from MyObject.

doesNotUnderstand:

If your code sends a message that is not understood, eventually the doesNotUnderstand: message will be sent. The default doesNotUnderstand:, implemented by Object, raises a Notifier window. You can override doesNotUnderstand: if you want to do anything specific, such as logging an error.

valueNowOrOnUnwindDo:

Suppose you have code that should be executed both after normal completion of a sequence of statements and if an exception is raised. You can wrap the regular code in a block and send it the message valueNowOrOnUnwindDo:, passing as the parameter a block containing the code you always want executed. A good example of this is closing a file. You'd like to close the file after successfully reading it, and also if an exception is raised while reading the file. Here's an example of how to use this technique:

```
stream := self myFilename readStream.
[self readFile: stream ]
    valueNowOrOnUnwindDo:
        [stream close ].
```

Emergency Exception Handler

If an exception can't be handled, the Emergency Handler will be invoked. The default Emergency Handler is defined during class initialization for Exception, and it raises a Notifier window. You can change the Emergency Handler by sending Exception the class message emergencyHandler:, where the parameter is a block that takes two arguments, the exception and the context. For example, try the following (after saving any changes you want to keep):

```
Exception emergencyHandler:
    [:ex :context |
        Dialog warn: 'Quitting: ', ex errorString.
        ObjectMemory quit].
3 next.
```

Once the emergency handler has done its thing, it attempts to re-execute the code that caused the exception. So, unless the emergency handler quits the Smalltalk image or starts a new thread of execution, you will end up in an infinite loop.

noHandlerSignal

As we saw earlier, if an exception can't find a signal to handle it, it asks Object noHandlerSignal to raise an unhandled signal exception. If this new exception can't find a handler, it invokes the Emergency Handler. However, the new noHandlerSignal exception is raised in the original context, so we still have an opportunity to trap it. To see an example of how this works, create a class with the following methods.

```
MyClass>>methodOne
    self methodTwo

MyClass>>methodTwo
    Signal noHandlerSignal
        handle: [:ex | Transcript cr; show: 'methodTwo - ', ex parameter errorString]
        do: [self methodThree]

MyClass>>methodThree
    self foo
```

If you now execute MyClass new methodOne, you will see the following on the transcript:

```
methodTwo - Message not understood: #foo
```

The way this works is that methodThree sends the message foo, which is not implemented and thus raises a messageNotUnderstood exception. The exception cannot find a handler for itself anywhere in the stack, so it raises a noHandlerSignal exception, with the original exception stored in the parameter instance variable of the new exception. In methodTwo we have a handler for the new exception, so we trap it and print out some information. Note that since the noHandlerSignal exception contains the original exception in its parameter variable, we have to print ex parameter errorString to get information about the original error.

Since the noHandlerSignal exception is raised only if no handler is found for the original exception, we should be able to add an exception handler in methodOne, and have this invoked instead of the handler in methodTwo. Modify methodOne to look like the following:

```
MyClass>>methodOne
    Object messageNotUnderstoodSignal
        handle: [:ex | Transcript cr; show: 'methodOne - ', ex errorString]
        do: [self methodTwo]
```

If you now execute MyClass new methodOne, you will see the following on the transcript:

methodOne - Message not understood: #foo

This technique gives us a way to create a "last resort" exception handler. By wrapping our code in a Signal noHandlerSignal exception handler, we in effect say "I'll give someone else an opportunity to handle any exception that is raised, but if no one else wants to handle it, I'll take care of it myself."

Exceptions and Processes

Unfortunately, Smalltalk doesn't do a good job of handling exceptions raised in forked processes. The problem is that, when a process is forked, it gets its own stack context. When an exception is raised in a forked process, it bubbles up the stack until it is either handled or it raises a Notifier window. Because the forked process has a different context than the process that forked it, the exception never gets into the stack of the forker.

This means that each forked process must have its own exception-handling code if you want to trap exceptions. What you do next, after trapping the exception, depends on the application and how it is structured. If you have an application in which there is a central dispatcher that gets requests and runs each request in its own forked process, each request could have an instance of SharedQueue, which it uses to communicate back to the forker. For an example of this, see the section named "Running tests that time out" in Chapter 30.

For a more complete discussion of handling exceptions in a multi-process environment, see the two-part article, "Cross-Process Exception Handling," by Ken Auer and Barry Oglesby in *The Smalltalk Report*, January 1994 and February 1994 (the first part is mistitled, being called "Cross-Purpose Exception Handling").

When to Look for Errors

There are different philosophies on when to look for error conditions. The idea that you should trap errors as soon as possible has made it into software engineering folklore. This makes sense when you are dealing with user interfaces, because it's reasonable to let users know about errors as soon as possible (of course, it's even better to write applications that prevent the making of errors by the users).

On the other hand, leaving aside user interface code, there's no reason to trap an error before it absolutely needs to be detected. There's no reason to have a whole hierarchy of methods, all checking the validity of the same parameters. Most of them won't even care what the value is and will simply pass it on. It makes a cleaner application to check the validity of things only when it's vital that they are valid. Then, and only then, raise an exception.

21

Debugging

This chapter is not so much about debugging as about debugging with Smalltalk. It won't necessarily help you become a better debugger, but it will help you learn what tools are available to help debug a Smalltalk application. One hint to becoming a better debugger is to explain the problem to someone else. The act of thinking the problem through clearly enough to put into words often leads you to a solution without the other person's having to say anything. If you can distill out the critical factors that make this so, you can become a better debugger even when no one else is present.

Bringing Up a Notifier Window

The basic mechanism for halting execution and giving you a Notifier window, as shown in Fig. 21-1, is to send the halt message in your code. The normal way of doing this is to send it to self. For example:

```
self halt.
```

When the halt message is sent, the halt method raises a signal (Object haltSignal), which eventually invokes the EmergencyHandler. The default emergency handler places a Notifier window on the screen, which gives you the option to debug the program. (Actually, it asks the class NotifierView to open. NotifierView opens a Debugger, which gives you the option of debugging, proceeding, terminating, etc. Because the window you get when you press Debug is what is usually thought of as the Debugger, it seems convenient to refer to the initial window as a Notifier window.) If you have a string you'd like displayed in the Notifier window, send the halt: message instead of halt. For example:

```
self halt: 'My string to display'.
```

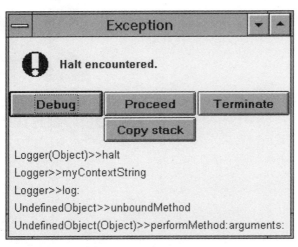

Figure 21-1. A Notifier window.

While sending one of the halt messages is the normal way to bring up a Debugger, you can also send notify: with a string parameter or error: with a string parameter. For example:

```
self notify: 'Count is now over 100'.
self error: 'Should not get here'.
```

Using a Debugger Window

From the Notifier window, you can press the Debug button to bring up a Debugger, as shown in Fig. 21-2. In the top window, the Debugger shows you several lines of the stack trace. By selecting one of the lines, you can see the source code for that method. You can examine all the parameters and temporary variables for the method, and all the class and instance variables for the message receiver. If the stack trace does not show enough methods, you can show more of the stack by selecting the more stack mouse menu option in the upper pane.

The main window shows the code. In this window you can highlight code segments and execute them, you can modify the code and accept it or you can execute the code one message at a time. To simply execute the next message send, press the step button. If you want to trace through the message send and go into the method that is executed, press the send button. The Debugger will stop at the first message in the new method.

If you modify the code and accept it, execution will start again at the beginning of the method if you press restart or proceed. This allows you to replay the application to try to recreate a problem (assuming that the application can be restarted). Go down the stack to a method that you can get useful debugging information from if you restart. Adding, then removing, a space forces recognition that a change has happened to the code, and you can then accept the method. Now you can use the step and send keys to step through the code and try to understand why the problem occurred.

A useful technique for writing new code is to write most of the code in the Debugger. Write your main method as a series of message sends that invoke supporting methods to do the real work. Each supporting method will initially consist of nothing more than self halt. When you run your application, you will get a Debugger on the first supporting method. You can now write the real code in the Debugger, using it to help you understand the context and the appropriate message sends, and to test out possible options.

Another use for the Debugger is to step through your code, one line at a time, when you first run your application. In doing this you will inevitably gain insights into the code. You'll see obvious mistakes that you made, and obvious ways to restructure your code. Stepping through your code in this way will almost always help you improve the code, making it less likely that you will need the Debugger to track bugs down later.

Inspectors

At the bottom of the Debugger are two Inspectors. The left one shows class and instance variables, while the right one shows parameters and temporary variables. When you click on a variable name, its value will

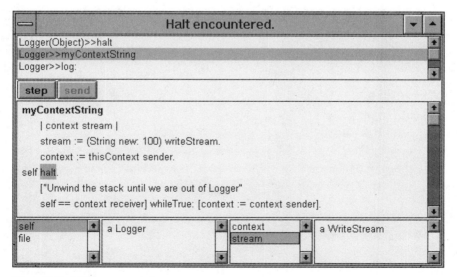

Figure 21-2. A Debugger window.

be displayed in the righthand window of the Inspector. To open a new Inspector, you can either highlight a variable name or a code sample in the code window, then choose inspect from the right mouse button menu, or you can select a variable name in an Inspector and choose inspect from the mouse menu.

(When you open an Inspector, the object you want to inspect is sent the inspect message. Most objects inherit inspect from Object, which opens a generic Inspector. However, some objects, such as OrderedCollection, Dictionary, and String override inspect to open a specialized Inspector.)

Modifying values in an Inspector

In the examples that follow, we will use a class called ModifyingValues, with three instance variables. The code for this example can be found in the file debug.st. To bring up the Debugger window, as shown in Fig. 21-3, evaluate ModifyingValues new initialize. The initialize method is as follows.

```
ModifyingValues>>initialize
    color := #blue.
    size := 5 -> 10.
    things := OrderedCollection with: 'one' with: 'two' with: 'three' with: 'four'.
    self halt: 'Use an inspector to modify the values'
```

If you want to replace a value in a variable, use the Inspector windows at the bottom of the Debugger. Highlight the variable, which causes the contents to be displayed on the righthand window of the Inspector. Replace the value in the window with the new value, and

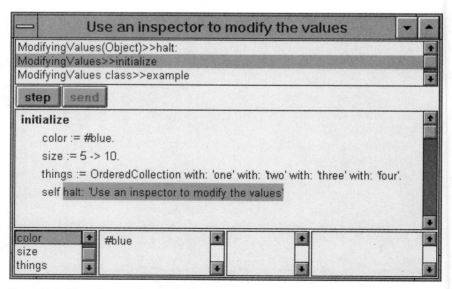

Figure 21-3. Changing a value in the Inspector.

choose accept from the mouse menu. In the preceding example, replace the value #blue with another value, then accept the change.

On the other hand, if you want to replace the *contents* of an object that is being referred to by a variable, you will need to bring up a new Inspector on the variable. You can do this to modify an instance variable of an object, or to modify the contents of a collection. In this example, we want to modify the things collection, removing one item and adding another. If we bring up an Inspector on the collection, we get a window like the one shown in Fig. 21-4. Now we select an item in the collection and use the mouse menu to delete it, or we can use the mouse menu to insert a new item.

In our example, the size variable is an Association. If we want to replace part of the contents of size, we again bring up a new Inspector on the variable, as shown in Fig. 21-5. We then select the variable we want replaced, change the value, and accept the new value.

Halting

If you have several occurrences of self halt in the code, it can be difficult to figure out where a particular Notifier window came from, especially if you are using forked processes. Sometimes you want to proceed a sequence of halts until you find a halt generated from a particular place. The Notifier windows do show some of the stack, but I find it easier to look at the text at the top rather than to scan the stack. There are two ways of doing this: you can modify system methods or you can write your own.

Modifying halt and halt:

The easiest way to provide context information is to modify halt and halt: for Object. Some people recommend against modifying Object, but this change is easy to reproduce when you get a new version of Smalltalk and it doesn't much matter if you don't make the change. Modifying the development tools and development environment tends to be less controversial than modifying system classes that will be used in the deployed application. In both of these examples we want to find the sender of the message, and we get this from thisContext sender.

In halt, modify the errorString: parameter to be 'Halt in ', thisContext sender printString.

In halt:, modify the errorString: parameter to be 'Halt in ', thisContext sender printString, ' - ', aString.

Writing your own myHalt and myHalt:

If you prefer not to modify system methods, or if you have organization rules that prohibit this, then you could instead write new methods on Object, myHalt and myHalt:, which you would use instead of halt and halt:.

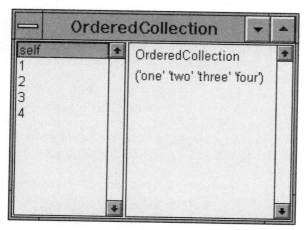

Figure 21-4. Inspecting an OrderedCollection.

```
Object>>myHalt
    Object haltSignal
        raiseRequestWith: thisContext
        errorString: 'Halt in ' , thisContext sender printString

Object>>myHalt: aString
    Object haltSignal
        raiseRequestWith: thisContext
        errorString: 'Halt in ' , thisContext sender printString , ' - ' , aString
```

Conditional halting

There are times when you don't want to halt every time through. One option is to conditionally do the self halt. Alternatively, you could write a haltIf: method on Object. Here are examples of the two approaches:

```
(some condition) ifTrue: [self halt]

Object>>haltIf: aBlock
    aBlock value ifTrue:
        [Object haltSignal
            raiseRequestWith: thisContext
            errorString: 'Halt in ' , thisContext sender printString]

self haltIf: [some condition]
```

Sometimes you don't have a specific condition you want to test for. You can see things happening on the screen or on the Transcript, and after a while you want to trigger the self halt. You need some stimulus to tell the debug code what you are ready, and one obvious way is to hold down a key or key combination that is not pressed in normal operations. For example, you might write an altCtrlHalt method that only halts when the Alt and Ctrl keys are held down at the same time (you could of course write a similar altHalt, ctrlHalt, shiftHalt, etc.):

```
Object>>altCtrlHalt
    "Note the two mechanisms we can use for detecting if the key is down.
    The first one is about 50% faster than the second."
    (InputState default altDown
        and: [ScheduledControllers activeController sensor ctrlDown])
        ifTrue: [Object haltSignal
            raiseRequestWith: thisContext
            errorString: 'Halt in ' , thisContext sender printString]
```

You could probably leave altCtrlHalt message sends in the code for long periods of time, and possibly leave them in customer code for over-the-phone debugging (assuming the stripped-down image contained the classes necessary to run the Debugger). If you don't want to halt, but would rather log something or display something to the Transcript, you can use altCtrlDo:.

```
Object>>altCtrlDo: aBlock
    (InputState default altDown and: [InputState default ctrlDown])
        ifTrue: [aBlock value]
```

Halting without adding a halt

A useful technique for stepping through code without having to add self halt to a method is to do the following. If you simply highlight the code and execute it, you will get a Debugger window and will be able to step into someMethod.

```
self halt.
someObject someMethod.
```

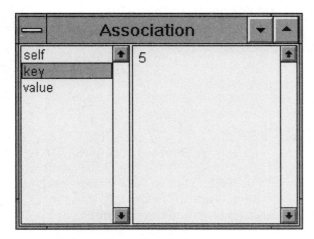

Figure 21-5. Inspecting an Association.

Writing Information to a File or the Transcript

Sometimes you might want to write information about the context to a file or to a Transcript for debugging. Here's an example of a class that does some simple logging. The code that follows prints a string followed by a printout of the stack, showing all the message sends that you made. It will log to either the Transcript or to a file, depending on whether the file variable has been set (the setting method is not shown here). This code can be found in the file debug.st (to run it, evaluate LoggerExample new run in the Transcript after filing it in).

```
Logger>>contextString
    |context stream |
    stream := (String new: 100) writeStream.
    context := thisContext sender.
    ["Unwind the stack until we are out of Logger"
    self == context receiver] whileTrue: [context := context sender].
    "Unwind the stack as far as possible, printing out as we go"
    [context notNil and: [context receiver notNil]]
        whileTrue:
            [stream cr; print: context.
            context := context sender].
    ^stream contents

Logger>>log: aString
    |contextString |
    contextString := self myContextString.
    Object errorSignal
        handle: [:ex |file := nil.
                ex restartDo: [self log: aString]]
        do: [self myWrite: self myWriteStream string: aString context: contextString]

Logger>>myWrite: aStream string: aString context: aContextString
    [aStream cr; cr; nextPutAll: aString; nextPutAll: aContextString; flush]
        valueNowOrOnUnwindDo:
            [aStream == Transcript ifFalse: [aStream close]]

Logger>>myWriteStream
    ^file notNil
        ifTrue: [file appendStream]
        ifFalse: [Transcript]
```

You can use the class NotifierView to give you stack information by doing the following message send, which returns a string containing a stack dump. The second parameter specifies the depth, or number of stack references to return. If the stack is not as deep as the depth you specify, the string contains the full stack. Note the that message is in the private protocol, which means it might be changed or removed.

```
NotifierView shortStackFor: context ofSize: 99
```

For more information on logging debug information, see the article, "A Trace Logger," by Alec Sharp and Dave Farmer, in *The Smalltalk Report*, Nov/Dec 1994.

Audible and Visible Information

Sometimes you might simply want to know when something is happening. If you are on a system that can make a bell sound, you can put the following code into methods to indicate that they are being executed:

```
Screen default ringBell.
```

If you don't want to ring a bell, you can flash a widget. Choose a widget (for example, a widget with the name saveAB), then send it the flash message. For example:

```
(self builder componentAt: #saveAB) flash.
```

Monitoring Activity of Objects

If you have an object that doesn't seem to be behaving itself but you can't figure out why, you can create an object to watch it and report on its behavior. To do this, create a Watcher class as follows. Notice that the superclass is nil. You'll get a warning message about a nil superclass when you accept the class definition for Watcher, and also if you fileIn the code. When you get the warning window, press the Proceed button.

```
nil subclass: #Watcher
    instanceVariableNames: 'watchedObject '
    classVariableNames: ''
    poolDictionaries: ''
    category: 'Debugging'

Watcher class>>on: anObject
    ^self new initializeWatcher: anObject

Watcher>>initializeWatcher: anObject
    watchedObject := anObject

Watcher>>doesNotUnderstand: aMessage
    |result |
    Transcript
        cr; print: thisContext sender; nextPutAll: ' sent ';
        print: watchedObject class; nextPutAll: '>>
        '; nextPutAll: aMessage selector asString.
    aMessage arguments size > 0 ifTrue:
        [Transcript print: aMessage arguments].
    result := watchedObject
        perform: aMessage selector
        withArguments: aMessage arguments.
    Transcript nextPutAll: ' ^'; print: result; flush.
    ^result
```

When you've defined the class and its methods, file out the code, remove the class, then file the code back in. This will create any additional needed methods. (In particular, it creates the method class. Because Watcher is subclassed off nil, it has some special needs.) To use the Watcher, instead of creating your object in the code, create a Watcher on the object by doing something like:

```
myObject := Watcher on: (MyClass new).
```

In your code, all the messages that are being sent to myObject will actually go to the Watcher, which keeps the "real" object in an instance variable. Because it's subclassed off nil, the Watcher doesn't understand many messages, so messages sent to it will end up invoking the doesNotUnderstand: method. In that method we log the message and its arguments, and who sent the message. We then pass the message on to its correct destination, log the return value, then return the return value. It would be easy enough to modify this code if you wanted to log to a file rather than to the Transcript. Here's an example, written on the class side of Watcher, followed by the results.

```
Watcher class>>example
    "self example"
    |array |
    array := self on: (Array new: 3).
    array at: 2 put: 'hello'.
    array at: 2.
    array printString.
    array size

Watcher class>>example sent Array>at:put:#(2 'hello') ^'hello'
Watcher class>>example sent Array>at:#(2) ^'hello'
Watcher class>>example sent Array>printString ^'#(nil ''hello'' nil)'
Watcher class>>example sent Array>size ^3
```

A brief aside

As an aside, the technique of overriding doesNotUnderstand: makes it possible to add instance-specific behavior to instances of a class. Suppose MyClass has an instance variable called methods (with accessors), which contains an IdentityDictionary. The Dictionary could contain associations of methods and blocks of code. MyClass would override doesNotUnderstand: as follows:

```
MyClass>> doesNotUnderstand: aMessage
    |codeBlock |
    codeBlock := self methods at: aMessage selector ifAbsent: [^nil].
    ^codeBlock valueWithArguments: aMessage arguments
```

Here's an example of how it might be used. When you execute this code, 'YES' is printed to the Transcript.

```
instance := MyClass new.
dictionary := IdentityDictionary new.
dictionary at: #yes put: [Transcript cr; show: 'YES'].
instance methods: dictionary.
instance yes.
```

This concept can be extended further to give roles to objects. To use an everyday example, most people have several roles during the day. For example, a woman might at different times play the role of wife, mother, employee, boss, shopper, and chauffeur. Each role has different behaviors. Smalltalk does not have multiple inheritance, but we can emulate the concept with roles. Suppose we have a RolePlayer with an instance variable of role. Instead of keeping a Dictionary of methods and blocks of code, we would create a Role object and pass the Role object to the RolePlayer. Then, if a message were not understood by the RolePlayer it would pass it on to the Role. For example:

```
RolePlayer>>doesNotUnderstand: aMessage
    role notNil ifTrue:
        [^role perform: aMessage selector withArguments: aMessage arguments]

ChauffeurRole>>pickUpKids
    Transcript cr; show: 'I am picking up the children'
```

Then, if we execute the following code, we see the message 'I am picking up the kids' printed to the Transcript.

```
person := RolePlayer new.
person role: ChauffeurRole new.
person pickUpKids.
```

You can find the code for this example in the file role.st. The topic of roles is quite a bit more involved than might be suggested here and is beyond the scope of this book. However, what we've just described might give you ideas for solutions to your own application problems.

Objects Not Being Garbage Collected

During development, the issue of objects not being garbage collected doesn't usually arise because your focus is getting the functionality written. However, as you approach shipping time, you often find that the memory used by your image keeps growing as the application is used. This usually means that there is a memory leak, because you have objects that are not being garbage collected. When an object is not garbage collected, it means that it is still being referenced by at least one other object. And this probably means that the other object is not being garbage collected either.

If you think you have objects hanging around longer than they should, start by doing a garbage collection. You can do this from the

File menu in the Launcher, or by doing one of the garbage collection operations in the collecting garbage class side protocol of ObjectMemory. Try one of the verbose operations, which give you information on the garbage collection done. Once you've cleaned up the garbage you can look at all instances of the class you think has unreclaimed instances, by inspecting:

```
SomeClassName allInstances.
```

If there are several instances, by inspecting the instance variables, you might be able to find one that you know should have disappeared. Otherwise, you'll have to select one at random. You can now look at the objects that reference this instance by inspecting self allOwners in the Inspector window. This is the classic approach, but it's not easy to use this technique to follow through the owners. A better approach is to inspect the following in the Inspector window.

```
self allOwnersWeakly: true
```

Sending allOwnersWeakly: true to an object returns a WeakArray of references rather than an Array, which means that the references can be garbage collected. Using allOwnersWeakly: usually gives you a smaller list of owners to look at. Below is some code that you can add to Inspector to inspect owners of an object, filtering out most of the uninteresting owners. It is based on a method written by Jan Steinman and documented by Alan Knight in *The Smalltalk Report*, May 1994. It appears to work, but I don't use it enough to guarantee anything!

```
Inspector>>inspectOwners
    ((self fieldValue allOwnersWeakly: true) reject:
        [:each | self shouldReject: each]) inspect

Inspector>>shouldReject: anObject
    "The WeakArray often gives an owner of 0"
    anObject == 0 ifTrue: [^true].
    "We don't want to see the object we are inspecting"
    anObject == object ifTrue: [^true].
    "We don't want to see this inspector"
    anObject == self ifTrue: [^true].
    "We don't want to see the methods that got us here"
    (anObject class == MethodContext
        and: [anObject selector == #allOwners
        or: [anObject selector == #allOwnersWeakly:]]) ifTrue: [^true].
    "We don't want to see the stack array that contains the object"
    (anObject class == Array
        and: [anObject size == 12
        and: [(anObject at: 3) == self fieldValue]]) ifTrue: [^true].
    "We want to see anything that's left after this filter"
    ^false
```

The Advanced Tools contains a class, ReferencePathCollector, whose purpose is to help find objects that are not being garbage collected. The class comment includes the following: "My purpose is to find what is hanging onto objects that can't be garbage collected, by finding reference paths to a given object." We can add another item to the inspect menu that uses the ReferencePathCollector. When you use it, be prepared for a long path; it can be several hundred references long.

```
Inspector>>inspectPaths
    (ReferencePathCollector allReferencePathsTo: self fieldValue) inspect
```

Once you've added these methods, you'll need to go to the fieldMenu method of Inspector and add the methods inspectOwners and inspectPaths to the menu. The labels string should now look something like 'inspect\owners\paths' withCRs. Accept the method, then evaluate Inspector flushMenus to make the change take effect. Here are a few lines of code from the modified fieldMenu.

```
ListMenu == nil ifTrue:
    [ListMenu := Menu
        labels: 'inspect\owners\paths' withCRs
        values: #(inspectField inspectOwners inspectPaths)].
```

For additional information on objects not being reclaimed, you might look at the article "Taking Out the Garbage," by Derek Williams, in the January 1996 issue of *The Smalltalk Report*.

Public Domain Debugging Software

A debugging enhancement is available from the *Smalltalk Archives*, written by Bob Hinkle. Called *Breakpoint*, its great virtue is that it allows you to add and remove breakpoints without affecting the change set and change log. You can add either an absolute breakpoint, which always causes a halt when encountered, or a conditional breakpoint, which causes a halt only when the associated condition evaluates to true.

A companion package, *Lightweight*, also written by Hinkle, allows you to add breakpoints to individual objects, rather than all objects of that class. That is, you can modify the behavior of just one object without affecting the behavior of any other object. There is more information on how to get files from the *Smalltalk Archives* in Chapter 35, *Public Domain Code and Information*.

Commercial Debugging Software

The Smalltalk Professional Debug Package

Also available for use with Objectworks\Smalltalk and VisualWorks is the *Smalltalk Professional Debug Package*. As with *Breakpoint*, adding a breakpoint does not affect the change set or the change log. However, where *Breakpoint* uses the compiler to add breakpoints, the *Smalltalk*

Professional Debug Package modifies the compiled code directly. This provides the capability for some nice features, such as the ability to add another breakpoint to a method without having to restart the method, having the breakpoints disappear when the method exits, and allowing skip-to-caret into and out of blocks. You can also use the package to add debugging code that does not cause a halt; for example to just collect data.

At the time of writing, the software cost is $89 plus shipping and handling ($149 for the ENVY version). To order or get additional information, you can send e-mail to traymond@craftedsmalltalk.com, or call Terry Raymond at (401) 846-6573. He also has a web site at http://www.craftedsmalltalk.com where you can get more information.

Object Explorer

Another package that might help you debug an application is *Object Explorer* from First Class Software. This software diagrams the interrelationships between objects, which can be quite a help when debugging a complex application that you are not familiar with. There is a review of Object Explorer by Steven Bilow in the June 1994 issue of *The Journal of Object-Oriented Programming*, which speaks very highly of the product; "It is a profound debugging tool and a great design aid."

At the time of writing, the software cost is $499. You can reach First Class Software at P.O. Box 226, Boulder Creek, CA 95006-0226, at (408) 338-4649, or by e-mail to Compuserve address: 70761.1216@compuserve.com.

22

Common Errors

This chapter describes some of the more common errors that Smalltalk programmers make, and gives suggestions on how to prevent the errors.

Notifier Window Messages

As you test your code you are likely to have exceptions raised. Here are a few exception messages you might run into, along with some text describing common causes of the exception.

Message not understood: #self (or some other object)

This occurs when you leave a period off the end of a statement. It tells you that the self with which you are starting a statement is being used as a message to the result of the previous statement. That is, there is no statement separator. You might be sending the message to an object other than self, in which case that variable name will be the message name that was not understood.

Message not understood: #do:

This often occurs in a printOn: method, if the parameter to nextPutAll: is not a string. To correct this, send printString or displayString to the parameter, or use the print: message instead of nextPutAll:.

Message not understood: #startingAt:replaceElementsIn:from:to:

This often occurs when you are creating a string using the comma (,) message but the object on the right side of the comma is not of the appropriate class. For example, 'abc', 3 would generate this exception.

Message not understood: #someArbitraryMessage

The most common cause of getting a message not understood exception is to send the message to nil. That is, your variable contains nil rather than the object you thought it contained.

Losing Code You Modified in a Debugger

A common mistake when debugging is to add self halt to a method and leave the method displayed in a Browser window. When you hit the halt, you step through the code, find the problem, and modify the code in the debugger. You then go back to the original window and make another change to the method. But because the Browser is still looking at the old version of the code, you lose the changes you made in the debugger. The easiest way to correct this problem is to deselect the method after adding a self halt. Then when you select it again, it has the changes.

Removing from a Collection You Are Iterating Over

If you are iterating over a collection using do:, and removing elements that satisfy some condition, you will probably get an exception. The invocation of do: sets up some boundary conditions that are no longer true when elements are removed, because the collection will be rearranged as you remove elements. When I do the following, I get a Message not understood exception:

```
collection:= OrderedCollection withAll: #(1 2 3 4 5 6).
collection do: [ :each | each even ifTrue: [collection remove: each]].
```

Instead, make a copy of the collection before iterating over it, such as shown below (of course, you should also consider using select: or reject:)

```
collection:= OrderedCollection withAll: #(1 2 3 4 5 6).
collection copy do: [ :each | each even ifTrue: [collection remove: each]].
```

It's also possible to have the same problem even if you are not deleting objects directly. For example, the following code closes any open files with the specified path. As the files are closed, they are removed from the OpenStreams collection of ExternalStream, so again, we need to iterate over a copy of the collection.

```
(ExternalStream classPool at: #OpenStreams) copy
    do: [ :each | each name = aPath ifTrue: [each close]].
```

Not Returning the Injection Variable in inject:into:

If you use inject:into:, you'll probably find that you sometimes forget to return the thing that is being injected. Remember that the value of a block is the value of the last statement executed, so you need to finish with something that guarantees the last thing is the injection variable. You can simply name the injection variable, or you can send it the yourself message. Here are examples of both:

```
self withAllSubclasses
    inject: OrderedCollection new
    into: [:coll :each | coll addAll: each allInstances; yourself]
```

```
#(3 $x 'hello' #mySymbol)
    inject: String new writeStream
    into: [ :stream :each |
        stream print: each class; nextPutAll: ' value '; print: each; cr.
        stream]
```

Missing Caret (^)

A very common bug for new Smalltalk programmers is to forget the caret (^) when returning a value. This is usually seen when writing a new method. For example, the following creates a new, initialized instance of MyClass, then returns the class rather than the instance:

```
MyClass>>new
    super new initialize
```

The correct version should have a caret to return the instance. (It might also be worth using the basicNew: message — see Chapter 5 for more information.)

```
MyClass>>new
    ^super new initialize
```

```
MyClass>>new
    ^self basicNew initialize.
```

Not Implementing =

If you create your own class, then compare two instances of it using =, the test will return false. For example, two separately created instances of a new Location class will not compare as equal, even if all the details of the location are the same. This is because the default implementation of = is to use ==, so = is actually checking to see if they are the *same object*. If you create your own class and will be doing tests for equality between instances of the class, you need to write your own = method that compares the instance variables.

If you write your own = method, you will also need to write your own hash method, because two objects that are equal should also have the same hash value. (Hash values are used when putting objects in collections that use hashing, such as Set and Bag.)

Assuming that Methods Return Self

A common bug is to assume that all methods return self, and in particular, to assume that add: returns self. The following will *not* give you what you expect, because add: returns the object added (similarly remove: returns the object removed, and at:put: returns the object put):

```
collection := OrderedCollection new
    add: objectOne;
    add: objectTwo.
```

The example above actually assigns objectTwo to collection. The following techniques all give you what you expected:

```
collection := OrderedCollection new.
collection
    add: objectOne;
    add: objectTwo.

(collection := OrderedCollection new)
    add: objectOne;
    add: objectTwo.

collection := OrderedCollection new
    add: objectOne;
    add: objectTwo;
    yourself.
```

The last example shows the use of the message yourself, which always returns the receiver. The use of yourself can make code a lot more robust. For example, both lines below should give you an employee object. However, the first line relies on the salary: accessor conforming to standards and returning self. The second line ensures that you always get the correct result.

```
employee := Employee new salary: aSalary.
employee := Employee new salary: aSalary; yourself.
```

Incorrect Messages to Booleans

You send ifTrue:, ifFalse:, ifTrue:ifFalse:, and ifFalse:ifTrue: to the Booleans true and false. These values might be the results of evaluating an expression in parentheses. On the other hand, you send whileTrue, whileFalse, whileTrue:, and whileFalse:, to instances of BlockClosure. That is, the if messages are sent to a Boolean and while messages are sent to a BlockClosure. For example:

```
(some condition) ifTrue: [some code].
(another condition)
    ifFalse: [this code]
    ifTrue: [that code].

[some code] whileTrue.
[some code] whileFalse: [more code].
```

Not Reinitializing Class Variables

A common error when using class variables to contain static information is to modify the information but to not reinitialize the variable. Class side initialize methods are invoked when code is filed into the image, but once the code is in the image, the initialize method is not automatically sent again.

A common partial solution is to have a comment saying "self initialize" at the start of the initialize method, which you select and execute after accepting the modified method. For example:

```
MyClass class>>initialize
    "self initialize"
    Messages := Dictionary new.
    Messages at: #notFound put: 'Not found'.
```

Problems with Copies

When you copy an object, the copy method does a shallow copy, which is a one-level-deep copy. The original object is copied, but no instance variables are copied — that is, the two objects have the same instance variable objects. Because of this, we have to be very careful about what we do with copies. Let's look at examples of modifying a copied collection and a copied non-collection object. In the examples below, we'll use a Person class, with the instance variables name and phone, and accessors for both variables:

Modifying copy of non-collection object

Suppose you make a copy of an Employee object for safekeeping while you modify the original. If you do the following, you'll see that personTwo now has a phone number of '444-5555', which is not what you wanted.

```
personOne := Person new name: 'Alec'; phone: '555-5555'; yourself.
personTwo := personOne copy.
personOne phone replaceFrom: 1 to: 3 with: '444'.
personTwo inspect.
```

Now, the chances are that you would not be replacing characters in a string, but rather the whole string, in which case there would be no problem. However, a Person object might contain an Address object. If you replaced the street address in personOne's address, you'd find this change reflected in personTwo. To overcome this problem, Person needs to implement postCopy. For more information, see Chapter 25.

Modifying copy of collection

Let's create a collection of Person objects, then copy the collection. We might expect that the Person objects in the second collection would be copies of the Person objects in the first collection. However, this is not the case. Even though we copied the collection, the objects in the copied collection are the *same* objects as the objects in the original collection. In this example, we modify the phone number of one person. If we inspect the copied collection, we'll see that the person has the new phone number, '222-2222'.

```
personOne := Person new name: 'Alec'; phone: '555-5555'; yourself.
personTwo := Person new name: 'Dave'; phone: '111-1111'; yourself.
collectionOne := OrderedCollection new add: personOne; add: personTwo; yourself.
collectionTwo := collectionOne copy.
personOne phone: '222-2222'.
personTwo inspect.
```

If we create the second collection by copying the Person objects, we solve this problem. For example, if we create collectionTwo by doing the following, then inspect collectionTwo, the phone number will still be '111-1111'.

```
collectionTwo := collectionOne collect: [:each | each copy].
```

If you have an object that contains a collection in an instance variable, there's a question of whether you should even give access to the collection. For more information, see the section on "Accessors for collections" in Chapter 4.

^ In Block Returns from Method

There is, unfortunately, no way to return from a block other than hitting the right square bracket. If you use a caret (^) to return, you will exit the method as well as the block. For example, the following will exit the method.

```
MyClass>>myMethod
    someCondition ifTrue:
        [self someCode.
        anotherCondition ifFalse: [^false].
        self moreCode.
        self otherCode].
```

For the code to work correctly, you'll have to structure the code so that the right end of the block is hit. The first example keeps the code in the original method. The second example shows how you might put the block code in a different method, to keep the methods simple and easy to understand.

```
MyClass>>myMethod
    someCondition ifTrue:
        [self someCode.
        anotherCondition ifTrue:
            [self moreCode.
            self otherCode]].
```

```
MyClass>>myMethod
    someCondition ifTrue:
        [self someCode.
        self checkConditionAndDoStuff].
```

Modifying a Literal Array

Modifying a literal array leads to unexpected behavior. For example, create a class MyClass and add the following method (the code can be found in the file literal.st).

```
MyClass>>methodOne
    |literalArray |
    literalArray := #(1 2 3 4 5).
    Transcript cr; show: literalArray printString.
    (literalArray at: 3) == 3
        ifTrue: [literalArray at: 3 put: 99]
        ifFalse: [Transcript cr; show: 'Oh no. It is already 99']
```

The first time you evaluate MyClass new methodOne you will see the following:

```
#(1 2 3 4 5)
```

If you then evaluate the same line again, you will see this instead:

```
#(1 2 99 4 5)
On no. It is already 99
```

Looking at the method, it appears that you are assigning #(1 2 3 4 5) each time you execute the method. However, if you hold down the Shift key when selecting the method, you will see that the assignment line looks like the following:

```
MyClass>>methodOne
    |t1 |
    t1 := #(1 2 99 4 5).
```

In other words, the literal array has been modified in memory. Let's look at another example, this time using a WriteStream. We use the with: message to position the stream pointer to the end of the collection.

```
MyClass>>methodTwo
    |stream |
    stream := WriteStream with: #(1 2 3 4 5).
    Transcript cr; show: stream contents printString.
    stream nextPutAll: #(6 7 8 9).
    Transcript cr; show: stream contents printString
```

The first time we execute methodTwo, the Transcript shows:

```
#(1 2 3 4 5)
#(1 2 3 4 5 6 7 8 9)
```

The second time we execute the method, the Transcript shows the following:

```
#(1 2 3 4 5 6 7 8 9 nil nil)
#(1 2 3 4 5 6 7 8 9 nil nil 6 7 8 9)
```

Again, the literal array has been modified in memory. This time it has actually grown rather than just having element values changed. As before, you can hold the Shift key down while selecting methodTwo in the Browser, and you'll see that the literal array is not what you thought it was.

How do we prevent this problem? The best way is to never do things directly with a literal array in your code. Always do things with a copy of the literal array. In the above two examples, if we had written the lines as below, there would be no problem:

```
literalArray := #(1 2 3 4 5) copy.
stream := WriteStream with: #(1 2 3 4 5) copy.
```

So, for example, if you have a method that returns a literal string, have it instead return a copy of the string, as shown below:

```
MyClass>>localName
  ^'Request' copy
```

User Interface

23

Model-View-Controller

The Model-View-Controller (MVC) paradigm is a way of splitting up your application so that it's easier to change parts of it without affecting other parts. Before we look at what this means, we need to define certain words, which we will do in the context of a user editing employee information on a screen. (See Fig. 23-1.)

The *model* is the object or objects that make up the underlying problem domain, and is therefore also known as the *domain model*. (The word domain is used a lot in Smalltalk applications, and means the realm, area, or field of the underlying problem you are trying to solve.) The model can exist without a user interface, and for the purposes of running regression tests, should probably be able to function without a user interface driving it.

In our example, the model is an employee object. The employee object can exist without a user interface, and in fact probably spends most of its time without a user interface, either in a database or taking part in report creation and paycheck creation.

The *view* is the presentation to the user of information contained in the model. This usually consists of screens containing information from the model. The data might be shown in fields, in editor windows, in tables, and so on. Also, the data might be read-only or it might be editable. In our example, the view is the employee edit screen, with fields to handle edits to the employee name, social security number, address, and so on.

The *controller* controls the input from the user. The default controllers handle input from the keyboard and from a mouse. Each of the fields on the screen has its own specialized controller, as does each action button, each menu button, and so on. Each type of widget has a controller that knows exactly how to handle keyboard and mouse input for that type of widget.

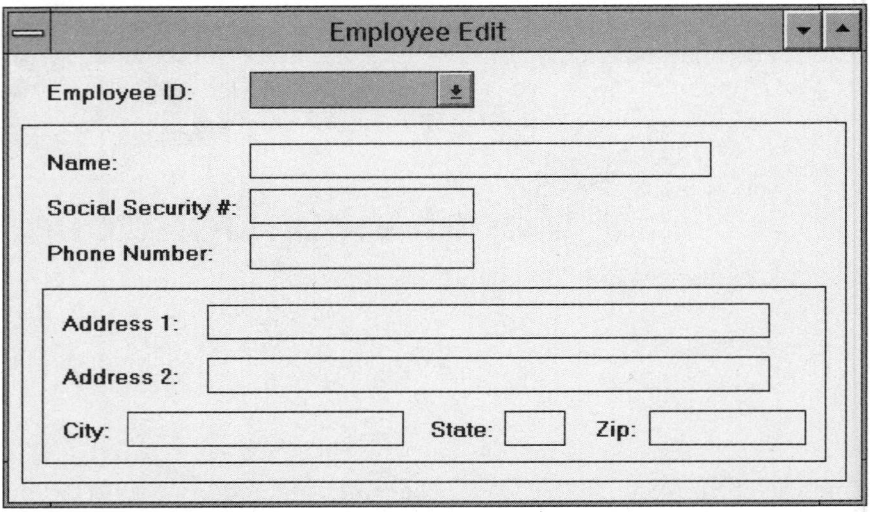

Figure 23-1. The Employee edit screen.

In a normal application, there is a tight coupling between the view and the controller, and for most purposes they seem to be simply different behaviors of the same thing. However, by separating the view and the controller it's possible to give them more powerful behavior, by giving them different inheritance hierarchies. It's also makes it possible to create customized controllers for more specialized applications.

Why Is Model-View-Controller Important?

Ignoring the controller, which seems to be the poor relative of the three, MVC allows us to separate our application into two major components that can be replaced or worked on in relative isolation. For example, by separating the model from the user interface, one set of developers can work on the underlying problem domain while others can work on the user interface. Obviously there has to be some connection, but MVC makes it a lot easier to separate the work areas. By separating the view from the model, it becomes possible to change the way the model is viewed, and even have multiple views of the model.

Because the view is separated from the model, there has to be a way for the view to tell the model that a user has made changes. Similarly, there has to be a way for the model to tell its view that the model has changed, and that the view needs to update itself with the latest information.

Because there is a separation between the model and the view, with a well defined way of communicating, this allows multiple views of the same underlying data. For example, suppose you have a spreadsheet open to do some modeling of revenue flows over the next year. Besides the spreadsheet, you also have open a graph showing revenues by month, and another graph showing cumulative revenues over the year. As you make changes to the spreadsheet (using a view and a controller), these changes are given to the model, which then tells *all* its views about the changes. The views get the new information and redisplay themselves appropriately. So, as you make changes to the spreadsheet the two graphs are automatically updated.

How Are the Model and View Tied Together?

The mechanism that ties the model and the view together is the *dependency* mechanism. Each view registers itself as a dependent of the model. The view knows about the model and can therefore send messages to the model directly, to update it. However, the model has no direct knowledge about any of the views. The model doesn't care if there are no views, one view, two views, or thousands of views. The only connection between the model and the views is that the model has a collection of dependents that it informs about changes. When the model changes, it sends out a message to each of its dependents about the change, but neither knows nor cares what the dependents will do with that information. Figure 23-2 illustrates this.

In effect, the model says, if you drop your business card in this box I will send you information about our new products. If you don't want to receive information, take your business card out of the box. So, when there is new information to distribute, the model goes to the box and sends the information to everyone whose card is in the box.

The Macro and Micro View

There are two ways of looking at MVC: macro, and micro. At a macro level, we might have a screen that allows a user to edit employee information. The employee object is the underlying model, while the screen is the view.

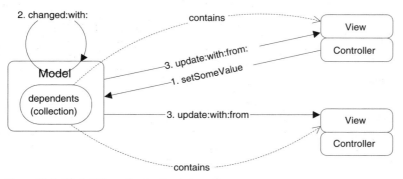

Figure 23-2. Model-View-Controller interactions.

At a micro level, the employee edit screen has several input fields — for name, social security number, phone number, address, and so on. It might have a menu button for pay grade and a text editor for general notes. Each of these fields is a miniature example of MVC. Each field has a controller associated with it that knows how to handle input to that type of field. Each field has an underlying model, an instance variable of the Employee object. One field might have the employee name as its model, while another field has the employee's social security number as its model. The view is obviously the input field.

So, when the user types an employee name, the controller updates the model, the model sends a changed message to its dependents, and the view is updated with the new name. This might seem a little redundant because the view is already showing the name (after all, the user just typed it in), but it allows us to manipulate the data. For example, the user enters the employee's hire date in one of several acceptable date formats. The date will be stored in the employee object as an instance of Date. When the view is informed of the change, it might change the date format to a standard display format.

The ApplicationModel Framework

VisualWorks provides a framework to help manage a user interface application with its many MVC components. This is the ApplicationModel. When we create a screen using the Canvas Tool, we have to specify a class to install the canvas on, and this class will usually be a subclass of ApplicationModel. In our example, we are using the screen to edit an instance of Employee, so let's call the class EmployeeUI. For each variable in the Employee object that we are editing, the EmployeeUI class has a corresponding instance variable. This allows us to separate out the underlying model (the instance of Employee) from the application (the instance of EmployeeUI).

By default, when the user edits data in an input field, the application will modify the data in its instance variable. Let's look at how this works, using an input field that is associated with an employee phone number. Remember that the mechanism at play is that the view (the input field) registers itself as a dependent of the model (the phone number), then gets informed about changes to the model.

ValueHolder

Our phone number is an instance of String. If the view adds itself as a dependent of the string '555-5555', it will never be told of changes. This is because we will not be *modifying* the string, but will be *replacing* it with another string, say '555-1212'. So if the view registers as a dependent of '555-5555', it will still be waiting for '555-5555' to change, which it will never do. In fact, the string won't even be garbage collected because the view is referring to it. This is illustrated in Fig. 23-3.

To solve the problem, we wrap the phone number in a ValueHolder and the view registers as a dependent of the ValueHolder. The ValueHolder has a single instance variable called value, which contains the object it is holding — in our case, the phone number. To get the phone number, we send the message value to the ValueHolder, and to set a new phone number, we send the message value:. When the ValueHolder receives the value: message it stores the new value, then sends itself a changed message, which informs all its dependents of the change. The value: method is implemented by a superclass, ValueModel and looks like this:

```
ValueModel>>value: newValue
    self setValue: newValue.
    self changed: #value
```

Figure 23-4 illustrates the ValueHolder mechanism, showing how dependents are informed when a value changes.

If you let the Canvas Tool Definer create the application model's instance variables, it will make them ValueHolders. Here's an example of the phone accessor that the Definer will create for you. Notice that the phone number is initialized to a ValueHolder on a new string (String new asValue).

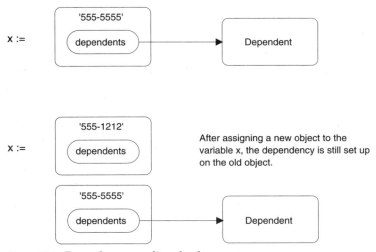

Figure 23-3. Dependency on a literal value.

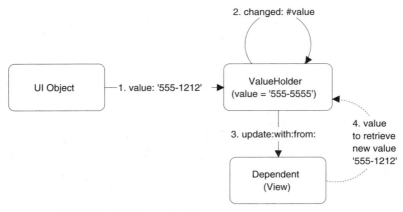

Figure 23-4. The ValueHolder mechanism.

```
phone
    "This method was generated by UIDefiner. Any edits made here
    may be lost whenever methods are automatically defined. The
    initialization provided below may have been preempted by an
    initialize method."

    ^phone isNil
        ifTrue:
            [phone := String new asValue]
        ifFalse:
            [phone]
```

Thus the EmployeeUI's phone variable contains a ValueHolder that is holding a phone string. However, in our Employee object, the phone variable contains a string, not a ValueHolder. Somehow we have to connect together the phone variable in our Employee object and the phone variable in our EmployeeUI object.

The easiest approach is to write two methods in EmployeeUI, called something like copyModelToView and copyViewToModel. When we get an Employee object to edit, we execute copyModelToView, which puts the employee values in the ValueHolders in EmployeeUI. Then, when the user is done editing and wants to save the changes, we execute copyViewToModel, which puts the new values into the Employee object.

AspectAdaptor

The ValueHolder mechanism suffers from one big disadvantage: The object you care about has to be wrapped in a ValueHolder. As we showed above, the easiest way to overcome this is to copy values from the Employee object into the ValueHolders, then copy them back when the user is finished editing. This means that we have to write specific copying methods.

The class AspectAdaptor eliminates this problem. AspectAdaptors act as middlemen, removing the necessity to copy values back and forth. The instance variable of our application (our EmployeeUI) contains AspectAdaptors. When we create each AspectAdaptor, we tell it what object we are interested in (the subject, or domain model), and what instance variable of that object (the aspect). In our example, we create an AspectAdaptor with the Employee object as its subject, and the phone number instance variable as its aspect. The phone input field then registers as a dependent of the AspectAdaptor. When the user changes the phone number, the input field tells the AspectAdaptor of the change, and the AspectAdaptor sets the new phone number in the employee object. Figure 23-5 illustrates this.

The change notification can then be done either by the Employee object or the AspectAdaptor. When you create the AspectAdaptor you can specify whether the subject (the employee) sends updates. The default is for the AspectAdaptor to send the update message, which is what we show in Fig. 23-5. If the subject sends updates, the AspectAdaptor registers as a dependent of the subject, receives the update messages, filters them, and sends the appropriate ones to its own dependents (i.e., the view). If the subject does not send updates, the AspectAdaptor does not register as a dependent. Instead, after setting the new value in the model, it sends the update message itself. Here's the code that does this (AspectAdaptor inherits the code from ProtocolAdaptor).

```
ProtocolAdaptor>>value: newValue
    self setValue: newValue.
    subjectSendsUpdates ifFalse: [self changed: #value]
```

Subject channels

An AspectAdaptor sets up a connection between an instance variable of a domain object and a view on a screen. If you are editing an Employee object, each AspectAdaptor is connected to a different instance variable of the Employee. To edit a different Employee object on the same screen

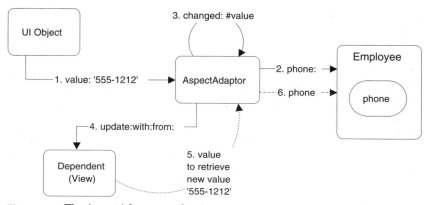

Figure 23-5. The AspectAdaptor mechanism.

means reconnecting each AspectAdaptor to the new Employee. Fortunately, VisualWorks makes it easy to do this using the subject channel. Instead of specifying a subject when creating the AspectAdaptor, we specify a subject channel. The subject channel should be a type of ValueModel, which in our example means that we will wrap the Employee in a ValueHolder and specify the ValueHolder as the subject channel.

Each AspectAdaptor registers as a dependent of the Employee ValueHolder, so when the ValueHolder is given a new Employee (by sending value: anEmployee to the ValueHolder), the AspectAdaptor is informed of the change in subject. Once it receives notification, it changes its subject. If all the AspectAdaptors are dependents on the Employee ValueHolder, they will all be informed when the Employee changes and will all set the new Employee to be their subject. Figure 23-6 illustrates how subject channels work. Note that step six is only done if the subject sends updates.

Using AspectAdaptors and the subject channel mechanism, we can easily associate individual fields on a screen with instance variables of the domain object, and the entire screen with the domain object as a whole. In the next chapter we'll go over examples of ValueHolders and different types of AspectAdaptor, using code to illustrate how they work.

Summary

The Model-View-Controller paradigm provides a way to separate out the components of a user interface-oriented application, allowing each component to specialize and to be developed in relative isolation. The VisualWorks user interface classes are all built around the MVC paradigm, so much of the work has already been done for you. At the

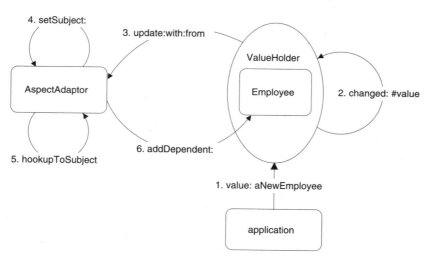

Figure 23-6. The subject channel.

micro level, all you really need to do is to use the provided classes until you need some specialized functionality.

It is at the macro level that the MVC paradigm really gives you something to think about. It encourages you to think about your domain problem to the point that you can separate out domain objects and domain functionality from the interface with the user. In most cases, the goal of such thinking should be to have a domain model that can be driven from an external source, such as a set of batch files, a socket interface, the Transcript, or a test tool. This makes it much easier to test the application. If the domain problem functionality can be driven by these mechanisms, then by adding a graphical user interface you are simply putting in a different view and a different controller.

Chapter

24

MVC Dependencies

In the previous chapter we talked about the Model-View-Controller philosophy, and about how it requires that we break the solution into *model*, *view*, and *controller* pieces, where each piece has relative independence from the others. A key part of MVC is that the views be separated from the model so that a given model can have multiple views looking at it, or different aspects of it.

To inform all the views of changes in the model, we use the dependency mechanism. In this chapter we take a look at some of the different ways that we can implement the dependencies. In most applications there is only one view, and the view and the controller are tightly tied. Some of the mechanisms we will look at only work in this tight environment and will not support additional views. The more general situation, of course, is one in which the controller and one view are tightly tied, but other views of the model also exist.

Our example will be a person with a name and an age. The person object is the underlying model. We will allow the user to set or change the name or age, using a window with input fields. We also create some additional windows that simply show the values of the person's name and age. The three superclasses for the MyPerson, MyInput, and MyView examples are as follows, showing only the important information:

```
Model subclass: #MyPerson
    instanceVariableNames: 'name age '

ApplicationModel subclass: #MyInput
    instanceVariableNames: 'person '

ApplicationModel subclass: #MyView
    instanceVariableNames: 'person '
```

All the code for these examples is shown in Appendix B at the end of the book. Enough code is shown in the following text to illustrate certain points, but for more details, you'll need to refer to the appendix. Additionally, you can find the code in the file mvcdep.st. Because we are just illustrating points in the text, we'll use only the age variable in our examples.

We will create one window that allows input, and several other windows that simply display the data. When we change the name or age in the MyInput window, we expect the MyView windows to update their displays. Unless otherwise noted, all input and view windows have one instance variable, person, to hold their model. We will not show any accessors for person to save space, and will reference it directly. Figure 24-1 shows how the windows look when you run the examples.

Shown are several examples of different dependency mechanisms. Each is numbered so that, for instance, Example One has a MyPerson1 model, a MyInput1 input window, and a MyView1 display window. Let's start by writing MyApp, an application that will run the various examples. Of course, we'll need to write the example code before this code will do anything.

```
MyApp class>>newExample: aNumber
    ^super new initialize: aNumber

MyApp>>initialize: aNumber
    |model window modelClass inputClass viewClass windowType num |
    num := aNumber printString.
    modelClass := Smalltalk at: ('MyPerson' , num) asSymbol.
    inputClass := Smalltalk at: ('MyInput' , num) asSymbol.
    viewClass := Smalltalk at: ('MyView' , num) asSymbol.
    model := modelClass new.
    1to: 4 do:
            [:index |
            windowType := (index == 4)
                    ifTrue: [inputClass]
                    ifFalse: [viewClass].
            window := (windowType open: model) window.
            window application: self.
            window bePartner]
```

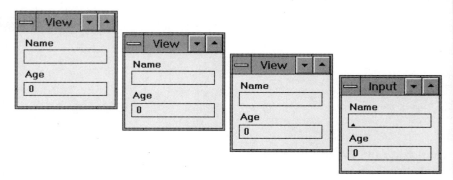

Figure 24-1. The view and input windows.

This code opens three MyView windows and one MyInput window and makes them peers, so that, if you close one they all close. For this to work, you must make sure that MyApp is subclassed off ApplicationModel. To start up Example1 when you've written the Example1 code, from a workspace evaluate:

```
MyApp newExample: 1.
```

Now we need to create the user interface for our examples. Using the Canvas Tool, create a small window with two input fields: a string field with aspect name and a numeric field with aspect age. Give the window the label Input. Install the window on class MyInput1 and define it as an Application. Modify the window label to be View, and make both fields read only, then install it on class MyView1, again defining it as an Application. All MyView and MyInput examples have a class side method open: as follows.

```
open: aPerson
    ^self openOn: (self new initialize: aPerson)
```

Example One: Using AddDependent:

The basic dependency mechanism is to register as a dependent using addDependent:, then to filter the change notifications in which you are interested. We will take a look at an example using this mechanism, but I don't particularly recommend it because VisualWorks provides much easier and more powerful mechanisms.

We'll start by looking at how data gets into the application, through the MyInput window. Below is the initialization code for MyInput1. We register ourself as a dependent of the age variable, so that when the age variable changes we'll be told about it (we'll see more about the onChangeSend:to: message in a later section).

We are assuming that the MyInput window is the only way that the age and name values can change. If the application can change a person's data behind the scenes, we would need to have the MyInput window register as a dependent of the parent, which means we would need extra code to prevent changes sent to us generating changes back to the model (which would lead to an infinite loop). In reality, we wouldn't be using this mechanism because better ones exist, as we will see in the other examples.

```
MyInput1>>initialize: aPerson
    person := aPerson.
    age := 0 asValue.
    age onChangeSend: #ageChanged to: self
```

When the user enters a new age, the MyInput1 object is sent the ageChanged message. It then sends a message to the model — the person — telling it to set its age.

```
MyInput1>>ageChanged
    person age: self age value
```

When we set a new age in our model, it sends itself a changed message to inform its dependents. We include the new value so that the dependents don't have to come back and ask us for it. Because no one asks us for the value, we don't need a get accessor. Note that, in Chapter 19, we adopted the convention of sending the *old* value in the changed message. In this chapter, we adopt the alternative convention of sending the *new* value.

```
MyPerson1>>age: aValue
    age := aValue.
    self changed: #age with: age
```

Figure 24-2 shows the mechanism used for notifying dependents when you use the addDependent: message.

The views all register as dependents of the person using addDependent:. This means that, when the person informs all its dependents of changes, the views will have to filter the update messages to see if they are interested in the change. The age variable contains a ValueHolder, because the input field widget expects to get an instance of a subclass of ValueModel when it sends the age message.

```
MyView1>>initialize: aPerson
    person := aPerson.
    person addDependent: self.
    age := 0 asValue.

MyView1>>update: aSymbol with: aValue from: anObject
    aSymbol == #name ifTrue: [self name value: aValue].
    aSymbol == #age ifTrue: [self age value: aValue]
```

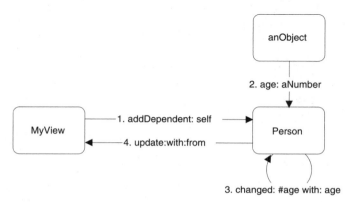

Figure 24-2. The addDependent: mechanism.

Example Two: ValueHolders

The problem with the basic dependency mechanism of addDependent: and update: is that we register an interest in hearing about any changes made to the model, then have to filter out the ones we are not interested in. If we had become dependent on the value of the instance variable we were interested in, we would have lost the dependency as soon as the instance variable had a new value. Instead of being dependent on the value, we can wrap the value in a ValueHolder, register a dependency on the ValueHolder, and be informed every time it gets a new value to hold.

As we explained in Chapter 19, we can register an interest in changes by sending onChangeSend:to: a subclass of ValueModel. In Example 2 we make the age and name variables into ValueHolders so that, when the actual value changes, the dependents of the ValueHolder will be sent the appropriate message. (See Fig. 24-3.)

```
MyPerson2>>age
    ^age isNil
        ifTrue: [age := 0 asValue]
        ifFalse: [age]
```

In MyView2 the initialize: method tells the person object's instance variables to send it a message when they change. It then has to implement the methods it has asked to be sent.

```
MyView2>>initialize: aPerson
    person := aPerson.
    person age onChangeSend: #ageChanged to: self.
    age := 0 asValue.
```

```
MyView2>>ageChanged
    self age value: person age value.
```

The model's instance variables are ValueHolders, which internally send the message changed: #value. This update message is trapped by a DependencyTransformer and transformed into the message we specified; in this case ageChanged. Because the new value is not passed back, we have to ask the person for the age ValueHolder, to which we sent the value message to get the new age that it is holding.

Again, I don't recommend using ValueHolders as the general mechanism for GUI dependency work, because VisualWorks provides an easier and more powerful mechanism, AspectAdaptors.

Example Three: AspectAdaptors

Using ValueHolders forces domain models to use artifical wrappers around their instance variables for the convenience of any potential GUI. The problem with using ValueHolders for the instance variables

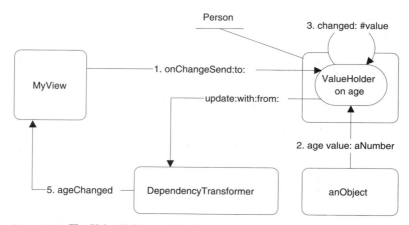

Figure 24-3. The ValueHolder mechanism.

of your model is that a model models some domain object. Conceptually, it has instance variables that are real data, rather than having instance variables that are wrappers of real data.

An AspectAdaptor is a powerful mechanism for handling GUI dependencies without forcing the model to use these artificial wrappers around its data. The model has various pieces of information, all contained in different instance variables. AspectAdaptors allow you to associate the GUI (ApplicationModel) with a particular subject (the model) and different aspects of the subject (the instance variables). (See Fig. 24-4.)

An AspectAdaptor is an easy way to set up an intermediary between the GUI and the model's data. When a user types something in a field in the GUI, the model's data is updated. Also, when the model's data is updated, the views of the data are updated. Let's see how we would code this:

```
MyInput3>>initialize: aPerson
    person := aPerson

MyInput3>>age
    ^(AspectAdaptor subject: person sendsUpdates: true)
        forAspect: #age
```

The code for MyView3 is exactly the same as that for MyInput3 (the only difference is that the fields are read-only).

There are two places we can define the AspectAdaptor, in initialize or in the accessor. To make the examples clearer, we will define it in the accessor. The normal approach to creating the AspectAdaptor is to use the CanvasTool and the Definer. If you select the input fields and press the Define button in the Canvas Tool, this will create the aspect methods for you, which you can then modify to use an AspectAdaptor. Here's an example of what the Definer will create.

age
"This method was generated by UIDefiner. Any edits made here
may be lost whenever methods are automatically defined. The
initialization provided below may have been preempted by an
initialize method."

^age isNil
   ifTrue:
      [age := 0 asValue]
   ifFalse:
      [age]

We would simply assign an AspectAdaptor to the age variable, rather
than a ValueHolder. In addition to creating the aspect method, the
Definer will also create instance variables with the same name. The
Definer approach has the advantage that you can send the age message
more than once with no harmful effects. However, in our application
the age message is sent only once, by the UIBuilder, when the window is
being built. In the interests of saving space we'll take the less safe
approach and simply create the AspectAdaptor. Note that, by doing this,
we don't need the MyInput3 or MyView3 class to have instance variables.
Look again at the AspectAdaptor in the age method:

MyInput3>>age
   ^(AspectAdaptor subject: person sendsUpdates: true) forAspect: #age

When we create the AspectAdaptor, we tell it what its subject is (the
person). We also get to specify whether the subject (the person) sends
update messages — that is, whether it does self changed:. An
AspectAdaptor provides a fairly tight coupling between a field in a
window and a value in the model. Because it knows when the model
changes, the AspectAdaptor can send the update message. However, the
only dependent of the AspectAdaptor is the one field it is tied to. This

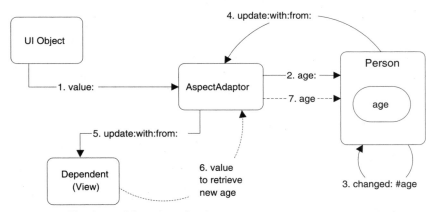

Figure 24-4. The AspectAdaptor mechanism.

means that none of the other views will find out about the change. Instead, we want the subject (the person) to send the update messages so that all the views are told the model has changed.

AspectAdaptors, by default assume that the aspect is #value. Once we have created the AspectAdaptor we tell it to look at the #age aspect. To get the age value the AspectAdaptor sends age to the model. To set the age value, it sends age:. In other words, when you tell it the aspect name, the AspectAdaptor assumes it can send get and set messages using the aspect name and the aspect name with a colon appended. It also assumes that the changed: message sends the aspect (i.e., the model sends self changed: #age).

Example Four: Subject Channels and Differently Named Accessors

Suppose we want our user interface to look at and be dependent on a different model. In our example, this means that one minute we might be looking at the name and age for John Doe, and the next minute at the data for Nikki Smith. If our AspectAdaptor is dependent on John Doe, we have no way of being informed about updates to Nikki Smith.

Also, the instance variables of the domain model might be accessed using different names than suggested by the aspect (in our example, the accessors will be something other than age and age:). In this section we will show two ways of modifying AspectAdaptors to handle these two problems. (See Fig. 24-5.)

To solve the first problem, remember that a ValueHolder is a way to wrap a value so that you can be dependent on the ValueHolder and be

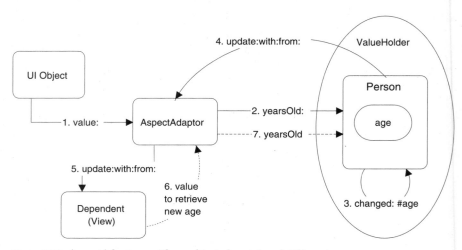

Figure 24-5. AspectAdaptors with a subject channel and different accessors.

informed when the value it is wrapping changes. In our example, we will wrap the model in a ValueHolder, and instead of creating an AspectAdaptor with our person as the subject, we will create an AspectAdaptor with the ValueHolder containing the person as the *subject channel*. That is, the ValueHolder is the channel through which the AspectAdaptor talks to the subject (the person). An analogy is the channel at a seance, through whom you can communicate with many different spirits, one at a time.

```
MyPerson4>>yearsOld
    ^age

MyPerson4>>yearsOld: aValue
    age := aValue.
    self changed: #age

MyInput4>>initialize: aPerson
    "Wrap the model in a ValueHolder"
    person := aPerson asValue

MyInput4>>age
    |adaptor |
    adaptor := AspectAdaptor subjectChannel: person sendsUpdates: true.
    adaptor
        accessWith: #yearsOld
        assignWith: # yearsOld:
        aspect: #age.
    ^adaptor
```

The code for MyView4 is exactly the same as that for MyInput4 (the only difference is that the fields are read-only). Note that we create the AspectAdaptor by sending subjectChannel:sendsUpdates: rather than subject:sendsUpdates:. This tells the AspectAdaptor that the subject is wrapped in a ValueHolder. Again, the subject sends the changed messages; otherwise, not all the AspectAdaptors will be informed.

Notice that we tell the AspectAdaptor what accessors to use to get and set the person's data. This solves the second problem we described above, that the accessors might have different names than the name suggested by the aspect.

Example Five: Delaying Updates

In the examples so far, whenever you changed the person's name or age, the change was immediately reflected in the other windows. However, in an application, you might want to present a screen with the data, let the user make changes to multiple fields, then update the model and other views all at once. (See Fig. 24-6.)

The MyInput5 ApplicationModel no longer has a simple AspectAdaptor sitting as intermediary between the field and its model's data. Instead,

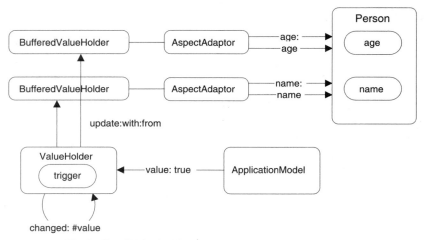

Figure 24-6. The BufferedValueHolder mechanism.

it adds a BufferedValueHolder between the field and the AspectAdaptor and talks to the BufferedValueHolder. The BufferedValueHolder registers as a dependent of a special trigger ValueHolder. When the trigger value changes, the BufferedValueHolder is informed, and if the trigger value is true the BufferedValueHolder talks to the AspectAdaptor, which then talks to the model (the person), setting the data appropriately.

```
MyInput5>>age
    |adaptor |
    adaptor := AspectAdaptor subject: person sendsUpdates: true.
    adaptor forAspect: #age.
    ^BufferedValueHolder subject: adaptor triggerChannel: trigger.
```

You will need to modify the MyInput5 canvas to also have an Accept button, with an action of accept (you can call it whatever you want as long as you give the action method the same name). Also, MyInput5 will now have an instance variable called trigger, which will hold a ValueHolder. MyInput5 sets the trigger value to false during initialization. When the value is set to true, the AspectAdaptors will do their work of taking the values in the user interface fields and using them to set the person's data. The trigger is set to true when the user presses the Accept button.

```
MyInput5>>initialize: aPerson
    person := aPerson.
    trigger := false asValue
```

```
MyInput5>>accept
    "The user has accepted the data. Set the trigger to true to update the model"
    trigger value: true
```

Because the view window is not setting the data, it doesn't need to have triggers and BufferedValueHolders. Instead, it uses a basic AspectAdaptor as in Example Four.

Using BufferedValueHolders, the user can now edit many fields on a form but not have the model updated until they commit the changes (for example, by pressing the Accept button). Unfortunately, a BufferedValueHolder suffers from a serious drawback: it does not get cleared or updated when its subject changes. A better mechanism for editing domain objects is to make a copy of the domain object and use AspectAdaptors to connect between the user interface and the domain object. We cover this briefly in Chapter 27.

Example Six: Aspect Paths

Despite the relative ease of setting up an AspectAdaptor, you might wonder why it's not easier still. In fact, it can be very easy. Using aspect paths, we can eliminate all the methods that created AspectAdaptors in the previous examples. Instead, we use the Canvas Tool to specify the aspect path. When building the window, we can specify in the Properties Tool the path to the variables we want associated with each field. (See Fig. 24-7.)

In the Aspect fields in the Properties Tool, type person age and person name. This specifies the paths to use to access the data in the model. The underlying model will be accessed through the accessor person. To get the age and name data, the user interface builder will generate

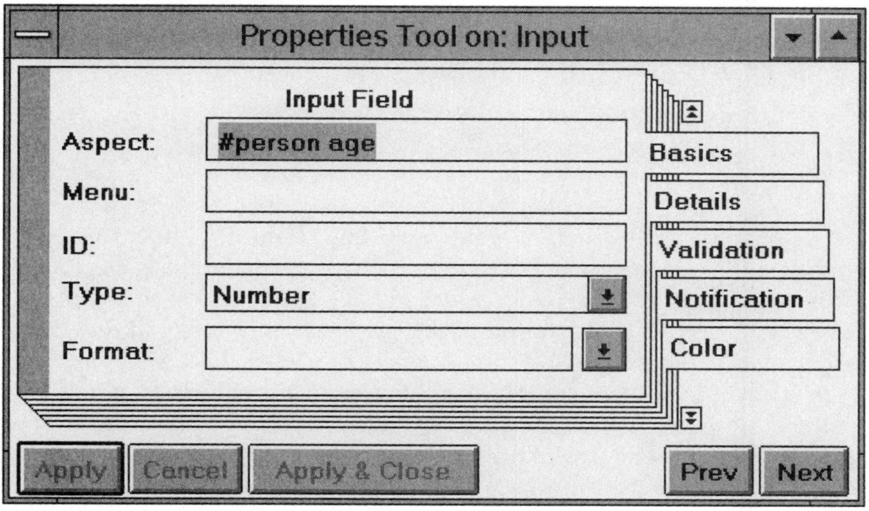

Figure 24-7. Specifying an Aspect Path.

code to send the messages age and name to the person. That is, it will send the messages person age and person name. To set the data, it adds a colon to the end of the message, and thus sends person age: and person name:. (You can specify a path that consists of several messages, if necessary. For example, if the person had an address object that consisted of street name and town, you could edit these fields by using an aspect path of person address street and person address town.)

Note that using aspect paths violates encapsulation, because you are giving the user interface knowledge of the domain model's methods. The more method names you specify in the path, the worse the violation.

If you ask the Definer to define these fields, it will create a single access method for the model, person. Below are all the methods that are needed. The code for MyView6 is the same as the code for MyInput6 apart from the read-only fields. Note that the model (i.e., the person) needs to be wrapped in a ValueHolder if you want to use aspect paths.

```
MyInput6>>initialize: aPerson
    person := aPerson asValue.

MyInput6>>person
    ^person

MyPerson6>>age
    ^age

MyPerson6>>age: aValue
    age := aValue.
    self changed: #age
```

When you run this, you will find that the view windows are *not* updated when you type in the the input window. Aspect paths are very easy to create, but the downside is that they provide very tight coupling between the model, view, and controller. When you type (using the controller), the model is automatically updated and the view is automatically informed and updated.

(When you use aspect paths, AspectAdaptors are created for you when the code runs. Because you have no control over how the AspectAdaptors are created, you can't get them to understand the update messages sent by the model. All the changed message code is done behind the scenes, out of your control. Thus the self changed: #age in the age: method doesn't do anything. However, it's worth leaving in because the model doesn't know how the views will register their dependency, and there might be some views that rely on it.)

The bottom line is that, if you have a user interface with a single view of the data (i.e., very tight coupling between the model, the view, and the controller), aspect paths are a very convenient way to go. If you want multiple views of the data, use another mechanism. (It's possible to use aspect paths for the input window and another mechanism for the read-only views.)

Example Seven: Buffered Aspect Paths

In Example Five, we saw how to use BufferedValueHolders to delay updating the model's data until the user indicates that everything is correct by pressing the Accept button. In Example Six, we used aspect paths to simplify the code and had very little software to write. Now we combine BufferedValueHolders and aspect paths to provide a way to buffer input with very little code writing.(See Fig. 24-8.)

In MyInput7, create an Action button labelled 'Accept' with an action of accept. In the Aspect fields in the Properties Tool, type person age | trigger and person name | trigger for the appropriate input fields. The message name after the vertical bar, trigger, is the message that is sent to get hold of the ValueHolder holding the trigger. We initialize the trigger to false, and when the user accepts the data, we set it to true. This tells the generated code to go ahead and update the model's data.

The code for MyView7 looks exactly like the code for MyView6, because we don't need to do buffering on the View windows. As in Example Six, the model (i.e., the person) needs to be wrapped in a ValueHolder. And, as in Example Six, when you run Example Seven, you will find that the view windows are *not* updated when you type in the the input window. Again, this is because of the tight coupling

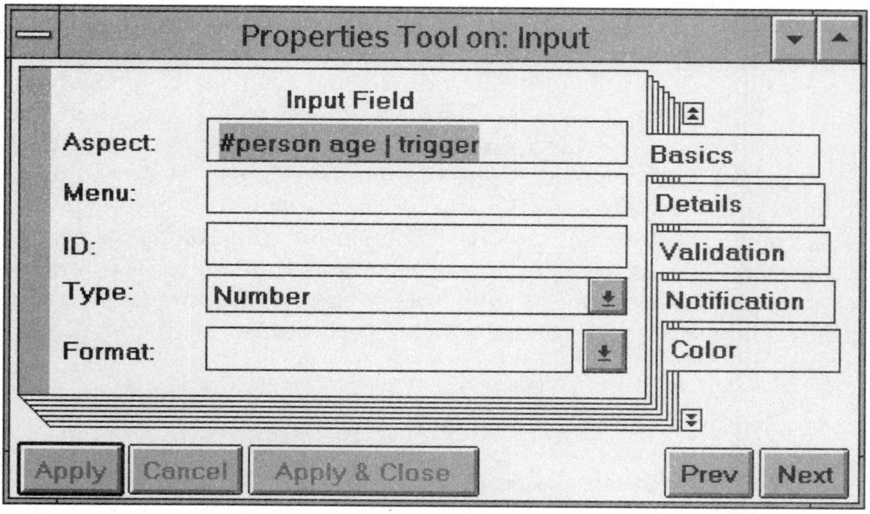

Figure 24-8. Specifying a Buffered Aspect Path.

between the model, view and controller that you get when you let VisualWorks generate all the AspectAdaptor code.

```
MyInput subclass: #MyInput7
    instanceVariableNames: 'trigger '

MyInput7>>initialize: aPerson
    person := aPerson asValue.
    trigger := false asValue.

MyInput7>>person
    ^person

MyInput7>>trigger
    ^trigger

MyInput7>>accept
    trigger value: true.
```

When you run this you will see no difference between Examples Six and Seven because, in both cases, the input window shows what you have typed but the views don't change. How can you tell whether the data really is being buffered until the user presses Accept? We show this by writing to the Transcript when the person's data changes

```
MyPerson7>>age: aValue
    age := aValue.
    Transcript cr; show: 'Age changed'.
    self changed: #age
```

Example Eight: PluggableAdaptors

A PluggableAdaptor is the most powerful type of adaptor, because it lets you manipulate the model's data when getting it from the model and when setting it in the model. Why would you want to do this? You might want to convert input to a standard format before storing it. Or perhaps you have stored a date and want to display it according to some user defined format. (See Fig. 24-9.)

Our model, the person, has basically the same methods we saw in the previous examples. The only difference is that we want to initialize the age to a meaningful value rather than letting it default to nil, because in our example we manipulate the data before displaying it.

```
MyPerson8>>age
    ^age isNil
        ifTrue: [age := 0]
        ifFalse: [age]

MyPerson8>>age: aNumber
    age := aNumber.
    self changed: #age
```

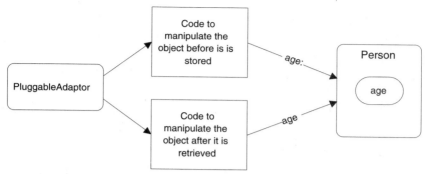

Figure 24-9. The PluggableAdaptor mechanism.

The Input window creates a PluggableAdaptor for each field (name and age). The subject of the PluggableAdaptor (the parameter to on:) is the model (the person), and the get and put blocks tell how to get and set the particular instance variable of the person. For the Input window we are doing some manipulation of the data before storing it in the model; we are multiplying the age by 3.

```
MyInput8>>initialize: aPerson
    person := aPerson.
```

```
MyInput8>>age
    ^(PluggableAdaptor on: person)
        getBlock: [:model | model age]
        putBlock: [:model :aValue | model age: aValue * 3]
        updateBlock: [:model :aspect :parameter | aspect == #age]
```

The update block tells the PluggableAdaptor whether to execute the get block and update the field in the user interface. The get block is executed if the block returns true. In the PluggableAdaptor above, because the PluggableAdaptor is interested in the person's age variable, it only cares when the age changes — that is, when the person does self changed: #age. So it tests to see if the aspect it received is the one it is interested in, #age. Similarly, the name PluggableAdaptor will check to see if the change was associated with the #name symbol.

The View window has exactly the same initialize: method as the Input window, but the PluggableAdaptors are slightly different because the View window can't change the data and so doesn't have to worry about the put block.

```
MyView8>>age
    ^(PluggableAdaptor on: person)
        getBlock: [:model | model age * 10]
        putBlock: [:model :aValue | ]
        updateBlock: [:model :aspect :parameter | aspect == #age]
```

The put block doesn't do anything because the View doesn't update the model. It still has to check for the aspect that changed so the update block is the same as for MyInput8. The get block multiplies the model's value by 10 before it gets displayed.

When you run Example Eight, the age will be multiplied by 3 before storing it in the model. Because the value has changed, the age field in the MyInput window will be updated, showing 3 times what you typed. In the MyView windows the age will be 10 times the value stored in the model — 30 times what you typed. The name you typed will be lowercased before being stored in the model, and will therefore display as lowercase in the MyInput window. In the MyView windows the name will be all uppercase.

One thing to note in this example is that we created the PluggableAdaptor on the model. When the model sends itself a changed message after one of its instance variables is changed, all the PluggableAdaptors get sent the update message. They use the update block to find the particular change they are interested in. So there is the potential for a lot of redundant message sends because each PluggableAdaptor will receive all the update messages even though it is not interested in most of them.

Summary

- The addDependent: message provides the basic dependency mechanism. It suffers from the disadvantage that all dependents get all update messages and have to filter out what they want. VisualWorks provides better mechanisms.

- ValueHolder provides a cleaner interface. It provides the ability to inform dependents of only the specific changes they are interested in. It has the disadvantage that models must wrap their data in ValueHolders.

- AspectAdaptor provides a still better interface, because it sits between the user interface widget and the model's data. The model does not have to wrap its data in ValueHolders.

- BufferedValueHolder provides a way to delay updating the model until the user chooses to commit the changes. It is a wrapper around all the ValueHolders or Adaptors that should be grouped together in a single update.

- Aspect Paths make it easy to set up AspectAdaptors using the CanvasTool rather than having to write methods. They have the disadvantage that there is a very tight coupling between the model, controller, and view, and they cannot update other views.

- Buffered Aspect Paths combine the buffering of BufferedValueHolder with the ease of creation of Aspect Paths. Again, there is a very tight coupling between the model, view, and controller.

- PluggableAdaptor provides a very powerful mechanism to modify data, either on its way from the view to the model or on its way from the model to the view.

25

Hooks into the System

Smalltalk provides various hooks into the system that allow you to do additional processing on top of the system-provided behavior. The two areas in which you are most likely to need these hooks are when copying objects and when opening and closing an application with a user interface. However, as you dig through the class library, you will inevitably find additional hooks, and these will give you ideas on new features you can add to your applications, or new ways of structuring your applications. Because most of this chapter describes user interface hooks it is located in the user interface section, despite the more general section on copying.

Copying

postCopy

When you send the copy message to an object, it returns a copy of itself. However, it returns what is known as a *shallow copy*. You have a new instance of the object's class, but the instance variables in the copy contain *exactly* the same object as in the original. So, if you change part of one of the instance variables in the copy, the original gets the same change.

Let's look at an example. Create two classes, Person and Address, as shown below (you can find the code in the file copydemo.st). Add accessors to all the instance variables. If you then run the code that follows, you will see that the street address of personOne is '221 Jones Court', which is not what you want.

```
Object subclass: #Person
    instanceVariableNames: 'name address '

Object subclass: #Address
    instanceVariableNames: 'streetAddress city '
```

```
(address := Address new)
    streetAddress: '916 Smith Avenue';
    city: 'Boulder'.
(personOne := Person new)
    name: 'Alec Sharp';
    address: address.
personTwo := personOne copy.
personTwo address streetAddress: '221 Jones Court'.
personOne address streetAddress inspect
```

The reason for the unexpected result is that Object basically implements copy as shallowCopy. The comment for shallowCopy says "Answer a copy of the receiver which shares the receiver's instance variables." Fortunately, copy also provides a hook so you can do further processing if a shallow copy is not adequate. The actual implementation of copy looks like the following.

```
Object>>copy
    ^self shallowCopy postCopy
```

This gives us an opportunity to get the behavior we want by implementing the method postCopy, in which we can make copies of the instance variables. When you implement postCopy you should always do super postCopy, in case one of your superclasses needs to do something. We want to make a copy of the address object so that we don't see the behavior shown above. If you implement the postCopy shown, then rerun the above code, you'll see that personOne still has a street address of '916 Smith Avenue'.

```
Person>>postCopy
    super postCopy.
    address := address copy
```

Other uses for postCopy include situations in which you need to reset something after copying an object. For example, when you copy an instance of Model, the copy does not get the list of dependents.

```
Model>>postCopy
    super postCopy.
    self breakDependents
```

(VisualWorks used to provide a deepCopy, which recursively copied the instance variables as well. However, the implementation could lead to problems when objects pointed to each other. In *The Journal of Object-Oriented Programming*, September 1994, Wilf Lalonde and John Pugh describe a partial implementation of a deepCopy.)

copyEmpty:

While it's not very common, you can create a class that is a subclass of a collection class and add new instance variables. As you add items to your collection, it might need to grow in size. The way this happens is that a new collection object is created, the collection items are copied across, then the old object *becomes* the new object. Unfortunately, your instance variables are not copied across into the new object.

Here's an example that illustrates this. The following code creates an instance of MyClass with a size of two, sets the two instance variables, then adds three items to the collection. Because the collection has a size of two, it has to grow. You'll need to write accessors for the variables.

```
Set variableSubclass: #MyClass
    instanceVariableNames: 'varOne varTwo '

coll := MyClass new: 2.
coll varOne: 1.
coll varTwo: 2.
coll add: 22; add: 33; add: 44.
coll inspect
```

When you inspect the collection, you will find that your instance variables no longer have the original values. Fortunately there is a hook that lets you copy them across. To get them, you must override Collection's copyEmpty: method. Here's an example of how you might do this:

```
MyClass>>copyEmpty: newCapacity
    ^(super copyEmpty: newCapacity)
        varOne: self varOne;
        varTwo: self varTwo;
        yourself
```

User Interface Opening

When you open an application (i.e., a subclass of ApplicationModel), there are several places where you can do additional processing. If you say MyApplication open, there are various hooks that give you the opportunity to set things up according to the needs of your application. In order, the following messages will be sent: initialize, preBuildWith:, postBuildWith:, and postOpenWith:.

We'll look at each in turn, but if you decide to override them, the first thing in your method should be a message send to super so that the inherited method is also invoked. Here's what the fundamental interface opening method looks like. Notice that this method directly does three of the message sends just mentioned.

```
ApplicationModel>>openInterface: aSymbol
    |spec |
    builder := UIBuilder new.
    builder source: self.
    spec := self class interfaceSpecFor: aSymbol.
    self preBuildWith: builder.
    builder add: spec.
```

```
self postBuildWith: builder.
builder window model: self.
builder openWithExtent: spec window bounds extent.
self postOpenWith: builder.
^builder
```

In what follows we will use the example of a window with two action buttons and two input fields. The action button actions are actionOne and actionTwo, and their IDs are actionOneAB and actionTwoAB. The input fields have aspects of inputOne and inputTwo, with IDs of inputOneIF and inputTwoIF. If you create the window and the appropriate methods, you can see that how this all works. The code can be found in the file hooks.st.

initialize

In the initialize method is where we usually set up the various ValueHolders for the aspects, assuming we don't want to use lazy initialization. In our example we will also set the field data.

```
MyClass>>initialize
    super initialize.
    inputOne := 'Text in input field one' asValue.
    inputTwo := 'Text in input field two' asValue
```

preBuildWith: aBuilder

The preBuildWith: method allows you to change the way the user interface will be built. The builder uses the spec that it is supplied with (usually #windowSpec, which is the symbol used if the open message is sent), but in this method you can override the description contained in the spec. For example, we want to change the way the action buttons work. Instead of invoking the specified method when the button is invoked, we want to invoke the same method but with a different parameter. We can set this up in preBuildWith:. We specify a block of code that should be executed when the button is pressed.

```
MyClass>>preBuildWith: aBuilder
    super preBuildWith: aBuilder.
    aBuilder actionAt: #actionOne put: [ self doAction: #one ].
    aBuilder actionAt: #actionTwo put: [ self doAction: #two ].
```

We could also set up blocks of code to build menus every time a menu button or a pop-up menu is selected. This would allow us to dynamically change the menu based on varying conditions. For example, we might have code such as the following, where buildInputOneMenu is invoked every time the user wants to see the menu:

```
aBuilder menuAt: #inputOneMenu put: [self buildInputOneMenu]
```

postBuildWith: aBuilder

In postBuildWith: we can make changes to the interface after it's built but before it is displayed. In our example, we will set the label of one button and the visibility of the other button. These actions can only be taken after the window is built.

```
MyClass>>postBuildWith: aBuilder
    super postBuildWith: aBuilder.
    self invisibleButton
        ifTrue:
            [(aBuilder componentAt: #actionOneAB) labelString: 'Yes'.
            (aBuilder componentAt: #actionTwoAB) beInvisible]
        ifFalse:
            [(aBuilder componentAt: #actionOneAB) labelString: 'No'.
            (aBuilder componentAt: #actionTwoAB) beVisible]
```

postOpenWith: aBuilder

In postOpenWith: we can do things that require the screen to already be displayed. In our example, we specify which input field should have the focus — that is, which field the cursor should appear in, and where to position the cursor in the field.

```
MyClass>>postOpenWith: aBuilder
    super postOpenWith: aBuilder.
    self invisibleButton
        ifTrue:
            [component := aBuilder componentAt: #inputOneIF.
            component takeKeyboardFocus.
            component widget controller selectAt: self inputOne value size + 1]
        ifFalse:
            [component := aBuilder componentAt: #inputTwoIF.
            component takeKeyboardFocus.
            component widget controller selectAt: 1]
```

Support methods

Here is sample code for the other methods we need to write:

```
MyClass>>invisibleButton
    "Requires an instance variable called invisibleButton"
    ^invisibleButton isNil
        ifTrue: [invisibleButton:= Dialog confirm: 'Invisible button?']
        ifFalse: [invisibleButton]

MyClass>>doAction: aSymbol
    Transcript cr; show: 'Action ', aSymbol

MyClass>>inputOne
    ^inputOne

MyClass>inputTwo
    ^inputTwo
```

User Interface Closing

Just as there are places you can add code during the creation and opening of windows, there are places you can add code when they are closing. In particular, we will look at how you are informed that someone wants to close the window, and that the window is closing. To close a window the usual way, you send the application a closeRequest message (if you add a Cancel button using the Canvas Tool, you can put closeRequest in the Action field in the Properties Tool). The closeRequest message puts a close event on the event queue, as if the user had used the native window manager facilities to close the window.

If you are writing a normal application subclassed off ApplicationModel, both changeRequest and requestForWindowClose messages will be sent by the window controller (an ApplicationStandardSystemController). The window will be closed only if both messages return true. The actual message sends are shown below, and although requestForWindowClose is sent to self (the controller), the requestForWindowClose method sends the same message on to the application model. Thus, the application model is sent both changeRequest and requestForWindowClose.

```
model changeRequest ifFalse: [^false].
self requestForWindowClose ifFalse: [^false].
```

Your application might need to add its own check to see whether it's okay to close the window. Typically, you will check that the user is not in the middle of editing data. If there are uncommitted changes, you'll probably prompt the user to save them. To do this checking, you can override either changeRequest or requestForWindowClose. Your method should first send the same message to its superclass, then do any application-specific checking, returning true if it's okay to close the window and false otherwise.

changeRequest

The changeRequest message is sent when something wants to change and is trying to find out if it's okay to change. In our case the change is quite drastic — we want to close the window. The window's controller sends changeRequest to the application model, asking if the application model gives permission for the change (i.e., the close). The inherited implementation of changeRequest sends an updateRequest message to all the dependents of the application model, asking whether they think that it's okay to change. So, changeRequest just checks with all the application model's dependents.

We can override changeRequest to add our application checks, making sure that the superclass's method is still invoked. Returning true now means that both the application model and its dependents agree to the change. Here's an example:

```
MyClass>>changeRequest
    super changeRequest ifFalse: [^false].
    ^self hasUncommittedChanges
        ifTrue: [self checkCloseWithUser]
        ifFalse: [true]
```

In fact, returning true simply says that, from the perspective of the application model and its dependents, it's okay to change. The controller will then check with the keyboard processor to make sure that there are no fields needing validation. So it's possible the window will not close even though you return true. In VisualWorks 1.0, overriding changeRequest was the standard technique for adding your own logic to see if the window might be closed. However, because the window might remain open even though you return true, it's a better technique to override requestForWindowClose, which was added in VisualWorks 2.0.

requestForWindowClose

After sending changeRequest, the window controller then sends the requestForWindowClose message to its application model, which checks to see if the keyboard processor thinks it's okay to close the window. If the keyboard processor returns true, no other checking will be done and the window will be closed. This is, therefore, a good time to do your application checking. Here's an example:

```
MyClass>>requestForWindowClose
    super requestForWindowClose ifFalse: [^false].
    ^self hasUncommittedChanges
        ifTrue: [self checkCloseWithUser]
        ifFalse: [true]
```

Overriding requestForWindowClose is now the recommended technique for adding your own checking to see if the window is allowed to close.

noticeOfWindowClose:

When a window closes, its application model will be sent the message noticeOfWindowClose:. If your application inherits this from ApplicationModel, the method simply returns self. However, you can override noticeOfWindowClose: if you want to do something specific when the window closes. For example, when I open windows from other windows I set up a parent-child relationship. This is different from the VisualWorks master-slave relationship because, in the master-slave relationship, a slave can't be a master in another relationship, whereas a window can simultaneously be the child of one window and the parent of another. When a parent window closes, it closes all its children. Here's an example of how this works, using the noticeOfWindowClose: message:

```
MyApplication>>requestForWindowClose
    ^super requestForWindowClose
        ifTrue: [self childApplicationsCanClose]
        ifFalse: [false]

MyApplication>>childApplicationsCanClose
    "We don't know if child applications will override changeRequest
    or requestForWindowClose, so we'll check both."
    |childrenThatCantClose |
    childrenThatCantClose := childApplications
        select: [:each | each changeRequest == false
                        or: [ each requestForWindowClose == false]].
    ^childrenThatCantClose isEmpty

MyApplication>>noticeOfWindowClose: aWindow
    super noticeOfWindowClose: aWindow
    self parentApplication notNil
        ifTrue: [self parentApplication removeChild: self].
    childApplications do:
        [:each | "Don't send closeRequest to subcanvases"
            each builder window == self builder window
                ifFalse: [each closeRequest]]
```

In Chapter 27, we talk about extending the VisualWorks
ApplicationModel. The code shown above extends the extensions we
discuss in Chapter 27, and can be found in the file framewrk.st.

26

Changing Widgets at Run Time

This chapter contains information on changing VisualWorks widgets while the application is running. For example, it describes how to change labels, how to disable action buttons, and how to make fields invisible. It is by no means a complete description of even this small aspect of VisualWorks, but it should give you some ideas of things you can do in your application, and places to look when you want to do more.

When we build a user interface, we place *widgets* on the canvas: action buttons, input fields, labels, etc. Each widget has a *controller* that handles input to the widget. The widget also has a wrapper that handles how the widget is presented to the user. The User Interface *builder* keeps track of all these wrappers, referring to them as *components*. Let's take a quick look at these four aspects of building an application.

The Builder

Every subclass of ApplicationModel (that is, every window-based VisualWorks application) has a user interface builder. This builder knows how to construct the user interface, but more important to us here, it keeps track of all the components of the user interface. Within the subclass of ApplicationModel the builder can always be referenced as:

```
builder := self builder.
```

Components

The canvas that you construct consists of a group of components. Each component is actually a *wrapper* around the widget that you added (such as an action button, a label, an input field, etc.). To reference one of these components it has to have an ID, which you specify in the ID field in the Properties Tool. I tend to give the component an ID that describes the type of the widget. For example, an action button might have the ID saveAB, where the AB specifies that it is an action button. Similarly, an input field might have an ID of employeeNameIF. To get the component, our application model asks its builder for the component at the ID we are interested in. For example:

```
component := self builder componentAt: #employeeNameIF.
```

Because the component is a wrapper around a widget, you will sometimes see the above code written as:

```
wrapper := self builder componentAt: #employeeNameIF.
```

Components/wrappers understand how to make themselves visible and invisible, or enabled and disabled. You can tell them to take the keyboard focus, you can change their label strings, and you can set their colors (via their look preferences). We'll see examples of these later.

Widgets

The widget is the object that you think of when you talk about things such as action buttons, input fields, and labels. For active widgets such as these, the widget is actually a view, such as an ActionButtonView. The component is the wrapper around the widget. To get the widget, you simply send the widget message to the component. For example:

```
widget := (self builder componentAt: #employeeNameIF) widget.
```

If you inspect a widget that is a view, you'll notice that it has instance variables for its model and controller.

Controllers

Each widget has a controller that handles the keyboard and mouse input. In particular, for input fields, the controller handles the text in the field, the cursor position, and the selection. To get the controller, you send the controller message to the widget. For example:

```
controller := (self builder componentAt: #employeeNameIF) widget controller.
```

If you use the Properties tool to set up a notification or validation method and specify a keyword method with one colon, the parameter to the method will be the controller. So, rather than having to get the controller via something like the above, you will be passed it directly as a parameter. You can then get the new text directly from the controller. For example, your validation method might look like:

```
MyClass>>validateName: aController
    newText := aController text.
    .... do some validation then return true or false...
```

Another thing to be aware of in validation methods is how to discover if user input has been accepted. If you set up an input field to be, say, a date or time, VisualWorks will flash the field if the data is invalid but will let the user proceed. To tell if the data is valid (i.e., it was successfully converted), send the controller the message hasEditValue, which returns a Boolean (you can also send this message to the widget). For example:

```
^aController hasEditValue
    ifTrue: [true]
    ifFalse:
        [Dialog warn: 'Invalid date'.
        false]
```

Before we leave the topic of validation, one thing I find frustrating about the validation mechanism is that there is no way to know which widget the user wants to pass focus to when you are in a validation routine. For example, suppose you have a field that requires valid input, such as a date field. If the user can't figure out what to enter and he or she presses the Cancel key, the application still tries to validate the input. So the user can't cancel until he either enters valid data or blanks out the field. One solution is to modify KeyboardProcessor. Add an instance variable called, say, controllerRequestingFocus, and a get accessor for it. In the method KeyboardProcessor>>requestFocusFor:, add the following line just before sending the requestFocusOut message to the current consumer:

```
controllerRequestingFocus := aController.
```

Now, in your validation routine you can have something like the following. Each validation method might want to check if the cancel key has been pressed, so we break out that code into a separate method. There is an example of this in the file focus.st.

```
MyApplication>>validateDate: aController
    self cancelPressed ifTrue: [^true].
    ^aController hasEditValue
        ifTrue: [true]
        ifFalse:
            [Dialog warn: 'Please enter a valid date'.
            false]


MyApplication>>cancelPressed
    ^self builder keyboardProcessor controllerRequestingFocus ==
        (self builder componentAt: #cancelAB) widget controller
```

Modifying Things

Now that we have a small amount of background, we can go ahead and show the code for doing various run-time changes. Examples of this can be found in the file widgets.st on the diskette. This first example is the class WidgetAttributes. (See Fig. 26-1.)

Enabling and disabling

To enable and disable a widget we send the enable and disable messages to the component. When a widget is disabled, it appears grayed out to indicate that it can't be used. For example:

```
(self builder componentAt: #saveAB) enable.
(self builder componentAt: #saveAB) disable.
```

Visible and invisible

We make a widget visible or invisible by sending the messages beVisible and beInvisible to the component. For example:

```
(self builder componentAt: #salaryIF) beVisible.
(self builder componentAt: #salaryIF) beInvisible.
```

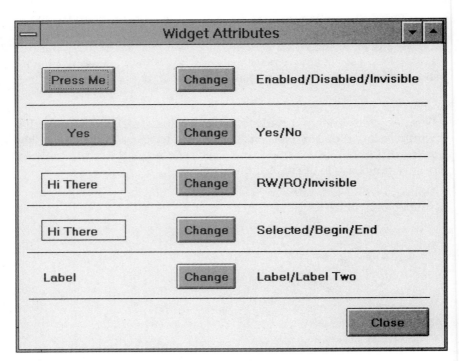

Figure 26-1. Dynamically modifying widget attributes

Changing labels

To change the label string on a widget, we send the labelString: message to the component. For example:

```
(self builder componentAt: #actionAB) labelString:
    (mode == #edit)
        ifTrue: ['Save']
        ifFalse: ['Add'].
```

Unfortunately, getting the label string is not quite as easy. We have to get it from the widget itself via several message sends. For example:

```
labelString := (self builder componentAt: #actionAB) widget label text asString.
```

Changing selections and cursor position

Selections and cursor position are associated with controllers, so to manipulate them we need to send messages directly to the controller. To make a widget be the active widget, send the takeKeyboardFocus message to the controller. In the case of an input field, this will also select and highlight all the text in the field. For example:

```
controller := (self builder componentAt: #salaryIF) widget controller.
controller takeKeyboardFocus.
```

If you send takeKeyboardFocus, you don't need to specifically select the text. However, you can alternatively select a range of characters, or position the cursor at a particular location. Here are some examples,

```
controller selectFrom: 3 to: 5.                      "Select and highlight from position 3 to 5"
controller selectAt: 1.                              "Position the cursor at the beginning"
controller selectAt: controller text size + 1.       "Position the cursor at the end"
controller find: 'and' startingAt: 1.                "Position the cursor before 'and' "
controller findAndSelect: 'and'.                     "Find the word 'and' after the current selection,
                                                      and highlight it"
```

Two additional messages, select and deselect, highlight and unhighlight the selected text. They do *not* change the selection. To retrieve the currently selected text, send selection to the controller.

Changing colors and fonts

In the following example class, WidgetText, we look at changing colors, fonts, and emphases. This class can be found in the file widgets.st. (See Fig. 26-2.)

There are several aspects to changing colors and fonts. To change *colors* such as the background colors and foreground colors of widgets, we have to get the component's look preferences (actually, the lookPreferences messages returns a copy of the look preferences). We then set the colors appropriately and give the new look preferences to the component. The lookPreferences: message tells the component that the look prefences have changed, so the component redisplays itself. For example:

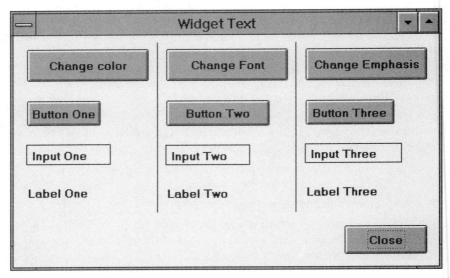

Figure 26-2. Dynamically modifying widget text

```
component := self builder componentAt: #saveAB.
lookPrefs := component lookPreferences.
lookPrefs setForegroundColor: ColorValue green.
component lookPreferences: lookPrefs.
```

To change the *text attribute* of a widget, we create an instance of TextAttributes. We'll use a default style named #large, although you get more flexibility by creating an instance of TextAttributes using CharacterAttributes. We replace the style rather than modifying the one we have because it might be one that this widget shares with other widgets. If we changed the style directly, the other widgets would also get the change. Note that we invalidate the widget afterwards, which causes it to redisplay itself.

```
widget := (self builder componentAt: #saveAB) widget.
widget textStyle: (TextAttributes styledNamed: #large).
widget invalidate.
```

To change the *text emphasis* for widgets with labels, such as an action button or a label, we can do something like the following. We get the label text and emphasize it by passing either an array of emphases or a single emphasis. Then we set the label's text to be the newly emphasized text.

```
widget := (self builder componentAt: #saveAB) widget.
emphasis := Array
    with: #italic
    with: #large
    with: #color -> ColorValue pink.
```

```
newText := widget label text emphasizeAllWith: emphasis.
widget label text: newText.
widget invalidate.
```

If we want to emphasize text in an input field, the approach is very similar, but we get the text from the controller rather than from the label. For example:

```
widget := (self builder componentAt: #nameIF) widget.
widget editText: (widget controller text emphasizeAllWith: #(#italic #large).
widget invalidate.
```

A shortcut for bold text is to send the message allBold to the text. Note that in the WidgetText class provided in widgets.st, the label fields have been lengthened. Without the lengthening, the old text is not completely cleaned up when the text size changes to a smaller size.

Changing Menus

In this section, we'll take a look at three different kinds of menus: menu bars, menu buttons, and text field menus. For each of these menu types we want to do three different things. First, we want to replace the menu with a completely different menu based on some event. Second, we want to dynamically select the menu to present when the user goes to select a menu item. Third, we want to modify the menus, disabling menu items, hiding items, changing colors, and adding items. Examples of the following can be found in MenuDynamicModify and MenuDynamicCreate in the file widgets.st. The first example, MenuDynamicModify, shows various modifications you can make to a menu. (See Fig. 26-3.)

Replacing menus

When we create a menu we specify a method in the Menu field in the Properties Tool. Usually this method is invoked once by the builder, returns a menu, and is never invoked again. To make it possible to replace the menu, we instead specify a method that returns a ValueHolder. The ValueHolder holds a menu, and by sending the value: aNewMenu message to the ValueHolder we can replace the menu completely. For example, in the initialize method we might have something like:

```
initialize
    menuButton := nil asValue.
    inputField := String new asValue.
    menuButtonMenuVH := self menuOne asValue.
    inputFieldMenuVH := self menuOne asValue.
    MenuBarVH := self class menuOne asValue.
```

Then, at any point in the program, we can install a new menu by doing the following:

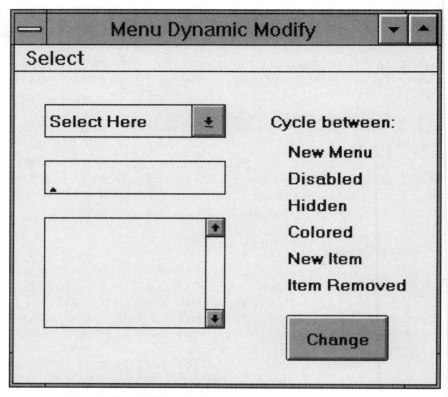

Figure 26-3. Dynamically modifying menus

```
menuButtonMenuVH value: self menuTwo.
inputFieldMenuVH value: self menuTwo.
MenuBarVH value: self class menuTwo.
```

Modifying menus and menu items

To modify a menu or menu item, we first need to get the menu (for the menu bar, I am assuming that we are modifying one of the pulldown menus). There are two basic ways to get the menu from the builder. One way gets it via the component; from the widget for a *menu button*, from the controller for a *text field*, and for a *menu bar* we get the submenu by specifying the main menu item, then asking for its submenu.

```
menu := (self builder componentAt: #departmentMB) widget menu.
menu := (self builder componentAt: #nameIF) widget controller menu.
menu := (MenuBarVH value menuItemLabeled: 'Select') submenu.
```

The other way of getting the menu is via the method specified in the Menu field of the Properties Tool. If the method gives back a menu, then we do the first line below. If the method gives back a ValueHolder, we do the second line. In both cases, the parameter to menuAt: is the name we specified in the Menu field of the Properties Tool.

```
menu := self builder menuAt: #menuButtonMenu.
menu := (self builder menuAt: #menuButtonMenuVH) value.
```

Once we have the menu, we get the menu item we want to change by sending the menuItemLabeled: message (we can also get the item by specifying its index or the value or selector associated with the item). For example:

```
menuItem := menu menuItemLabeled: 'One'.
menuItem := menu menuItemAt: 3.
menuItem := menu menuItemWithValue: aValueOrMethodSelector.
```

Here are some of the changes you can make to a menu or a menu item while your application is running:

```
menuItem disable.                              "Disable a menu item"
menuItem enable.                               "Enable a menu item"
menu hideItem: menuItem.                       "Hide a menu item"
menu unhideItem: menuItem.                     "Make visible a hidden menu item"
menu backgroundColor: ColorValue green.        "Change the menu color"
(menu menuItemLabeled: 'Three')
     color: ColorValue red.                    "Change the color of a menu item"
menu
addItemLabel: 'New Item'
     value: #someMessageSelector.              "Add a menu item to the end"
menu removeItem:
     (menu menuItemLabeled: 'New Item').       "Remove a menu item"
```

Creating the menu at selection time

We can dynamically choose the menu to display when the user goes to select a menu item. Before any items are shown, we figure out what the menu should look like and display the newly created menu. To make this work, we install a block of code in the preBuildWith: method, rather than creating a method that will return the menu. This block of code will be executed each time the user tries to select the menu. (Note that this technique does not work for menu bars.) An example of this technique can be seen in the class MenuDynamicCreate in the file widgets.st.

```
preBuildWith: aBuilder
    aBuilder menuAt: #menuButtonMenu put: [self selectMenu].
    aBuilder menuAt: #inputFieldMenu put: [self selectMenu].
    aBuilder menuAt: #textEditorMenu put: [self selectMenu]

selectMenu
    mode == #menuOne
        ifTrue: [^self menuOne]
        ifFalse: [^self menuTwo]
```

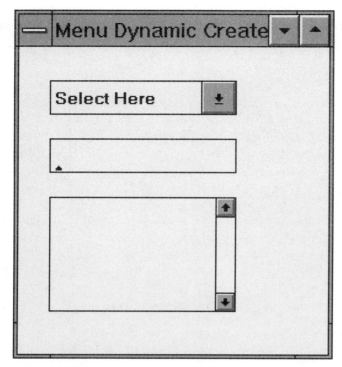

Figure 26-4. Dynamically creating menus

Keyboard Events and Double-Clicking

All active widgets (widgets that accept keyboard input) allow you to intercept keystrokes by specifying a block of code as a keyboard hook. List and Table widgets also allow you to specify actions to take when the user double-clicks a selection using a mouse. You specify the double-click method in the Notification page in the Properties Tool. Alternatively, you can programmatically specify a block of code or a method to invoke, which overrides any method you specified in the Properties Tool.

Let's look at an example using a List box (you can find the code in the file listdemo.st on the diskette). Create an application class called ListDemo with two instance variables, list and keyboardSelectors. (See Fig. 26-5.)

We'll specify the double-click action in two ways, with a method and a block of code to execute. We'll write code to delete the selected item when the user presses the Delete key, and to show a dialog box when the user presses the right arrow key. To make the keyboard hook general, we'll record the the keys and the methods they should invoke in a Dictionary. We set this up during initialization.

```
ListDemo>>initialize
    pets := SelectionInList new.
    pets list: #('dog' 'cat' 'mouse' 'parrot') asList
    self mySetUpKeyboardSelectors

ListDemo>>mySetUpKeyboardSelectors
    keyboardSelectors := Dictionary new.
    keyboardSelectors
        at: Character del put: #deleteSelection;
        at: #Right put: #expandSelection
```

Here are the methods that will be executed when the user presses
the delete key or the right arrow key:

```
ListDemo>>deleteSelection
    |collection index |
    index := self pets selectionIndex.

List Demo>>deleteSelection
    | index |
    index := self pets selectionIndex.
    index > 0 ifTrue: [self pets list removeAtIndex: index]

ListDemo>>expandSelection
    self pets selectionIndex == 0
        ifFalse: [Dialog warn: 'Details of selection']
```

Now we want to specify a keyboard hook that will allow us to intercept keystrokes. We'll also specify a block of code that will be executed

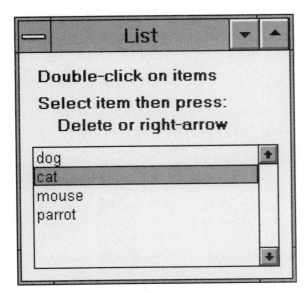

Figure 26-5. The ListDemo window

when the user double-clicks on a list selection. We tell the controller about the keyboard hook and the controller's dispatcher about the double-click block or method.

```
ListDemo>>postBuildWith: aBuilder
  |listController |
  super postBuildWith: aBuilder.
  listController := (self builder componentAt: #petsLB) widget controller.
  listController keyboardHook: self myKeyboardHookBlock.
  listController dispatcher doubleClick: [self blockDoubleClick].
```

A keyboard hook is a block of code taking two parameters, the event and the controller. It should return the keyboard event or nil (nil meaning that no further processing should be done on the keyboard event). We'll always return the event so that the list can do its usual processing. Because we store the actions in a Dictionary we can change the keystrokes that we are looking at, and the actions they should perform, based on the current context.

```
ListDemo >myKeyboardHookBlock
  ^
  [:event :controller |
  |selector |
  selector := keyboardSelectors at: event keyValue ifAbsent: [nil].
  selector notNil ifTrue: [self perform: selector].
  event]
```

When the block is executed in response to a double-mouse-click on a selection, we'll change the double-click mechanism to specify a method to be executed rather than a block. Then, when the method we specify is invoked, we'll change the mechanism back to using a block.

```
ListDemo>>blockDoubleClick
  Dialog warn: 'Block double click'.
  (self builder componentAt: #petsLB)
    widget controller dispatcher doubleClickSelector: #selectorDoubleClick

ListDemo>>selectorDoubleClick
  Dialog warn: 'Selector double click'.
  (self builder componentAt: #petsLB)
    widget controller dispatcher doubleClick: [self blockDoubleClick].
```

Extending the Application Framework

The basic VisualWorks ApplicationModel framework is an excellent way to approach building an application with user interface screens. However, as with most things, it's possible to extend the framework to make the development of user- interface-oriented applications easier. In particular, Tim Howard has written extensions to the ApplicationModel framework that he has described in various articles, and in a book.

The extensions consists of several new classes: ExtendedApplicationModel, ExtendedSimpleDialog, DomainObject, DomainAdaptor, and CollectionAdaptor. The code for all these extensions is in the Smalltalk Archives. It's worth spending some time looking into using these extensions in your applications.

Advantages of the Extended Framework

If you subclass your applications off ExtendedApplicationModel rather than ApplicationModel, you get a lot of benefits in terms of cleaner and simpler code. Let's look at a few of them here.

Simpler code

ExtendedApplicationModel allows you to do everything you could do with ApplicationModel, but makes much of it a lot easier. Here are some examples written first with ApplicationModel functionality, and second with ExtendedApplicationModel functionality.

```
ApplicationModel
(self builder componentAt: #saveAB) enable.
(self builder componentAt: #editAB) enable.
(self builder componentAt: #cancelAB) disable.
```

```
ExtendedApplicationModel
self enable: #(saveAB editAB).
self enable: #(saveAB editAB) disable: #cancelAB
```

```
ApplicationModel
component := self builder componentAt: #employeeNameIF.
widget := (self builder componentAt: #employeeNameIF) widget.
controller := (self builder componentAt: #employeeNameIF) widget controller.
```

```
ExtendedApplicationModel
component := self component: #employeeNameIF.
widget := self widget: #employeeNameIF.
controller := self controllerFor: #employeeNameIF.
```

Eliminating instance variables

ApplicationModel keeps an instance variable for each widget on the screen that will be handling input. Each input field, each list, each table, and so on will require at least one instance variable. However, the builder also keeps track of the data, so the instance variables are actually redundant.

ExtendedApplicationModel uses the builder's variables, allowing you to write applications without all the usual instance variables. To do this, it provides new methods for creating ValueHolders and SelectionInLists. Here is an example of an access method using the new functionality:

```
colors
    ^self
        selectionInListFor: #colors
        collection: self domain colors
        selectionChange: #colorChanged
```

Notice that we are not initializing or returning an instance variable. The code is also smart enough to return the SelectionInList if it exists, and to create a new one if it doesn't exist. It also registers as a dependent of the SelectionInList, removing the necessity to set up the dependency using onChangeSend:to:.

DomainAdaptors

Recall that, in Chapter 23, we noted that the ApplicationModel framework provides the concept of a *subject channel*, which makes it possible to replace one domain object with another and have all the AspectAdaptors now refer to the new object. The DomainAdaptor class provides additional mechanisms for associating screens with domain objects. A DomainAdaptor is, in effect, an editor for a single domain object. You can open a DomainAdaptor on a domain object, or simply open a DomainAdaptor, which creates a new domain object. DomainAdaptors allow you to replace a domain object with a new domain object, and they update the data in the views when you do so.

```
employeeDA := EmployeeUI open.
employeeDA := EmployeeUI openOn: anEmployee.
employeeDA domain: anotherEmployee.
```

DomainAdaptors make it easy to create AspectAdaptors using no instance variables, and to register for change messages at the same time. For example:

```
name
    ^self aspectAdaptorFor: #name changeMessage: #nameChanged
```

They also let you edit collections that are part of the domain object. For example, if the employee has a set of skills that you want to add to or remove from as part of editing employee information, your skills method might look like the following:

```
skills
    ^self
        collectionAdaptorFor: #skills
        addSelector: #addSkill
        removeSelector: #removeSkill
        changeMessage: #skillSelectionChanged
```

Other useful mechanisms

The ExtendedApplicationModel allows you to keep track of your parent application, which gives you the opportunity to send it messages if necessary. You can open an application as a single instance, which ensures that only one instance of the application will be created. If you try to open the application again, the single instance will be expanded or raised if it was collapsed or behind another window. There are extensions to Dialogs, and applications can be opened either as a Dialog (modal) or as an Application window (non-modal). There are many, many more features than we've discussed here; this chapter simply touches on the extensions to the ApplicationModel framework.

How to Get the Extended Framework

Tim Howard has written articles on his framework extensions in several issues of *The Smalltalk Report*, and his code is available in the *Smalltalk Archives* (the file domain.st contains all the classes mentioned above). For information about retrieving software from the *Smalltalk Archives,* see Chapter 35. However, I recommend that you purchase his book, *The Smalltalk Developer's Guide to VisualWorks.* It's published by SIGS Books (ISBN 1-884842-11-9) and Prentice Hall (ISBN 0-13- 442526-X).

The book covers the same material as his articles in *The Smalltalk Report*, plus a lot more. It comes with a diskette containing all the framework extensions, and a significant amount of example code. In particular, it contains an excellent tutorial that is run as a Smalltalk application, and which is invaluable in learning the VisualWorks application framework and application widgets, as well as Howard's extensions to the framework. To me, the tutorial itself is easily worth the price of the book.

Advanced

28

Eliminating Procedural Code

In procedural programming, we write a lot of code that gets information, then makes a decision based on the information. In C, we see a lot of if/else if/else blocks, and a lot of switch statements. If we wrote the same type of code in Smalltalk we might see the following:

```
MyClass>>myDoLoop
    [self myProcessObject: self myGetObject] repeat

MyClass>>myProcessObject: anObject
    anObject isSuccessResponse
        ifTrue: [^self myProcessSuccess: anObject].
    anObject isFailureResponse
        ifTrue: [^self myProcessFailure: anObject].
    anObject isHeartbeat
        ifTrue: [^self myProcessHeartbeat: anObject].
    self myProcessUnknown: anObject
```

The trouble is that this code demonstrates procedural thinking. In fact, if you start writing code like this, the logical question is, "Why is there no switch statement in Smalltalk?" At one time, we wrote a Switch class, but each time we used it we got into trouble. Eventually we realized that while a switch statement was seductive, it caused us to think procedurally and our objects got messed up. We finally removed the class and rewrote all the code that used it.

Tell, Don't Ask

How might we write the above code if we use the OO *Tell, don't ask* approach? The classic solution is use polymorphism to simply tell the object to process itself, and to rely on each type of object being able to do this in its own way. Give the object responsibility and make it responsible for carrying out the action. For example:

```
MyClass>>myProcessObject: anObject
    anObject processYourself
```

Sometimes, however, this approach doesn't work because some or most of the behavior and knowledge is in MyClass. If the work will be shared between MyClass and the object it is processing, we can give the objects knowledge of each other. For example:

```
MyClass>>myProcessObject: anObject
    anObject processYourselfWith: self

OtherClass>>processYourselfWith: anObject.
    self myDoSomeStuff.
    anObject doSomeStuffWith: self.
    self myDoMore Stuff

MyClass>>doSomeStuffWith: anObject
    ....
```

If all the work will be done in MyClass, we need a mechanism to figure out what method in MyClass to execute. The classic answer to this problem is *double dispatching*, wherein the first object tells the second object to tell the first object what to do. In our example, MyClass doesn't know what method to execute, so it tells the other object to tell it what method to execute.

```
MyClass>>myProcessObject: anObject
    anObject processUsing: self
```

Then, in each class that the object could belong to, we see the following:

```
SuccessResponse>>processUsing: anObject.
    anObject processSuccessResponse: self

FailureResponse>>processUsing: anObject.
    anObject processFailureResponse: self

Heartbeat>>processUsing: anObject.
    anObject processHeartbeat: self
```

We also add processUsing: to Object to trap all the situations in which we come across an object that doesn't understand processUsing:; that is, an object for which we haven't yet written processUsing:.

```
Object>>processUsing: anObject
    anObject processUnknown: self.
```

Back in MyClass, we implement the code that knows how to handle the different types of objects we might be processing.

```
MyClass>>processSuccess: anObject
    .. do success stuff ..
```

```
MyClass>>processFailure: anObject
   .. do failure stuff ..

MyClass>>processHeartbeat: anObject
   .. do heartbeat stuff ..
```

We also add processUnknown: to handle those situations in which the other object inherited processUsing: from Object. That is, where we forgot to write processUsing:.

```
MyClass>>processUnknown: anObject
   self error: anObject printString, " does not understand processUsing:'.
```

Processing External Objects

Another type of object we might need to deal with is an object we get from an outside source, such as a socket or a serial line. For example, we might be talking with an external device and getting back status codes. Or we might be getting requests sent in over sockets, each request telling the program to do something different.

Typically, we will get information in the form of a string and we'll have to figure out what to do based on the contents of the string. An obvious procedural answer is to compare the data with known strings and do different things for different data. However, we want an OO answer, so let's look at ways to deal with this type of object without having to make explicit decisions.

perform:

One way is to use one of the perform: family of messages. When you write a Smalltalk method, you usually specify all the messages that it will send. So, although the arguments won't be known until run time, all the message names are known at compile time (when you accept the method). The perform: family of messages give us the ability to create a symbol and use this symbol as a message name. By using perform:, we don't have to specify the message names when we write the method, and can delay this knowledge until run time. The perform: family has several members, depending on how many keywords there are in the message to be performed. For each keyword, you need one argument.

```
self perform: selector.
self perform: selector with: argument.
self perform: selector with: argument1 with: argument2.
self perform: selector with: argument1 with: argument2 with: argument3.
self perform: selector withArguments: argumentArray.
```

Suppose that from an external device we get back status codes as numeric strings, and we take different actions for different status codes. We could prefix the code with a string, then perform this as a method. For example:

```
MyInterface>>handleResponse
    statusCode := self myDeviceResponse.
    selector := ('msg', statusCode) asSymbol.
    self perform: selector.
```

In a production system you would pass in additional information to the performed method, so let's assume that we get back a status code followed by a space followed by some real data.

```
MyInterface>>handleResponse
    response := self myDeviceResponse.
    selector := ('msg', (response copyUpTo: Character space)) asSymbol.
    self perform: selector with: response.
```

Instead of having meaningless methods, such as msg0215, let's keep a dictionary of message selectors (alternatively, you could keep a dictionary of code blocks). The relationship between status codes and selectors could be set up in the class side initialize method, storing the relationships in an instance of Dictionary. We might have to take the same action for several status codes so this technique has the added benefit that we don't have to write several methods to do the same thing.

```
MyInterface class>>initialize
    "self initialize"
    StatusCodeDictionary := Dictionary new.
    StatusCodeDictionary
        at: '0215' put: #performDeviceOffline;
        at: '0216' put: #performInvalidParameters

MyInterface>>myStatusSelector: aString
    ^StatusCodeDictionary
        at: aString
        ifAbsent: [#performUnknownStatusCode]

MyInterface>>handleResponse
    response := self myDeviceResponse.
    selector := self myStatusSelector: (response copyUpTo: Character space).
    self perform: selector with: response.
```

Notice that we've prefixed the method names in the dictionary with perform. A drawback to performing methods is that, if the method name is created programatically, there will be no references to the method. If you run Class Reports (a tool in the Advanced Tools that offers some lint-like capabilities), it will tell you that the method is implemented but not sent. Unsent messages are always candidates for removal, so having a distinct prefix for performed methods reduces that likelihood that you will unknowingly remove methods that are needed.

Dictionary of Classes

The technique shown above can be useful when we get some data and want to execute different methods based on the data. Sometimes, however, we will want to create a new object and have the object do the processing. For example, from a socket we get a string representing a request, and the various request parameters. We want to create a request object of the right type, then tell the request object to process itself.

One approach is to have a set of request classes, with a superclass of MyRequest. On the class side, MyRequest has a dictionary containing relationships between strings and class names. To create a request object, we ask the superclass, MyRequest, to create the appropriate type of request. An instance of InvalidRequest is created if the string does not correspond to a valid request type. This InvalidRequest should respond with error information when sent the message processYourself.

```
MyInterface>>handleRequest
    input := self mySocketInput.
    request := MyRequest newFrom: input.
    request processYourself

MyRequest class>>newFrom: aString
    requestType := aString copyUpTo: Character space.
    requestClass := RequestDictionary
        at: requestType
        ifAbsent: [#InvalidRequest].
    ^requestClass new initialize: aString.
```

The dictionary could be built explicitly, as in the previous example. However, this has the disadvantage that, every time you add a new request class, you have to remember to update the RequestDictionary. You're taking responsibility away from the objects themselves and putting it somewhere else.

Another approach is for each request class to know the string that is associated with it. In MyRequest we write an initialization method, initializeRequests, which asks all the subclasses of MyRequest for their strings. Depending on whether you fileIn your code or keep it in the image, you could have initialize send initializeRequests or you could do MyRequest initializeRequests during product startup.

```
MyRequest class>>initializeRequests
    "self initializeRequests"
    RequestDictionary := Dictionary new.
    self allSubclassesDo:
        [:each | each requestName notNil
            ifTrue: [RequestDictionary
                at: each requestName
                put: each]]
```

```
MyRequest class>>requestName
    "Don't inherit the name. Make sure the request explicitly implements it"
    ^(self class includesSelector: #myName)
        ifTrue: [self myName]
        ifFalse: [nil]
```

```
SomeRequestSubclass class>>myName
    ^'register'
```

We don't want a request class to inherit its request name from a superclass, so we have code to handle classes that don't implement myName. We simply don't put them in the dictionary. If we get a string for which there is no entry in the dictionary, the code in newFrom: returns the InvalidRequest class, which generates the appropriate error code when instantiated and sent the processYourself message.

An alternative approach is to use a class instance variable to store the name. We use this technique in Chapter 30.

Summary

To eliminate procedural code we should *tell rather than ask*. Ideally, we use polymorphism and simply tell the object to process itself in some way. We might have to split the responsibility, in which case we might tell the object to process itself using us. Or we might use *double dispatching* to avoid a pseudo-switch statement. With certain types of object we can use the perform: family of messages, or we can build dictionaries that store relationships between classes and other objects, such as a string or a symbol.

Meta-Programming

In Smalltalk, we usually write code that creates objects then makes the objects interact by sending each other messages. Sometimes, however, you will want to do a different type of programming, one that makes use of the internal structure of classes and objects. You might want to find out what variables a class defines, what methods it implements, or whether it defines a particular protocol. You might want to do some operation for each subclass of a class. This type of programming is called *meta-programming*.

Meta programming is not for the faint of heart or for the inexperienced. However, as you become more comfortable with Smalltalk, you might find it useful to know something about how things are done behind the scenes. The main classes to look at are Behavior, ClassDescription, Class, and Metaclass, all of which reside in the Kernel-Classes category. We'll talk a little about how these classes interact, but for a fuller description see the Purple book, *Smalltalk-80, The Language*, by Adele Goldberg and David Robson, published by Addison-Wesley.

Classes and Metaclasses

Let's start by taking a look at classes and their metaclasses. Just as an OrderedCollection is an instance of the class OrderedCollection, the class OrderedCollection is an instance of another class. A class whose instances are classes is called a *metaclass*, so OrderedCollection is an instance of its metaclass. When you define a new class, a new metaclass is automatically created for it — the metaclass has exactly one instance, the class you created. The metaclass is an instance of the class MetaClass and it has no name, so you can't look at it in a Browser. If you inspect the two statements below that were evaluated in a plain VisualWorks 2.5 image, you'll see that the number of subclasses of

Object is about twice the number of class names in Smalltalk.[1] This illustrates the point that each class has a unique metaclass.

Object allSubclasses size.   1903
Smalltalk classNames size.   960

Since a class is an instance of its metaclass, what we think of as class side methods are really instance side methods of the class's metaclass. Every class has an instance variable, methodDict, that stores the methods that have been defined by the class for invocation by instances of the class. So in the methodDict variable of a class's metaclass are stored the methods that have been defined on the metaclass for invocation by its instances — in this case, the single instance which is the class. Thus all methods are really instance methods. To see a concrete example for yourself, inspect OrderedCollection and look at the methodDict variable. This shows all the instance side methods of OrderedCollection. Now inspect OrderedCollection class and look at methodDict. You will see the class side methods of OrderedCollection. Figure 29-1 shows the two inspectors.

So, if you send initialize to an instance of a class, you are invoking the instance method of the class. If you send initialize to the class, you are invoking the instance method of the class's metaclass. For example, to count the number of methods defined for OrderedCollection on both the instance and class side, you can do the following. This counts the number of methods defined by OrderedCollection, plus the number of methods defined by OrderedCollection's metaclass:

OrderedCollection selectors size + OrderedCollection class selectors size.

Because class side methods are actually defined on the class's metaclass, the notation for class side methods of MyClass class>>myClassMethod

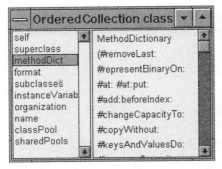
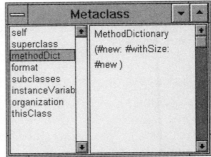

Figure 29-1. The methods of a class and its metaclass

---

[1]The first number is not exactly twice the second, since a few classes are not subclassed off Object. Also, the number of subclasses of Object is an odd number, because Metaclass is a strange oddity, having a metaclass of Metaclass.

is more than just a notation convention. It actually correctly describes the structure, since MyClass class returns the metaclass.

Just as instance side methods are defined by the class, and class side methods are defined by the metaclass, instance variables are defined by the class, and class instance variables are defined by the metaclass. A class has a variable named instanceVariables, in which are stored the names of the instance variables of the class's instances. Similarly, the class's metaclass stores the names of the instance variables of *its* instances; that is, of the class itself. To make all this talk of method dictionaries and instance variables clearer, take a look at the code in the file metademo.st. Figure 29-2 shows inspectors looking at instance variables of a class and its metaclass, in which the class has defined instance, class, and class instance variables.

Adding General Class Side Behavior

In Chapter 32, we will see examples of adding general instance side behavior to Object so that all instances inherit the behavior. In this section, we will look at adding general class side behavior that is inherited by all classes. The obvious place to add general class methods is the class side of Object. However, if you look at the class side methods of Object you will see that there are very few of them, and that most of them are associated with the signals that Object keeps in its class variables. Methods such as new and new: are conspicuously absent. So if methods associated with class side behavior of subclasses is not found in Object, where are they found?

Just as instances execute methods defined either on their class or a superclass of their class, classes execute methods defined either on their metaclass or a superclass of their metaclass. So, if you want a class side method that all classes will inherit, you can either write in on the class side of Object (where it is implemented on Object's metaclass), or on the instance side of one of the superclasses of Object's metaclass.

The superclass of Object's metaclass is Class — that is, Object class superclass is Class. Class has a superclass of ClassDescription, which has a superclass of Behavior. So, to add general class side behavior, we can add it to the class side of Object or we can add it to the instance side of Class, ClassDescription, or Behavior. Both Class and ClassDescription are associated with the internal workings of classes and instances, with the handling of classes, variables, protocols, etc. Behavior provides additional behavior and is where new and new: are defined. The class comment for Behavior includes the following: "Most objects are created as instances of the more fully supported subclass, Class, but Behavior is a good starting point for providing instance-specific behavior." Thus, based on the purpose of these three classes, the instance side of Behavior is the most appropriate place to add general class side methods.

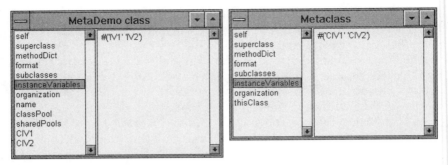

Figure 29-2. Instance variables of a class and its metaclass

As an interesting note, the superclass of Behavior is Object. So, to add new class side behavior, we could actually add the method to the *instance* side of Object. We can demonstrate this by sending a method defined on the instance side of Object to a Class (for example, OrderedCollection basicSize). Try the following. Define the method foo on the instance side of Object, then send it to the class OrderedCollection and to an instance of OrderedCollection.

```
OrderedCollection new foo.
OrderedCollection foo.
```

```
Object>>foo
    Transcript cr; show: thisContext printString.
```

Of course, the problem with defining new class side behavior on the instance side of Object is that it will be inherited by both instances and classes, which is not what we want. Figure 29-3 illustrates the parallel instance and class side hierarchy.

Examples We've Seen in Other Chapters

We've seen examples of meta-programming in other chapters. For example, in Chapter 15 we wrote printAllOn: using the messages allInstVarNames, instVarIndexFor: and instVarAt: to find the names and values of instance variables. In Chapter 30 we send the message includesSelector: to find out if a particular message selector is defined by a specified class. In the same chapter we send the messages organization and listAtCategoryNamed: to get the names of all the methods in a specified method protocol. In Chapter 33, we show how to count the number of classes and methods in the image, using the classNames and selectors messages.

Examples We Promised in Other Chapters

Finding classes with a specified protocol

In Chapter 20, we mentioned that we would write code to find all the classes that contain a specified protocol. If you follow the convention mentioned in Chapter 32, you will put additions to system classes in a protocol named (additions). When we get a new release of VisualWorks, we might need to find all the system classes to which we've added methods, so let's write our code to look for all classes that include the protocol (additions).

```
Object allSubclasses select:
    [:each | each organization categories includes: #'(additions)'].
```

The above example finds all the classes that contain the (additions) protocol on either the class or the instance side. It works because the subclasses of Object include both the regular classes and their meta-classes. If we just wanted to find the classes that include the protocol on the class side we would look only at metaclasses, as in the example below. (Correspondingly, to find classes that include the protocol on the instance side we would replace each isMeta with each isMeta not.)

```
Object allSubclasses select:
    [:each | each isMeta and: [each organization categories includes: #'(additions)']].
```

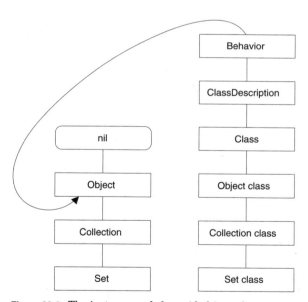

Figure 29-3. The instance and class side hierarchy

The top-level classes in Smalltalk have nil as their superclass, with Object being the main top-level class. To find all the classes that have nil as their superclass, inspect Class rootsOfTheWorld. If you want to see *all* the classes that include the (additions) protocol, including Object and other class hierarchies that are subclassed off nil, do the following.

```
collection := OrderedCollection new.
Smalltalk allBehaviorsDo:
    [:each | (each organization categories includes: #'(additions)')
        ifTrue: [collection add: each]].
collection inspect.
```

The Browser makes heavy use of meta-programming, and you can find some interesting methods on its class side. For example, to find the names of all the methods in all the class side (additions) protocols, inspect the first example. To browse all the methods in these protocols, do the second example.

```
Browser allClassMethodsInProtocol: #'(additions)'.
Browser browseAllClassMethodsInProtocol: #'(additions)'.
```

To look at all methods rather than just class side methods, create a new method, allMethodsInProtocol:, which tells you all the classes with the specified protocol, regardless of whether the protocol appears on the class side or the instance side. Base the new method on allClassMethodsInProtocol: but remove the isMeta test. Also, create a new method, browseAllMethodsInProtocol:, basing it on browseAllClassMethodsInProtocol: but sending the allMethodsInProtocol: message instead of allClassMethodsInProtocol. You can now browse *all* your additions to system classes by doing the following.

```
Browser browseAllMethodsInProtocol: #'(additions)'.
```

allInstancesAndSubInstances

In Chapter 16, we mentioned that, if you subclass off Process, you will need to modify code reading Process allInstances to now read Process allInstancesAndSubInstances. Here's the definition of this new method. Note the yourself in the into: block which guarantees that the block value is the collection that will be injected in the next iteration.

```
Behavior>>allInstancesAndSubInstances
    ^self withAllSubclasses
        inject: OrderedCollection new
        into: [:coll :each | coll addAll: each allInstances; yourself]
```

Creating accessors for instance variables

In Chapters 3 and 4, we mentioned that we would write code to automatically create accessors for our instance variables. To do this we add the following methods to Class. This mechanism will create public and private (my prefixes) accessors for each instance variable. You can then remove the ones that you don't need. To save space, we show only two of the methods that return the string used to create the accessing methods, and have compressed cascades and other messages. We also make use of the capitalize method we wrote in Chapter 12.

```
Class>>mySubclass: t instanceVariableNames: f classVariableNames: d
poolDictionaries: s category: cat
    | newClass |
    newClass := self
        subclass: t instanceVariableNames: f classVariableNames: d
        poolDictionaries: s category: cat.
    newClass instVarNames do:
        [:each |
        newClass compile: (self getAccessor: each) classified: #accessing.
        newClass compile: (self setAccessor: each) classified: #accessing.
        newClass compile: (self myGetAccessor: each) classified: #'private-accessing'.
        newClass compile: (self mySetAccessor: each) classified: #'private-accessing'].
    ^newClass

Class>>getAccessor: aName
    | stream |
    stream := String new writeStream.
    stream nextPutAll: aName.
    ^self getAccessor: aName stream: stream

Class>>mySetAccessor: aName
    | stream |
    stream := String new writeStream.
    stream nextPutAll: 'my'.
    stream nextPutAll: aName capitalize.
    ^self setAccessor: aName stream: stream

Class>>getAccessor: aVariableName stream: aStream
    ^aStream crtab; nextPut: $^; nextPutAll: aVariableName; contents

Class>>setAccessor: aVariableName stream: aStream
    | value prefix |
    value := aVariableName capitalize.
    prefix := (value at: 1) isVowel ifTrue: ['an'] ifFalse: ['a'].
    value := prefix, value.
    ^aStream
        nextPutAll: ': '; nextPutAll: value; crtab; nextPutAll: aVariableName;
        nextPutAll: ' := '; nextPutAll: value; contents
```

To use this mechanism, when you define a new class, replace the subclass: keyword with mySubclass:. When you accept the class definition, the new protocols will be created and public and private accessors will be created for every instance variable. For example, the first two lines of the class definition might look something like the code shown below. Following is an example of one of the accessors that was created for age.

Object mySubclass: Person
    instanceVariableNames: 'name age address '

Person>>myAge: anAge
    age := anAge

A Brief Overview of Other Capabilities

There are a wealth of methods that do interesting things. You can find all the immediate subclasses of a class (subclasses), the whole hierarchy of subclasses (allSubclasses), the class itself with all it subclass hierarchy (withAllSubclasses), and the corresponding superclass methods (superclass, allSuperclasses, and withAllSuperclasses).

You can see if a class is identically equal to another class or is a subclass of it (includesBehavior:), if it is simply a subclass (inheritsFrom:), or if it is an immediate subclass (isDirectSubclassOf:).

You can look at all the instances of a particular class (allInstances), all the objects that reference a particular object (allOwners and allOwnersWeakly:). (If you do either of these, you might want to do ObjectMemory garbageCollect beforehand, to eliminate any unused objects that are waiting to be garbage collected.) You can iterate over all the subclasses of a class (allSubclassesDo:), all the instances of a class (allInstancesDo:), and all the instances of a class's subclasses (allSubInstancesDo:).

You can look at all the methods a class defines (selectors), and all the methods it understands, including inherited methods (allSelectors). You can see if an object understands a particular message (respondsTo:) and whether a particular method is defined by a class (includesSelector:). You can even find which class in the hierarchy defines a method that your object responds to (whichClassIncludesSelector:).

You can look at all the instance variable names defined by a class (instVarNames), all the instance variable names that it both defines and inherits (allInstVarNames), and you can do the same for class variable names. You can find the number of instance variables (instSize), the index for a particular instance variable name (instVarIndexFor:) and the value of an instance variable for a given index (instVarAt:).

Tread lightly when doing programming that involves knowledge of class structure. It can be useful, but should not be used as a substitute for good application design.

30

Testing

It seems easier to write error-free code in Smalltalk than in other languages. I suspect that this is partly because it's difficult to have off-by-one errors, the garbage collector takes care of memory management, there is a very rich class library, and there are no pointers. However, we still do create errors, both coding errors and functionality errors — that is, we didn't code the correct functionality. So we need to test the software. Smalltalk code is easy to test and debug because it is so interactive. However, as with any other language, once we've done our initial development and testing, it is psychologically difficult to thoroughly retest after making changes. What we need is a way to develop test cases that can be retained and replayed after changes.

In this chapter we will look at a way to develop tests, and a user interface to run the tests. I want to acknowledge Kent Beck and his article, "Simple Smalltalk Testing," from *The Smalltalk Report*, October, 1994, for presenting some interesting ideas that I used in developing the testing scheme that follows. This chapter contains a lot of code. If you work through it, by the end of the chapter you should have a working test facility. I hope you also will have learned some useful ideas for other problems you are working on. As in other chapters, to save on space I won't generally use accessors for instance variables, and the formatting is sometimes tighter than usual. The code can also be found in the file testing.st.

The testing scheme here is not designed to test user interfaces. Specialist products are available to capture and replay keystrokes and mouse actions. A good application will separate out the user interface from the domain model, and it should be possible to test the domain model in isolation from the user interface. This is where the classes described in this chapter can help. The scheme described uses a test manager to runs tests. Rather than embed the tests within the classes

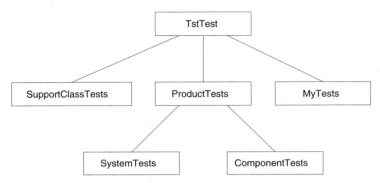

Figure 30-1. The TstTest class hierarchy.

that we want to test, we have separate test classes that exist in a well-defined hierarchy. The test manager makes use of this hierarchy when figuring out which tests to run.

The Test Class

The basic concept is that we have a *TstTest* class (Tst is the prefix I am using for my testing classes) that provides the behavior for running tests cases. We organize our tests by subclassing off TstTest. Each test class can have both individual tests to run, and subclasses that have their own individual tests and their own subclasses.

This hierarchy mechanism gives us a way to organize our tests in some logical fashion. For example, you might have the immediate subclasses of TstTest be ProductTests, SupportClassTests, and MyTests. Subclassed off ProductTests you might have SystemTests and ComponentTests. Under MyTests could be tests that you have written in conjunction with new code you are developing. When you are satisfied with the code and have officially blessed it, you might move the tests you wrote into the ProductTests or SupportClassTests hierarchy. Figure 30-1 illustrates the hierarchy.

We run the tests using a test manager that organizes the test classes by their inheritance hierarchy. There are two ways to run tests. The first way runs a hierarchy of tests and reports on the results in a TstResult. The second way runs individually selected tests and raises an exception when a failure occurs, allowing you to go into the debugger and look at the values.

Building the TstTest class

```
Object subclass: #TstTest
    instanceVariableNames: 'selector '
    classVariableNames: 'TestFailedSignal '
```

```
poolDictionaries: ''
category: 'TST-Test'
```

```
TstTest class
    instanceVariableNames: 'DisplayName '
```

If a test fails, our code raises a TestFailedSignal. Rather than create a signal for each test we create it for the class, which means we need a class initialization method. In this method we also set the name to be displayed by the Test Manager.

```
TstTest class>>initialize
    "self initialize"
    DisplayName := 'All Tests'.
    TestFailedSignal := (self errorSignal newSignal)
            notifierString: 'Test failed: ';
            nameClass: self message: #testFailedSignal;
            yourself
```

```
TstTest class>>testFailedSignal
    ^TestFailedSignal
```

We don't really need to send the nameClass:message: message when creating the signal, but it's good practice to include it when creating a signal, because it allows other methods to create their own instances of a TestFailedSignal.

The general idea is that a subclass of TstTest can have its own subclass hierarchy and some individual tests to run. The test manager will find all the individual tests for a given test class, and will create an instance of the class for each test to run. The individual tests each have their own method names in the tests protocol. So when an instance is created, the method selector to run is specified.

```
TstTest class>>newTest: aSelector
    ^self new initialize: aSelector
```

```
TstTest>>initialize: aSelector
    selector := aSelector
```

```
TstTest>>printOn: aStream
    aStream
        print: self class;
        nextPutAll: '>>';
        print: selector
```

What does an individual test look like? Below is an example. Notice that it does some work, then sends the expect:string: message. This tells the test code that it expects the code in the block to evaluate to true. If the code evaluates to false, the test fails. The string that is sent as a parameter is simply a way of making it easier to find the part of the test that failed. If you only have one result, you can do self expect: [some code].

```
SomeTest>>driveBusy
    |request response |
    request := self myMountRequest: 'PAYROLL' drive: 'DRIVE2'.
    response := self mySendMessage: request.
    self expect: [response isSuccessResponse] string: 'Mount first volume'.
    request := self myMountRequest: 'BKUP950524' drive: 'DRIVE2'.
    response := self mySendMessage: request.
    self expect: [response isFailureResponse] string: 'Mount second volume'
```

Let's take a look at what expect: and expect:string: do:

```
TstTest>>expect: aBlock
    self expect: aBlock string: nil
```

```
TstTest>>expect: aBlock string: aStringOrNil
    aBlock value ifFalse:
        [self class testFailedSignal raiseErrorString: aStringOrNil]
```

If the block evaluates to false, we ask our TestFailedSignal to raise
an exception. If we specified a string, then it raises the exception using
our string as the error string. I'm not going to show them, but you can
write the corresponding reject: and reject:string: methods that reject the
result — that is, raise the exception if the block evaluates to true.

Now we need to see how the exception is handled. To do this we look
at how the tests are run. Remember that we specified the selector (or
method) to run when we created the instance of the test, and stored
the selector in an instance variable. To run the method we have to perform the selector.

```
TstTest>>performTest
    self perform: selector
```

We have two ways of performing the test. We can send the run message or the run: message to the test instance. If we send run, there is no
exception handling and, if a test fails, the exception will raise a notifier window, allowing us to immediately debug the code that failed. If we
send run:, we specify a test result object in which we will record information about the test.

```
TstTest>>run
    self performTest
```

```
TstTest>>run: aTestResult
    self errorSignal
        handle: [:ex | aTestResult error: ex localErrorString in: self]
        do: [self class testFailedSignal
            handle: [:ex | aTestResult failure: ex localErrorString in: self]
            do:
                [aTestResult incrementCount.
                self performTest]]
```

Two things can go wrong with a test: a failure, wherein the result is
different from what we expected, and an error, in which an error is in

the test (for example, the test might send a message that is not understood). We trap both conditions in the run: method.

The innermost exception handler looks specifically for the TestFailedSignal exception that we raise if we get an unexpected result. If it comes across one, in the handle: block it logs the failure in the test result. The outermost exception handler traps all exceptions other than those raised by TestFailedSignal. So, if we send a not-understood message, or do a division by zero, or try to access a nonexistent array element, they will all be handled in the handle: block, which logs the error in the test result.

Finally, on the class side, we write several methods that will be used when interacting with the test manager. The first method specifies the protocol that contains all the individual test case selectors. The second method uses meta-programming to return the names of all the individual test cases in sorted order, and the third method returns the actual test cases.

```
TstTest class>>testProtocol
    ^#tests

TstTest class>>individualTestNames
    ^(self organization listAtCategoryNamed: self testProtocol) asSortedCollection

TstTest class>>individualTests
    ^self individualTestNames
        collect: [:each | self newTest: each]
```

The next two methods are used to return a collection of the test superclasses of the test that has been selected to run. This collection will be used for doing setup and cleanup work prior to and after running the test.

```
TstTest class>>rootTestClass
    ^TstTest

TstTest class>>testSuperclasses
    "Returns a collection of the superclasses up to the root test class"
    |collection class |
    collection := OrderedCollection new.
    class := self.
    [class == self rootTestClass]
        whileFalse:
            [class := class superclass.
            collection add: class].
    ^collection
```

The Test Result

The test result is the object that stores information about the errors and failures.

```
Object subclass: #TstResult
    instanceVariableNames: 'test startTime stopTime count failures errors '
    classVariableNames: ''
    poolDictionaries: ''
    category: 'TST-Test'

TstResult class>>newFor: aTest
    ^super new initialize: aTest

TstResult>>initialize: aTest
    test := aTest.
    count := 0.
    failures := OrderedCollection new.
    errors := OrderedCollection new

TstResult>>incrementCount
    count := count + 1
```

The failure:in: method below stores the test case and string in the failure collection. There is an equivalent (but not shown) method for error:in:. Because there are only two parameters, the test case and the string, we store them in an Association. If we ever wanted to record more than two pieces of information, we would create a new class.

```
TstResult>>failure: aString in: aTestCase
    failures add: aTestCase -> aString

TstResult>>start
    startTime := Timestamp now
```

There is a corresponding stop method. The final thing is to provide a printOn: method for TstResult. Figure 30-2 shows how a test result might appear when displayed in an inspector window. Following the figure is the code that generates the output.

```
TstResult>>printOn: aStream
    aStream nextPutAll: 'Name: '.
    test printOn: aStream.
    aStream
        cr; nextPutAll: 'Tests run: '; print: count;
        cr; nextPutAll: 'Start time: '; print: startTime;
        cr; nextPutAll: 'Stop time: '; print: stopTime.
    self myPrintFailuresOn: aStream.
    self myPrintErrorsOn: aStream

TstResult>>myPrintFailuresOn: aStream
    failures isEmpty ifFalse:
        [self
            myPrintCollection: failures
            label: 'Failures'
            on: aStream]
```

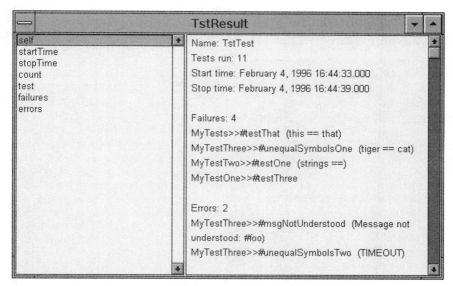

Figure 30-2. The output of a test result.

```
TstResult>>myPrintCollection: aCollection label: aString on: aStream
    aStream
        cr; cr;
        nextPutAll: aString;
        nextPutAll: ': ';
        print: aCollection size.
    aCollection do:
        [:each |
            aStream cr.
            each key printOn: aStream.
            each value notNil
                ifTrue:
                    [aStream nextPutAll: ' ('.
                    aStream nextPutAll: each value.
                    aStream nextPut: $)]]
```

The Test Manager

Now that we have the test class, let's look at how we might create a
user interface to run the tests. First, create a window with a read-only
input field, three action buttons, a check box, and two list widgets.
Figure 30-3 shows the window.

The read-only input field at the top left displays the currently selected test. To the right is another window showing all the immediate subtests of the current test. Below is a pane showing all the individual
tests associated with the current test. There are three action buttons:

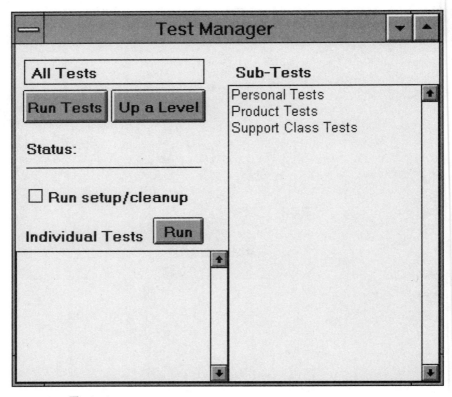

Figure 30-3. The test manager.

Run Tests, which runs the hierarchy of tests from the displayed test down; *Up a Level*, which makes the next higher test in the hierarchy the current test; and *Run*, which runs the tests that have been selected in the Individual Test pane. Below are the class definition and initialize method. In the aspects protocol we also need to write methods to get the instance variables (we won't show the getters here).

```
ApplicationModel subclass: #TstTestManager
    instanceVariableNames: 'mainTest subTestList individualTestList doSetupCleanup '
    classVariableNames: ''
    poolDictionaries: ''
    category: 'STBE-Testing'

TstTestManager>>rootTestClass
    ^TstTest

TstTestManager>>initialize
    mainTest := self rootTestClass asValue.
    doSetupCleanup := false asValue.
    subTestList := SelectionInList new.
```

```
subTestList selectionIndexHolder onChangeSend: #changedSubTest to: self.
individualTestList := MultiSelectionInList new.
self myBuildLists.
```

Now, let's take a look at what we are doing in the initialize method. First, we set our main test from the root test class. Next we set our subTestList variable to be a SelectionInList, and we register the Test Manager as a dependent of the SelectionInList, asking to be sent the changedSubTest message if the user selects or deselects a test in the righthand pane. Finally, we initialize the individual test list to be a MultiSelectionInList, which allows the user to select multiple individual test cases to run. Finally, after setting up the variables, we build the subtest and individual test lists for the current main test.

In the initialize method we told the SelectionInList object to send us a message if the selection index changes. Here's what we do in the changeSubTest method. If the user selected a test in the righthand pane, we want to make it the main test then display its subtests and its individual tests, if any.

```
TstTestManager>>changedSubTest
    self subTestList selection notNil
        ifTrue:
            [self mainTest value: self subTestList selection.
            self myBuildLists]
```

If the user wants to go back up a level in the test hierarchy, and presses the *Up a Level* button, we execute the method showSuperclass, which sets the main test to be the superclass of the current test (unless we are already at the root test class) and rebuilds the subtest and individual test lists.

```
TstTestManager>>showSuperclass
    |mainTestClass |
    mainTestClass := self mainTest value.
    mainTestClass == self rootTestClass
        ifFalse:
            [self mainTest value: mainTestClass superclass.
            self myBuildLists]
```

We've now seen several references to myBuildLists, so let's take a look at the method.

```
TstTestManager>>myBuildLists
    |test |
    test := self mainTest value.
    self subTestList list: test subclasses asSortedCollection.
    self individualTestList list: test individualTestNames
```

There are several points to note when looking at this method. When we create the list of subtests, we want to display the subtests in alphabetic order, so we send the asSortedCollection message to the collection. For this to work, we need to make sure that our test case classes respond to the <= message, which is used to sort a collection.

```
TstTest class> <= anObject
    ^self displayString <= anObject displayString

TstTest class>>displayString
    ^DisplayName notNil
        ifTrue: [DisplayName]
        ifFalse: [self name]

ProductTests class>initialize
    "self initialize"
    super initialize.
    DisplayName := 'Product Tests'
```

Note that these methods are all written on the class side because we are displaying classes in the input field and in the subtest list. The displayString message is sent to an object by a SelectionInList and by an Input field (for the input field to work, in the Properties Tool you must define it as holding an Object). We override the default displayString to return the display name, assuming that the DisplayName class instance variable has been set in the class. This allows us to display something more reasonable than the class name. If we haven't set the DisplayName, the class name will be displayed instead. The third method shown here gives an example of how a class would set its DisplayName.

Running Tests

All tests

When you press the *Run Tests* button, you run all the individual tests associated with the displayed test, then recursively go through the subtests, running all the individual tests associated with each subtest and all their subtests. The action associated with the *Run Tests* button is the runTests method.

```
TstTestManager>>runTests
    |testClass  testResult |
    testClass := self mainTest value.
    testResult := self myTestResultFor: testClass.
    self myDoHierarchySetupFor: testClass.
    testResult start.
    self myRunTestsForClass: testClass result: testResult.
    testResult stop.
    self myDoHierarchyCleanupFor: testClass.
    testResult inspect.
```

We start by creating a test result, which we use to record the results of the tests. The code to return a test result is shown here.

```
TstResult>>myTestResultFor: aTest
    ^TstResult newFor: aTest
```

We then do any setup for higher level classes, run the test hierarchy, and do any cleanup for higher level classes. Each test class in the hierarchy can do setup before and cleanup after running the tests. This allows the classes to set up any conditions that are required for the test. Typically, this involves such things as populating classes with needed data or making sure that databases have the correct records. We give each class in the hierarchy the opportunity to do any setup and cleanup. For setup we start at the root test class and work down to our immediate superclass. For cleanup we do this in reverse, starting at our superclass and working up to the root test class. We'll run setup and cleanup for the current test and its subtests later.

(One thing to note is that we assume the setup and cleanup will work. This test manager doesn't have the ability to handle problems in setup and cleanup, or handle exceptions raised there.)

We have a method that determines whether any setup should be done, and another method that does the setup for all the superclasses in the hierarchy. We won't show them, but there are similar methods for doing cleanup.

```
TstTestManager>>myDoSetupFor: aClass
   (aClass class includesSelector: #setUp)
      ifTrue: [aClass setUp]

TstTestManager>>myDoHierarchySetupFor: aClass
   aClass testSuperclasses
      reverseDo: [:each | self myDoSetupFor: each]
```

A feature of our setup is that we don't want to inherit setup methods from superclasses. If we allowed inheritance, we would do the same setup more than once if a particular class in the hierarchy didn't need to do any setup. We handle this with the code:

```
each class includesSelector: #setUp
```

This code checks to see if the named selector has been defined by the class. We can't use respondsTo: because this will also return true if the method is inherited from a superclass, which we specifically don't want. The cleanup methods looks very similar except that they use cleanUp rather than setUp, and because cleanup should occur in the opposite order to setup, myDoHierarchyCleanupFor: sends do: rather than reverseDo:.

A point to note is that we define the setUp and cleanUp methods on the class of the test classes side rather than the instance side. This is because we might want to invoke these methods for several classes in the test case hierarchy. The only way we could do this on the instance side would be to create an instance of each class in the hierarchy, then send it the message. It's a lot cleaner to put the behavior on the class side.

Here is another method for which we need to look at the code:

```
TstTestManager>>myRunTestsForClass: aClass result: aTestResult
    self myDoSetupFor: aClass.
    aClass individualTests
        do: [:each | each run: aTestResult].
    aClass subclasses do:
        [:each | self myRunTestsForClass: each result: aTestResult].
    self myDoCleanupFor: aClass
```

When we run tests for a class we do any setup for the test class we are running, we run any individual tests defined on the test class, we go through all our sub tests (asking them to do exactly what we are doing), then we do any cleanup for the test class. So, in this method, we recursively ask all our subclasses to execute this same method. This gives us a depth-first recursion through the whole subtest hierarchy for this test. Well, that's it for running a hierarchy of tests. The other way to run tests is by selecting individual tests to run.

Selected tests

The Test Manager has a different philosophy when running individual tests. Rather than going through all the setup and cleanup of classes higher in the test hierarchy, it assumes that any setup has already been done (you can change this by clicking the Run setup/cleanup check box). However, it *does* do setup and cleanup for the current test class. It also runs the tests without a test result wrapper, which means that, if an individual test fails, it will raise a Notifier window and let you start debugging. You can select multiple tests to run in the individual test window; then, when you press the *Run* button, the runSelected method is executed.

```
TstTestManager>>runSelected
    |selectedTests testClass testCollection |
    selectedTests := self individualTestList selections.
    selectedTests isEmpty ifTrue: [^self].
    testClass := self mainTest value.
    testCollection:= selectedTests collect: [:each | testClass newTest: each].
    self doSetupCleanup value ifTrue: [self myDoHierarchySetupFor: testClass].
    self myRunSelectedCases: testCollection forClass: testClass.
    self doSetupCleanup value ifTrue: [self myDoHierarchyCleanupFor: testClass]].
```

If any individual tests have been selected we create a collection of test objects, one for each test selected. We then run the selection in another method:

```
TstTestManager>>myRunSelectedCases: aCollection forClass: aClass
    self myDoSetupFor: aClass.
    aCollection do: [:each | each run].
    self myDoCleanupFor: aClass
```

At this point we do setup for the class we are in, we run each test without a test result wrapper, then we do any cleanup. Because we are not using a test result, any failure will cause a Notifier window to be displayed.

Running Tests That Never Complete

Some tests might never complete because they are waiting for something that doesn't happen. This presents a problem in the current scheme, because the rest of the tests will never run and you will not see the test result. If you have such a situation, you can replace the performTest method with the following code. However, a more likely scenario is that you will have only a few tests with the potential to wait forever. For example, your System Tests might have the potential to hang, but other tests will always complete. In this case, you would override performTest in the SystemTest class. Or, you could set up a two-branch hierarchy under TstTest, one branch for tests that have the potential to hang and one branch for those that don't.

```
TstTestManager>>performTest
    |testProcess timeoutProcess sharedQueue exceptionOrNil |
    super class showContext: thisContext.
    sharedQueue := SharedQueue new.
    testProcess :=
        [self errorSignal
            handle: [:ex | sharedQueue nextPut: ex]
            do:
                [self perform: selector.
                sharedQueue nextPut: nil]] fork.
    timeoutProcess :=
        [(Delay forSeconds: self timeoutValue) wait.
        sharedQueue nextPut: (self errorSignal newException errorString: 'TIMEOUT')] fork.
    exceptionOrNil := sharedQueue next.
    testProcess terminate.
    timeoutProcess terminate.
    exceptionOrNil notNil ifTrue:
        [exceptionOrNil propagateFrom: thisContext]
```

We run the test in a forked process and create another forked process that will wait for some timeout period. Both forked processes put something on a SharedQueue when they have done their work, and the main flow waits until it can read something from the queue. It then takes action based on what it gets off the queue. Let's look at the details.

In testProcess we run the test, wrapped in an all-encompassing signal handler. If the test succeeds, we put nil on the shared queue. Seeing nil tells the main flow that the test succeeded. If the test does not succeed, an exception is raised as we saw earlier in the chapter. We trap the exception and put it on the shared queue. In timeoutProcess we simply wait for some timeout period, then we create an exception and put it on the shared queue. Because we are using a message send to get the timeout value (you'll have to write the timeoutValue method and have it return a number), subclasses can override the value if they need a different timeout period.

The main flow of control waits for one of the processes to put something on the shared queue. This will either be nil, which means the test succeeded, or an exception, which we raise again so that the code in the run or run: method can handle it appropriately. It also terminates both forked processes because they are no longer needed (sending terminate to an already terminated process is benign).

We do things this way because when a process is forked it gets its own context. A signal handler in one context can't trap an exception raised in another context, so we trap the signal in the forked process, give it to the main process, and let the main process start it up again as though it came from the main process.

Loading in the Tests

Besides having a mechanism for filing in all the tests or a subset of the tests, you might find it useful to have each class responsible for filing in tests that test it. A mechanism for doing this is to have fileIn code in a class-side method, such as:

```
MyClass class>>fileInTests
    "self fileInTests"
    #(  'MyTest1.st'
        'MyTest2.st'
    ) do: [:each | (self myTestDir construct: each) fileIn]
```

Summary

In this chapter, we looked at a test scheme that makes use of a test manager to run the tests. We could extend this scheme and give each class the ability to test itself, using the TstClass functionality. For example, we might write a method such as the following on the class side of classes we wish to test:

```
MyClass class>>runTests
    "self runTests"
    #(  MyTestOne
        MyTestTwo
    ) do: [:className | (Smalltalk at: className) individualTests do: [:test | test run]]
```

However, the technique shown still relies on the existence of separate classes to do the testing. An alternative scheme would be to keep the test cases completely within the classes to be tested, but such a scheme goes beyond the scope of this chapter.

31

Customizing Your Environment

One of the things that makes Smalltalk development so much fun is that you can easily modify the development environment. If you don't like something, change it. This chapter contains examples of such changes. They are preferences of mine but not necessarily those of everyone (if they were so good, they'd be part of the standard image). To make the changes part of your standard environment, you can either save the image with your changes or file the changes in every time you start up the image. For more information on filing in changes, see Chapter 33.

Keyboard

In VisualWorks the, delete key and the backspace key work identically, both deleting the character to the left of the cursor. To change the delete key so it deletes to the right of the cursor, evaluate the following.

```
LookPreferences deleteForward: true.
```

Another change I like to make is to map Ctrl-X, Ctrl-C, and Ctrl-V to Cut, Copy, and Paste, as is standard in Windows applications. I also map Ctrl-A to Accept. One way to remap your keyboard is to modify the class side method initializeDispatchTable in ParagraphEditor. If you make the following changes, you must execute ParagraphEditor initializeDispatchTable after accepting the method. This is most easily done by selecting the text in quotes at the top of the method and executing do it. The will take effect in the next Browser you open, so close your current Browsers and open new ones.

```
ParagraphEditor class>>initializeDispatchTable
    ....
    Keyboard bindValue: #cutKey: to: Ctrlx.
    Keyboard bindValue: #copyKey: to: Ctrlc.
    Keyboard bindValue: #pasteKey: to: Ctrlv.
    Keyboard bindValue: #acceptKey: to: Ctrla.
    ....
```

This approach is a reasonable one if everyone will be getting the same keyboard mapping. An alternative way, which allows developers to easily customize their own keyboard maps, is to create a new class method, keyboard, for ParagraphEditor that returns the class variable, Keyboard. Once you have this method, you can modify the keyboard bindings by sending bindValue:to: messages to the keyboard. This scheme has the advantage that programmers don't have to change the initializeDispatchTable method, or reinitialize it. As before, the changes will only take effect when new Browsers are opened. Here's some code showing how this approach might work:

```
ParagraphEditor class>>keyboard
    ^Keyboard

ParagraphEditor keyboard
    bindValue: #cutKey: to: (TextConstants at: #Ctrlx);
    bindValue: #copyKey: to: (TextConstants at: #Ctrlc);
    bindValue: #pasteKey: to: (TextConstants at: #Ctrlv);
    bindValue: #acceptKey: to: (TextConstants at: #Ctrla).
```

The wonderful thing about Smalltalk is that there are many ways to do things. If you don't want to add methods to system classes, there is yet another approach to take. We can directly get hold of the Keyboard class variable, then send it the relevant messages. For example:

```
(ParagraphEditor classPool at: #Keyboard)
    bindValue: #cutKey: to: (TextConstants at: #Ctrlx).
```

Ctrlx, etc., are found in the TextConstants pool dictionary. ParagraphEditor has specified TextConstants as a pool dictionary, but if you evaluate the above line in a workspace you have to specify where to find Ctrlx. At this point we are not quite done, because by default Ctrl-C is the interrupt key, which takes precedence over Copy. We need to remap the interrupt key to something else. I choose Ctrl-Q because it is easily remembered (Q = quit).

```
InputState interruptKeyValue: (TextConstants at: #Ctrlq).
```

If you don't like to remap Ctrl-C but would still like these changes, an alternative technique would be to map the keys to a double key combination. For example, we might map Cut, Copy, and Paste to Esc-x, Esc-c, Esc-v. Here's an example of doing this, assuming we have a keyboard method.

```
ParagraphEditor keyboard
    bindValue: #cutKey: to: (TextConstants at: #ESC) followedBy: $x;
    bindValue: #copyKey: to: (TextConstants at: #ESC) followedBy: $c;
    bindValue: #pasteKey: to: (TextConstants at: #ESC) followedBy: $v.
```

Besides these changes, I also remap the Replace and Search keys and include several emacs key bindings such as Ctrl-D for delete-character, Ctrl-K for delete-to-end-of-line, and Ctrl-E for end-of-line. The emacs key-bindings code is available from the *Smalltalk Archives* (see Chapter 35). If you have a Sun keyboard, you can map the keys on the left by using #L1, #L2, etc., as the names. For example:

```
Keyboard bindValue: #copyKey: to: #L6.
Keyboard bindValue: #pasteKey: to: #L8.
Keyboard bindValue: #cutKey: to: #L10.
```

VisualWorks 2.5 change

In VisualWorks 2.5, the TextEditorController gets its own copy of the keyboard table from ParagraphEditor, its superclass. If you make changes to ParagraphEditor's keyboard table, you will need to reinitialize TextEditorController after making the changes and before opening new windows.

```
TextEditorController initialize
```

Launcher

There are several changes I like to make to the Launcher. However, rather than changing the class VisualLauncher, we'll create a MyVisualLauncher as a subclass of VisualLauncher. Here are some examples of what we might add to it. Because the launchers are created differently in VisualWorks 2.0 and 2.5, we'll show the differences where appropriate. (You can find the source code in the files launch20.st and launch25.st.) After making the changes, open a MyVisualLauncher and close the old VisualLauncher. Figure 31-1 shows the customized Launcher.

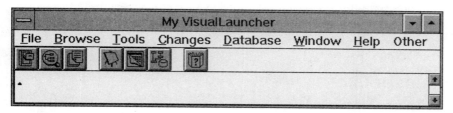

Figure 31-1. The customized Launcher

Window label

The first thing we'll do is modify the window label so that it's obvious we're not using a standard Visual Launcher. We change the label after the window is built, but before it is displayed.

```
MyVisualLauncher>>postBuildWith: aBuilder
    super postBuildWith: aBuilder.
    aBuilder window label: 'My VisualLauncher'
```

Other menu

Next, we add a new menu to the menu bar, the *Other* menu. This is where we will put most of the additional actions that we'd like to invoke from the Launcher. The Other menu will look like Fig. 31-2.

We'll add the new Other menu to the end of the menu bar, which we do by overriding the newMenuBar method and adding a new menu item to the end.

```
MyVisualLauncher>>newMenuBar
    |menuItem |
    menuItem := MenuItem labeled: 'Other'.
    menuItem submenu: self class otherMenu.
    ^(super newMenuBar) addItem: menuItem; yourself
```

VisualWorks 2.0

Copy the browseMenu method in the class side resources protocol of VisualLauncher to the new MyVisualLauncher class. Modify the name to otherMenu both in the method name and in the comment. Accept the method, then highlight the text inside the comment and do it, which brings up a menu editor.

Modify the menu text and method names to look like the following, then press the *Build* button followed by the *Install* button. Press *OK* when given the Install screen. Note that a Tab separates the menu

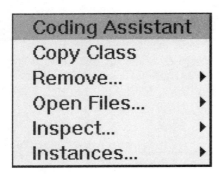

Figure 31-2.
The Other menu

item name from the method name. What follows are some items that I like to include in my Other menu. Obviously you can add your own favorite actions and modify or remove the ones shown here.

Coding Assistant	otherOpenCodingAssistant
Copy Class	otherCopyClass
Remove...	nil
Window	otherRemoveWindow
Dialogs	otherRemoveDialog
Open Files...	nil
Inspect	otherInspectOpenFiles
Close	otherCloseFile
Inspect...	nil
Smalltalk	otherInspectSmalltalk
Undeclared	otherInspectUndeclared
Instances...	nil
Inspect	otherInspectInstances
Remove	otherRemoveInstances

VisualWorks 2.5

In VisualWorks 2.5 you can directly edit the menu bar using the menu editor, placing the Other menu wherever you think appropriate. However, you must first select Settings from the File menu, then choose Use Enhanced Tools in the UI Options tab. If you don't use the Enhanced Tools, the menu will not be correctly built and you will get an exception when you open the new Launcher.

However, we will add the Other menu to the end of the menu bar without modifying the menuBar method, which allows us to inherit the VisualLauncher menu bar. In the ResourceFinder, highlight MyVisualLauncher, then select New Menu from the Resources menu. Add the items shown above, then install your changes by selecting Install from the Menu menu.

Both

Moving to the instance side of MyVisualLauncher, in a new actions protocol write the following methods. Once you've added this code, open a new Launcher by executing MyVisualLauncher open in a workspace, and close the old Launcher.

```
MyVisualLauncher>>otherInspectSmalltalk
    Smalltalk inspect

MyVisualLauncher>>otherInspectUndeclared
    Undeclared inspect

MyVisualLauncher>>otherOpenCodingAssistant
    CodingAssistant open
```

The following methods inspect and close open files. It's possible to lose a reference to a file without having closed it, especially if an exception is raised in the file reading or writing code. The garbage collector will collect your file object, but won't close the file on disk.

```
MyVisualLauncher>>otherInspectOpenFiles
    (ExternalStream classPool at: #OpenStreams) copy inspect
```

```
MyVisualLauncher>>otherCloseFile
    |path count |
    count := 0.
    path := Dialog request: 'Full path for file you want to close?' initialAnswer: ''.
    (ExternalStream classPool at: #OpenStreams) copy
        do: [:each | each name = path
            ifTrue:
                [each close.
                count := count + 1]].
    Dialog warn: 'Closed ' , count printString , ' files'
```

The next methods remove windows that are on the screen but which you can't remove in the normal way. Sometimes windows won't close, and sometimes dialogs are left orphaned if the code associated with them raises an exception.

```
MyVisualLauncher>>otherRemoveDialog
    "Close orphan dialogs"
    ScheduledControllers scheduledControllers
        do: [:each | (each isKindOf: ApplicationDialogController)
            ifTrue: [each closeAndUnschedule]]
```

```
MyVisualLauncher>> otherRemoveWindow
    |label |
    label := Dialog request: 'Label for window you want to remove?' initialAnswer: ''.
    ScheduledControllers scheduledControllers
        do: [:each |
            (each view label = label or: [each view label = label asSymbol])
                ifTrue: [each closeAndUnschedule]]
```

The next methods inspect and remove instances of a class. Sometimes you will have instances that won't disappear. This indicates a problem with your application, in that some object is still referencing the instance. However, you might still want to get rid of the instances. Be careful of this feature, though; if you remove instances of system classes, such as OrderedCollection, your system will no longer function correctly, if at all. (Also, don't plan on saving the image because there is something wrong with your application and it is not releasing objects correctly.)

We use the become: message to change each instance of the class to a new instance of String. In VisualWorks, become: swaps all references to the receiver and to the argument. So, every object that referenced the instance of the specified class now references a new instance of String. Also, every reference to this new instance of String now holds onto the instance of the specified class. Because the string is new there are no objects holding onto it, so your instances will now be garbage collected. (If you try to make something become nil, you will swap the references so that every place that referred to nil will now refer to the instance of the specified class, which will cause untold problems.)

```
MyVisualLauncher>>otherInspectInstances
    |class className |
    className := Dialog request: 'Inspect instances of which class?' initialAnswer: ''.
    class := Smalltalk at: className asSymbol ifAbsent: [nil].
    class notNil
        ifTrue: [class allInstances inspect]
        ifFalse: [Dialog warn: 'This class does not exist']
```

```
MyVisualLauncher>>otherRemoveInstances
    |class className count |
    className := Dialog request: 'Class for which to remove instances?' initialAnswer: ''.
    class := Smalltalk at: className asSymbol ifAbsent: [nil].
    class notNil
        ifTrue:
            [count := class allInstances size.
            class allInstancesDo: [:each | each become: String new].
            Dialog warn: 'Removed ' , count printString , ' instances']
        ifFalse: [Dialog warn: 'This class does not exist']
```

Sometimes you will decide that a class has too much responsibility and will split it into two classes. The easiest way to do this is to start with two identical classes and remove the methods that are not needed. One way to create a copy of the class is to file it out, change the class name, then file the original class back in (in Envy, you can't rename classes so you'll have to change the name in the disk file). Another approach is to add a menu item to the Launcher.

```
MyVisualLauncher>>otherCopyClass
    |sourceName sourceClass destinationName writeStream newSourceCode |
    sourceName := Dialog request: 'Class to Copy?'.
    sourceClass := Smalltalk at: sourceName asSymbol ifAbsent:
        [^Dialog warn: 'This class does not exist'].
    destinationName := Dialog request: 'New Class?' initialAnswer: ''.
    destinationName = '' ifTrue: [^self].
    (Smalltalk at: destinationName asSymbol ifAbsent: [nil]) notNil
        ifTrue: [^Dialog warn: 'This class already exists'].
    writeStream := (String new: 1000) writeStream.
    sourceClass fileOutSourceOn: (SourceCodeStream on: writeStream).
    newSourceCode := writeStream contents
        copyReplaceAll: sourceName
        with: destinationName.
    newSourceCode readStream fileIn
```

Changes

Let's make a couple of changes to the Changes menu. I like to have Inspect Change Set at the top, and I like to add a Condense Changes option. All the code that you write is compiled into byte-codes, and these byte-codes stay in the image when you save it. However, the source code goes into the change file, which records all the modifications to classes and methods. Because the change file grows as you make changes to your application, it's a good idea to periodically condense it, removing all but the most recent version of your code. (Alternatively, you could periodically start with a fresh image and save it under your name.) Figure 31-3 shows what the new Changes menu will look like.

VisualWorks 2.0

For VisualWorks 2.0, go to the resources protocol on the class side and copy changesMenu from VisualLauncher to MyVisualLauncher. In the changesMenu method, highlight the text inside the command, and do it. Change the order of the menu items to put Inspect Change Set at the top, then add the entry shown below.

VisualWorks 2.5

For VisualWorks 2.5, you'll need to make sure that you have selected Enhanced Tools in the Settings. Copy over the menuBar method from the VisualLauncher class side resources protocol to MyVisualLauncher. Change the order of the menu items to put Inspect Change Set at the top of the Change menu, then add the entry shown below.

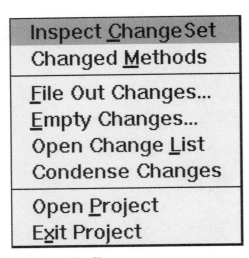

Figure 31-3. The Change menu

Both

For both VisualWorks 2.0 and 2.5, add the following to the Changes menu:

Condense Changes   changesCondenseChanges

Now you need to write the changesCondenseChanges method in the instance side actions protocol, and open a new Launcher.

```
MyVisualLauncher>>changesCondenseChanges
    SourceFileManager default condenseChanges
```

The condenseChanges message removes all but the most recent versions of the methods and classes in the changes file. A similar message, condenseChangesOntoSources, adds the most recent changes to the sources file (visual.sou), removing *all* changes from the changes file. This latter message is useful after you get a new release of the software and you want to add code that will be part of the base image, such as the Advanced Tools. If you add the new code then do SourceFileManager default condenseChangesOntoSources, the changes will be added to the source file and will be available to everyone. You could certainly leave the changes in the change file, but then everyone would get a larger change file than necessary. In regular use you definitely do *not* want developers to condense their changes onto the source file. General usage should be to condense changes within the changes file.

If you simply wanted to add a group of menu items to the end of the menu, you wouldn't need to override the changesMenu method. Instead you could add items to the end of the menu by adding more code to the newMenuBar method.

```
MyVisualLauncher>>newMenuBar
    |menuItem menuLabels menuSelectors changesMenu newMenuBar |
    newMenuBar := super newMenuBar.
    menuItem := MenuItem labeled: 'Other'.
    menuItem submenu: self class otherMenu.
    newMenuBar addItem: menuItem.
    menuLabels := #('Condense changes').
    menuSelectors := #(#changesCondenseChanges).
    changesMenu := newMenuBar menuItemLabeled: 'Changes'.
    changesMenu submenu addItemGroupLabels: menuLabels values: menuSelectors.
    ^newMenuBar
```

Default browser

I prefer to use the Full Browser rather than the System Browser, so I'd rather have the Browser button bring up a Full Browser. To do this, we simply override browseAllClasses as follows:

```
MyVisualLauncher>>browseAllClasses
    self openApplicationForClassNamed: #FullBrowser
```

Adding VisualLauncher Menus to a Mouse Button

If you use a virtual desktop such as mvwm or HP Dashboard®, you might find yourself moving Browsers and other windows onto other virtual screens. Then you might find yourself either moving between desktops whenever you want to use the Launcher, or creating additional Launchers for your other desktops.

Below is some code that will add the Launcher menus to the mouse window menu. This is the righthand mouse button on a three-button mouse (eg, for UNIX workstations), or Ctrl-Righthand mouse button on a two-button mouse (eg, for PCs). We use the window menu rather than the operate menu, because the window menu is defined only in one place, whereas the operate menu is context sensitive and is defined in many places.

```
windowMenu := StandardSystemController classPool at:
    #ScheduledBlueButtonMenu.
launcherItem := windowMenu menuItemLabeled: 'Launcher' ifNone: [nil].
launcherItem notNil ifTrue: [windowMenu removeItem: launcherItem].
menuItems := MyVisualLauncher new newMenuBar menuItems.
subMenu := Menu new addItemGroup: menuItems.
windowMenu addItem:
    ((MenuItem labeled: 'Launcher') submenu: subMenu)
```

You will also need to make a change to StandardSystemController, to redirect execution from the controller to a MyVisualLauncher. It is definitely a hack, but it also works quite nicely. In StandardSystemController>>blueButtonActivity, find the code at the bottom that says self perform: choice. Modify this to be the following:

```
(self respondsTo: choice)
    ifTrue: [self perform: choice]
    ifFalse: [MyVisualLauncher new perform: choice]
```

If you are using ENVY, you could extend the window menu by executing:

```
windowMenu :.= StandardSystemController classPool at: #ScheduledBlueButtonMenu.
windowMenu menuItemLabeled: 'ENVY'
    ifNone:
        [windowMenu addItem:
            ((MenuItem labeled: 'ENVY') submenu: VisualLauncher browseMenu)].
```

You would then modify blueButtonActivity to read as follows. This works because the ENVY menu returns a block rather than a method to perform.

```
(choice isSymbol)
    ifTrue: [self perform: choice]
    ifFalse: [choice value].
```

Templates

To change the method template (the thing you see if you have a protocol selected but no method selected), modify sourceCodeTemplate for class Behavior. To put in a date and copyright, do something like the following. If you want anything more sophisticated, it might be clearer to use a Stream to build up the string.

```
Behavior>>sourceCodeTemplate
    ^'methodName
    "Copyright My Company: ', Date today printString, ' ', Time now printString, '"
    '
```

Another change that you might want to make for methods is to record each modification to a method. The starting point for this is TextController>>doAccept, but the modifications are non-trivial.

If you want to change the class comment template so that it gives a specific layout for the comments you want developers to write, you can modify ClassDescription>>commentTemplateString. Take a look at the comments for a few of the system classes (such as Date and KeyedCollection) and use them as guidelines for building your own template.

Screen Color

If you want to change the colors of the development environment, the easiest way to do so is to go to the appropriate WidgetPolicy class. If you are using Motif widgets on a Unix workstation, you can modify the class side method initializeDefaultGenericColors to specify the colors you want, such as shown below, then execute MotifWidgetPolicy initializeDefaultGenericColors.

```
MotifWidgetPolicy class>>initializeDefaultGenericColors
    ...
    matchAt: SymbolicPaint background put: (background := ColorValue lightCyan);
    matchAt: SymbolicPaint selectionBackground put: ColorValue pink;
    matchAt: SymbolicPaint selectionForeground put: ColorValue black.
    ...
```

Alternatively, you can change the colors by sending messages rather than modifying a system method, which is more appropriate if you want to change the colors using a fileIn. To do this, send matchAt:put: messages to the appropriate object. Again, if it is a Motif widget, you would do the following:

```
MotifWidgetPolicy defaultColorWidgetColors
    matchAt: SymbolicPaint background put: ColorValue lightCyan;
    matchAt: SymbolicPaint selectionBackground put: ColorValue pink.
```

Once you've done this, you need to update the default screen and refresh the display. You can execute the following lines to accomplish this.

```
Screen default updatePaintPreferences.
ScheduledControllers restore.
```

If you are not on a platform that runs X, VisualWorks pays attention to the color scheme you chose for the platform (on Windows, these are the colors specified in the Control Panel). To disable this and make VisualWorks pay attention to the colors you specify using the mechanism above, comment out the line that says self installPlatformPreferencesFrom: aGraphicsDevice on: colors in the method WidgetPolicy class>>defaultWidgetColorsOn:.

Speed Up Startup

On a UNIX system, VisualWorks takes a long time to come up. One of the reasons is that, during startup, VisualWorks looks at every font on the system. When we modified this code to look only at the fonts that were necessary, we found that the startup time went from about thirty seconds down to seven seconds. To do this change, modify the FontPolicy>>initializeFor: method. In it, change the following line to the three lines below:

```
availableFonts := aDevice listFontNames collect: [:name | fontClass parse: name].
```

```
availableFonts := false
    ifTrue: [aDevice listFontNames collect: [:name | fontClass parse: name]]
    ifFalse: [self necessaryFonts collect: [:name | fontClass parse: name]]
```

To get the list of fonts that should be returned in the necessaryFonts method, inspect Screen default. From the inspector, inspect openFonts. Highlight the array of Associations and move it into the necessaryFonts method. You'll need to remove the value part of each association and make the strings into a literal array. You should end up with something like the method shown here.

```
necessaryFonts
    ^#('-adobe-helvetica-medium-r-normal—12-120-75-75-p-67-iso8859-1'
    ...
    '-adobe-helvetica-medium-r-normal—14-140-75-75-p-77-iso8859-1')
```

These changes will take effect the next time you load the image, so save the image, exit, and restart VisualWorks. If you want to revert back to reading all the fonts (perhaps you are going to run the image on another type of computer), simply change the false to true in FontPolicy>>initializeFor:.

32

Changes to System Classes

Sometimes it is useful to modify system classes. To be able to add a method to Object that everyone can inherit can make life much easier. In fact, in several chapters in this book we've seen new methods added to system classes. There are several kinds of change you can make, and we'll look at them in this chapter.

Some people feel it is inappropriate to modify system classes for various reasons. The arguments listed below are all valid arguments, and after reading this chapter you will have to decide where your own beliefs lie.

- If you change a system class, then get a new release of the system software, your change will not be there. It might be difficult to put back in because of possible restructuring of system classes. You might simply forget to reimplement the change and this might not be discovered until a customer uses the software.

- The system classes are highly reliable. Any change you make could detract from that reliability.

- Programmers won't know that certain behaviors were added and will expect to find the changes in other projects they work on.

- Programmers might expect a method to behave a particular way, then discover too late that the method was modified to behave a different way.

Subclass Where Possible

It's better to subclass off a system class than to add a method or modify a method. It's not always possible to subclass, as we'll see, but the failure to subclass is often a result of not attempting to do so. For example, when I originally extended the VisualLauncher with a few changes, I simply added new methods. Only later did it dawn on me to subclass from VisualLauncher. Besides the virtues of not modifying system classes, subclassing has the additional virtue that it is obvious when programmers are using a nonstandard class.

If you want to add behavior to Object that you want inherited by all your application objects, consider creating a new class, MyApplicationObject, that is subclassed off Object. If you subclass all your application objects from MyApplicationObject you can add application-specific behavior that all your objects will inherit, without having to modify Object in any way. We saw an example of this in Chapter 5.

Types of Changes to System Classes

There are two facets to consider when talking about changing system classes. First is that some changes will be to classes used in the development environment, while others will be to more fundamental classes that are used in your deployed application. The other facet is that there is a difference between adding methods to system classes and modifying existing methods.

Development environment versus deployed classes

You can make changes to your development environment that will never be executed in a deployed application. More important, you can make changes to your development environment that don't have to be incorporated into the production application. For example, you might make changes to remap your keyboard for development, to allow resizing of Browser panes or to add more sophisticated breakpoints. None of these changes have to be included when building the application for testing and deployment.

Added versus modified methods

Adding methods to system classes is a lot less risky than modifying existing methods. When you modify a method, you have to be very careful that your change will not cause harm to any of the senders of the message. Sometimes this is easy to determine, sometimes difficult. Avoid modifying a method in a way that will confuse programmers who expect certain results from message sends. To use an extreme example, if someone modified add: to return self rather than the object added, the result would probably be confusion and code that no longer worked.

Adding functionality by subclassing is the right thing to do when possible, but even when possible it's not always easy. Suppose we want to add trimWhiteSpace to remove leading and trailing white space from a string. It's not easy to add a subclass of String because String new actually returns an instance of a subclass of String, and creating a literal string, such as 'hi there', will not create an instance of our new subclass. So, it's much easier to add trimWhiteSpace to String.

In fact, I'm in favor of adding methods as long as they are well thought through and well tested. I'm also in favor of modifying methods to extend functionality as long as the old expected behavior is preserved. For example, in Chapter 16, we looked at the idea of subclassing off Process. Unfortunately, the method Process>>anyProcessesAbove: assumes that there are no subclasses of Process. So, in order to subclass off Process we had to modify this method to operate on instances of Process and its subclasses.

If you do have to modify a system method, try to put the smallest possible change in the modified method and most of the processing in another method (on one of your objects, if possible). You might end up with something like the following:

```
SystemClass>>someModifiedMethod
    ...
    self doNewThing.
    anInstanceOfMyClass doAnotherNewThing.
    ...

SystemClass>>doNewThing
    "Here's where most of the new code might be"

MyClass>>doAnotherNewThing
    "Here's another place where most of the new code might be"
```

Summary

- Subclass where possible.

- Be comfortable adding well-tested methods to system classes.

- Don't worry too much about modifications to system classes for development environment changes, if you don't need those changes in the deployed image.

- Selectively modify fundamental system classes, as long as you are extending functionality rather than modifying functionality.

Distinguishing Your Additions and Modifications

For two reasons, it's important to be able to distinguish system methods you've added and modified from base-system methods. First, it's only fair to tell programmers that they are using nonstandard methods.

Second, when you get a new release you need to be able to identify the changes you've made, so you can add them to the new image.

I use two mechanisms. The first is to group all added methods into protocols called (additions), and to move all modified methods to protocols called (modifications). Yes, the parentheses are part of the name — it makes the name stand out. Chapter 29 tells you how to find all classes with protocols named (additions) or (modifications).

However, I don't do this for development environment changes that I get from the *Smalltalk Archives* or similar places. Some of these fileIns make such extensive changes to system classes that it's more important to make sure they are only in development environments and not in production applications.

The second mechanism I use to distinguish my changes from the standard classes is to place one of the following statements as the first executable line in the methods (the method definitions are shown later in the chapter). By noting new methods and changed methods in this way, it's easy to find all the new or changed methods by browsing references to either newMethod: or changedMethod:.

```
self newMethod: 'Date. Author. Why'.
self changedMethod: 'When. Who. Why'.
```

Why use both the message sends and the protocol name? In part, to increase my chances of tracking all the changes that I have to carry forward to new releases. However, the two mechanisms do serve different purposes. When I want to find a method I wrote but can't remember the details of, looking for message references will get me there quickly. If I'm browsing a class, the special protocol names tell me immediately that there are extensions or modifications to the class. By grouping added and modified methods, I can easily file out all the changes to system classes by choosing the file out menu option from the protocol window.

Some Useful Additions

This next section shows a few minor additions to Object that I've found useful. We've seen additions and changes to system classes in other chapters, but we are not repeating them here.

The following methods make it much easier to print information to the Transcript. Some people find it easier conceptually to use the echoYourself methods, but once you get used to the idea of objects printing themselves to the Transcript, it's less typing to use the echo methods. The code is based on Ernest Micklei's echo.st contribution to the *Smalltalk Archives*.

```
Object>>echo
    Transcript cr; nextPutAll: self displayString; flush
```

Object>>echo: anObject
    Transcript
        cr; nextPutAll: self displayString;
        space; nextPutAll: anObject displayString;
        flush

Object>>echoYourself
    self echo

Object echoYourselfAnd: anObject
    self echo: anObject

The next few methods don't do anything. They exist simply so that you can find all references to them.

Object>>newMethod: aString
    "Does nothing. Used to find methods added to system classes"

Object>>changedMethod: aString
    "Does nothing. Used to find system class methods that have been changed"

Object>>obsoleteMethod: aString
    "Does nothing. Used to find obsolete methods"

Object>>optimizePoint: aString
    "Does nothing. Used to find methods that need additional work"

33

Managing Source Code

In the description that follows, I am assuming that you are not using a product such as ENVY to manage your source code and configurations. Instead, you are using some combination of filing out your changes, saving your image, and filing in your changes. We'll talk more about ENVY in Chapter 34.

As you work, you are probably saving your changes in some way, whether by filing out categories, classes, or methods, or by periodically saving your image. Certainly you'll need to file out your changes if other developers are to incorporate them. Whatever technique you use to protect your work from crashes and to distribute your changes to others, it's important to be able to rebuild your image with all the correct code.

The technique that I've usually used is to rely on developers filing out changes, usually at the class category level, then every day starting up a clean image — one containing no source code — and filing in all the latest code. If you choose to save your image periodically instead of filing out your changes, then I recommend that you also have available a clean image you can start from, again filing in the latest code. In what follows we'll look closely at some of the aspects of filing out code and filing in code.

What we describe is certainly not the only way to manage your source code and might not even be the best way. If you have a very large application, it might take too long to do what is shown here more than perhaps once a week. It might be a better option to maintain an *application base image* that contains all the needed system class additions and modifications, using a fileIn such as shown below to build the application base. Derived from the application base might be a *developer base image* that also contains development environment changes that are expected to be in the images of all developers.

Again, this could be maintained using some of the code shown below. Derived from the developer base might be *individual base images* that contain the preferences of individual developers. Again, the code below can help track those changes. Periodically the developers would file in all the latest application code, then would save their new *working image*. Also periodically, the latest application code would be filed into the application base image and saved as a *testing image*.

Treat the code shown as possibility code. Take what you like, discard what you don't like, and above all, use it to generate ideas that work for your development environment.

Change Set

The Change Set is a wonderful tool for keeping track of what changes you are making. Every change you make gets recorded in the Change Set so rather than writing down your changes on paper (as I did when I first started programming in Smalltalk), you can simply look at the Change Set. By doing two small things you can make it truly useful. We show how it might be done later in this chapter, but basically, when you have filed in your changes you do ChangeSet noChanges to empty the change set. After all, you know that there have been a lot of changes due to filing in all those classes and methods; what you are interested in is changes made since then.

The second change is Browser removeChangesOnFileOut: true. This tells the Browser that when you file out changes, those changes should be removed from the Change Set. So, by looking at the Change Set, you can tell what changes you have made but have not yet saved. As you file out the relevant categories or classes, the Change Set gets smaller. When you get to an empty Change Set, you have filed out all the changed code. (Unfortunately there is one small gotcha. If you rename classes using the rename menu option, that change is not recorded in the Change Set, so you'll have to remember it.)

Filing in Code

It's important to periodically file in the latest code — application code, necessary changes to system classes, and development environment code. In the subsections that follow, we'll look at a mechanism for filing in all three types of code. Whether you do this daily, more frequently, or less frequently, it's something that you'll need to do at times in order to keep the images of all developers synchronized. In the fileIn examples that follow, I'll intersperse text with the fileIn code to explain what each section is doing. The code can be found in the manage directory in the file install.st.

Filing in the application

```
"install.st - Install the Application software
Created: When. Who. Why
Changed: When. Who. Why

|sourceDir sysAddDir sysModDir localFile
beforeClassCount beforeMethodCount afterClassCount afterMethodCount |
```

The next section sets up the various directories and files that we will need later on. In this example, we are assuming that development is done on both UNIX and MS-Windows platforms, so the code determines which platform we are currently on and sets the names for that platform.

```
"Figure out the various directories. We allow development to be done on different
platform"
Window platformName = 'X11'
    ifTrue:
        [sourceDir := '/product/src' asFilename.
        sysAddDir := '/visual/sys/additions' asFilename.
        sysModDir := '/visual/sys/modifications'.
        localFile := '/home/', (CEnvironment getenv: 'LOGNAME'), '/.vwlocal' asFilename]
    ifFalse:
        [sourceDir := 'c:\alec\st\source' asFilename.
        sysAddDir := 'c:\alec\st\sysadds' asFilename.
        sysModDir := 'c:\alec\st\sysmods' asFilename.
        localFile := 'c:\visual\local\local.st' asFilename].
```

If the directories are subdirectories of a base directory, we could write code without hard-coding the base directory. In the example that follows, we assume that install.st is being filed in from the base directory. The idea is that we trace the context back until we find a stream, which we assume is the stream filing in this file. Once we have the base directory, we can build up the subdirectories. An example of this code can be found in the manage directory in the file install2.st.

```
context := thisContext.
[context receiver isKindOf: Stream]
    whileFalse:
        [context := context sender].
baseDir := context receiver name asFilename head asFilename.
sourceDir := baseDir construct: 'source'.
```

The next section files in any system additions and system modifications that are required for the application. It makes the assumption that it should file in all the .st files in these directories. In other words, if you don't want something filed in, don't put it in one of these directories.

```
"File in any required system additions and modifications that we find"
(sysAddDir filesMatching: '*.st') do: [ :each | each asFilename fileIn].
(sysModDir filesMatching: '*.st') do: [ :each | each asFilename fileIn].
```

We now file in any development environment changes that are specific to the programmer. If there is a named file and the file is readable we go ahead and read it. The intention is that each developer will have a file with a known name in a known, but unique to them, directory, and that if this file exists, it will be filed in. The names of the directory and file will depend on what type of platform you are working on, and how your computers are networked. This scheme will work also for building the deployed application image, because you don't need to set up a local file for the user that creates the application image.

```
"File in any programmer-specific changes that we find"
(localFile notNil and: [localFile isReadable])
    ifTrue: [localFile fileIn]
    ifFalse: [Transcript cr; show: 'No local file'].
```

Before we file in the application code we want to count the number of classes and methods in the image. We'll do the same after filing in the code, then we'll be able to report how many classes and methods our application contains.

```
"Count the number of classes and methods in the image before filing in the application
code"
beforeClassCount := Smalltalk classNames size.
beforeMethodCount := Smalltalk classNames
    inject: 0
    into:   [:subtotal :each | | class|
            class := Smalltalk at: each.
            subtotal + class selectors size + class class selectors size].
```

Now we create any necessary pool dictionaries and add all the pool dictionary variables. We need to do this in a fileIn; otherwise, there will be problems. If the pool dictionary doesn't exist, the fileIn will raise an exception; if the pool dictionary variables don't exist, then references to them will fail when you try to accept a method or run the code.

```
"Create any necessary pool dictionaries and add all the pool dictionary variables"
Smalltalk at: #MyPoolDictionary put: Dictionary new.
MyPoolDictionary at: #PoolVariableOne put: nil.
MyPoolDictionary at: #PoolVariableTwo put: nil.
```

The next section files in all the application code. In this example, we specify exactly what application code we want in the image, unlike the system additions where we took all the files in the directory. We also assume that you filed out by class category. If you file out by class or by method, it would probably be too painful to specify all the files and would be easier to file in every file in the directory.

```
"File in all the named categories"
#( 'CatgOne.st'
   'CatgTwo.st'
   'CatgThree.st'
) do: [ :each | (sourceDir construct: each) fileIn ].
```

Now we count the number of classes and methods in the image after filing in the application code, and report on the counts.

```
"Count the number of classes and methods in the image after filing in the application
code, then report on the counts."
afterClassCount := Smalltalk classNames size.
afterMethodCount := Smalltalk classNames
    inject: 0
    into:   [:subtotal :each | | class|
            class := Smalltalk at: each.
            subtotal + class selectors size + class class selectors size].

Transcript
    cr; nextPutAll: 'Before loading in:';
    crtab; nextPutAll: 'Class count = '; print: beforeClassCount;
    crtab; nextPutAll: 'Method count = '; print: beforeMethodCount;
    cr; nextPutAll: 'After loading in:';
    crtab; nextPutAll: 'Class count = '; print: afterClassCount;
    crtab; nextPutAll: 'Method count = '; print: afterMethodCount;
    cr; nextPutAll: 'New:';
    crtab; nextPutAll: 'Classes = '; print: (afterClassCount - beforeClassCount);
    crtab; nextPutAll: 'Methods = '; print: (afterMethodCount - beforeMethodCount);
    endEntry.
```

The last section does any final system changes that need to be done. In particular, we empty the change set so that the Change Set just reflects changes we make after filing in our application code, and make sure that the delete key deletes in a forward direction.

```
"Do any final system changes"
LookPreferences deleteForward: true        "Make the delete key delete forwards"
ChangeSet noChanges.                        "Empty the change set"
```

Filing in development environment changes

Let's now look at an example of a local file that files in development environment changes. Again, explanatory text will be interspersed with the code. The code can be found in the manage directory in the file local.st.

```
"local.st - Alec's specific environment changes
When. Who.     Why.
"

|genericDir localDir |

Window platformName = 'X11'
    ifTrue:
        [genericDir := '/visual/generic'.
        localDir := '/home/alec/st/fileIns']
    ifFalse:
        [genericDir := 'c:\visual\generic'.
        localDir := 'c:\alec\st\fileIns'].
```

In this section we file in everything we find in two directories. The first one is our own personal fileIn directory. This allows us to include any other enhancements we need. After we've done our personal changes to the image, we then fileIn everything in the generic directory. These are changes that everyone should be picking up. The reason for having this is that there might be modifications to the development environment that are standard across the organization, and which a programmer can expect to see in another programmer's environment.

```
"Do any personal and generic development environment fileIns"
(localDir asFilename filesMatching: '*.st') do: [ :each | each asFilename fileIn].
(genericDir asFilename filesMatching: '*.st') do: [ :each | each asFilename fileIn].
```

The code that follows could easily be in one of our personal fileIns, but instead, we'll show it here. The code shown is described in detail in Chapter 31, so we won't explain it in depth. The next section remaps the keyboard (assuming that you have defined a keyboard method on ParagraphEditor), remaps the interrupt key, then changes the window colors.

```
"Remap the keyboard"
ParagraphEditor keyboard
    bindValue: #cutKey: to: (TextConstants at: #Ctrlx);
    bindValue: #copyKey: to: (TextConstants at: #Ctrlc);
    bindValue: #pasteKey: to: (TextConstants at: #Ctrlv);
    bindValue: #acceptKey: to: (TextConstants at: #Ctrla).

"If this is not VW2.0, initialize the TextEditorController so it gets the new keyboard
mappings"
(Smalltalk version findString: '2.0' startingAt: 1) == 0
    ifTrue: [TextEditorController initialize].

"Change the Interrupt key from Ctrl-C to Ctrl-Q"
InputState interruptKeyValue: (TextConstants at: #Ctrlq).

"Change my window colors"
Win3WidgetPolicy defaultColorWidgetColors
    matchAt: SymbolicPaint background put: ColorValue lightCyan;
    matchAt: SymbolicPaint selectionBackground put: ColorValue pink;
    matchAt: SymbolicPaint selectionForeground put: ColorValue black.
Screen default updatePaintPreferences.
ScheduledControllers restore.
```

Windows created before we remapped the keyboard still use the old keyboard bindings, so we create some new windows that use the new key bindings. We want the windows to be created automatically rather than waiting for us to position them, so we tell the ScheduledWindow class not to prompt us when opening the window. We also create a SystemWorkspace-like window, which contains useful statements that can be highlighted and executed.

```
"Create some new windows with my new key bindings"
prompt := ScheduledWindow promptForOpen.
ScheduledWindow promptForOpen: false.
FullBrowser open.
ComposedTextView
    open: (ValueHolder with: ('c:\alec\st\useful' asFilename contentsOfEntireFile))
    label: 'Useful Things'
    icon: nil
    extent: 500@200.
ComposedTextView open.
ScheduledWindow promptForOpen: prompt.
```

Generic development environment changes

In the directory containing changes to the generic development environment, we have at least one file. This file tells the Browser that when developers file out code, the changes should be removed from the Change Set.

```
"general.st - General Development Environment changes
Created: When. Who. Why
"
```

```
"Remove changes from the change set after doing a file out"
Browser removeChangesOnFileOut: true.
```

Using a Class to File in the Code

Besides filing in from a text file, we could use a class to control what gets filed in. For my personal customization I use a class rather than a file because I find it easier to make changes to a class. Here's an example of the main flow of my Customizer class. The code for this class can be found in the file custom.st.

```
Customizer>>customize
    "self new customize"
    self myFileInSystemAdditions.
    self myFileInSystemModifications.
    self myFileInNewClasses.
    self myKeyboardChanges.
    self myLauncherMenu.
    self myResetChangeSet.
    self myOpenWindows.
```

Filing Out

Depending on how you manage your fileOuts, you might want to run programs like diff to find the differences between two versions. Unfortunately methods are filed out in a seemingly random order, which makes it difficult to discover the real differences. By changing self selectors to self selectors asSortedCollection in ClassDescription>> fileOutMethodsOn: you can have the methods file out in sorted order.

Creating a Production Image

When you rely on people to do things there is always a chance of error. People are creative, but also prone to making errors, which is why make schemes are so popular.[1] They apply rules to determine what to build, and then automatically compile and link any files that are out of date. The process of building and saving a Smalltalk image is usually somewhat manual. We might have a fileIn that gets the right code in, but a person usually has to decide that an image needs building and then do the manual steps of invoking the fileIn and saving the image. Here is a scheme that allows the building of a Smalltalk image to be done automatically, possibly as part of a make scheme. In VisualWorks 2.0, it was difficult to create a production image and this process makes it a lot easier. VisualWorks 2.5 has a new facility, the ImageMaker, that makes it much easier to create a production image. Below are two schemes to automate the image creation, one for VisualWorks 2.0 and one for 2.5. The code can be found in the files imcr20.st and imcr25.st.

Common to VisualWorks 2.0 and 2.5

The basic idea is that we start with a clean image that has either the Stripper or the ImageMaker code loaded, and has a new ImageCreator class loaded. It does *not* have the application code loaded. The Undeclared dictionary should be cleaned up apart from the reference to your main application class (the ImageCreator will start your application, but because the application code is not yet loaded the ImageCreator will be referring to a class that doesn't yet exist in the image).

We then save the image under a descriptive name such as makeIm. When we run makeIm, it files in the application code, removes unnecessary classes, opens the application, closes the VisualLauncher, sets up a new emergency handler, and then saves the application image. We start by creating ImageCreator, a new subclass of Object with no instance or class variables.

In the ImageCreator class initialization, we register ourself as a dependent of ObjectMemory. This means that, when ObjectMemory

---

[1]*Make* is a standard UNIX utility for building programs from source, header, and object files. It checks dates on the various files to determine which object files need to be rebuilt, and which executable files need to be relinked.

sends changed: messages, the ImageCreator class will receive them. Because it is the class that is registered as a dependent, we write update:with:from: on the class side. In this method, the only thing we want to hear is that we have just returned from a snapshot — that the image has just come up. When this is the case, we create a new instance of ImageCreator and tell it to make a new application image by sending the createImage message.

```
ImageCreator class>>initialize
    "Register ourselves to receive an update message when the image comes up."
    "self initialize"
    (ObjectMemory dependents includes: self)
        ifFalse: [ObjectMemory addDependent: self]

ImageCreator class>>update: anAspect with: arguments from: anObject
    (anObject == ObjectMemory and: [anAspect == #returnFromSnapshot])
        ifTrue: [self new createImage]
```

VisualWorks 2.0

In VisualWorks 2.0 we need to first load in the Stripper code. We will create a subclass of Stripper called MyStripper, in which we will override a few methods to prevent dialogs coming up and to initialize variables. However, let's first look at createImage and its support methods. Most of the methods are short, so it would be possible to put all the code in one method. However, by having several methods it makes it easier to modify and tailor. In this section we show the methods that are specific to VisualWorks 2.0; methods common to both 2.0 and 2.5 are shown later. Two things to note are that we run MyStripper after filing in the application because we need the compiler when filing in, and we install the application emergency handler at the end in case something goes wrong and we want a regular Notifier raised.

```
ImageCreator>>createImage
    ObjectMemory globalGarbageCollect.
    self myRemoveSelfAsDependent.
    self myFileInApplication.
    self myRunStripper.
    self myOpenApplication.
    self myCloseLauncher.
    self myInstallEmergencyHandler.
    self mySaveImageAndQuit

ImageCreator>>myRunStripper
    "Run the stripper to remove any unnecessary system classes."
    MyStripper new
        doRemoveOfSubsystems;
        stripSystem.
```

```
ImageCreator>>myCloseLauncher
    "Close any open Launchers "
    self myLauncherClass allInstances do:
        [:each | each builder window controller closeAndUnschedule]
```

```
ImageCreator>>mySaveImageAndQuit
    "Do a final garbage collect then save the image and quit.
     Saving as a snapshot means that no change file is created.
    The loadPolicy parameter specifies that objects in old space are loaded in perm space."
    ObjectMemory globalGarbageCollect.
    ObjectMemory
        snapshotAs: self myImageName
        thenQuit: true
        withLoadPolicy: 1
```

Besides the methods that do the real work, we have some methods in the names protocol. These are the methods that should be modified for different applications, because they provide the image name, the main application class, and so on. As mentioned above, only the methods that are specific to VisualWorks 2.0 are shown here; the common methods are shown later.

```
ImageCreator>>myImageName
    "Return the name of the image to save"
    ^'myApp' copy
```

```
ImageCreator>>myLauncherClass
    "We may be using a subclass of VisualLauncher as our Launcher"
    ^VisualLauncher
```

There are several changes you must make to the stripper code for it to work in this environment. So that the stripping can run automatically, without human intervention, you'll need to override doRemoveOfSubsystems and stripSystem in MyStripper to remove the dialogs. Depending on which subsystems you want removed, you should set the appropriate options to have a value of true in initialize. For example, we want to also remove the database tools, the printing facility, and extra classes that we specified.

```
MyStripper>>initialize
    super initialize.
    doDbtools := true asValue.
    doPrinting := true asValue.
    doExtras := true asValue.
```

If there are classes that you know you want to strip, add them to MyStripper class>>initExtras, making sure you reinitialize the array. Alternatively, you could strip the basic image down before creating the makeIm image, keeping just enough to be able to file in the application code and save the image. You'll still need to strip the compiler later, but creating the application image would be faster if you started from a basic image that had already been stripped of a lot of classes.

If you want more than a VisualLauncher open in the builder image, you can add a message send of myCloseOtherWindows before filing in the application code.

```
ImageCreator>>myCloseOtherWindows
    "Close any open windows that aren't Launchers"
    ScheduledControllers scheduledControllers
        do: [:each | each model class ~~ self myLauncherClass
            ifTrue: [each closeAndUnschedule]]
```

VisualWorks 2.5

In VisualWorks 2.5 you need to first load in the ImageMaker code. You then run the ImageMaker (ImageMaker open) and select the removal options you want. To remove other classes in addition to the subsystems specified, select Set Additional Removals from the Classes menu, and select the Remove Additional Classes button. Once you have made all your choices, select File Out Choices from the File menu. We'll use the choices file later in one of the ImageCreator methods.

As before, we'll start by looking at createImage and its support methods, showing the methods specific to VisualWorks 2.5 here, with methods common to both 2.0 and 2.5 shown later.

```
ImageCreator>>createImage
    self myRemoveSelfAsDependent.
    self myInitializeImageMaker.
    self myFileInChoices.
    self myFileInApplication.
    self myOpenApplication.
    self myInstallEmergencyHandler.
    self myRunImageMaker

ImageCreator>>myInitializeImageMaker
    "Create a new ImageMaker and make it the current one"
    MyImageMaker current: MyImageMaker new.

ImageCreator>>myFileInChoices
    "File in the ImageMaker choices that we previously saved"
    self myChoicesFile fileIn

ImageCreator>>myRunImageMaker
    "Remove unneeded classes and save the new image"
    MyImageMaker current makeDeploymentImage

ImageCreator>>myChoicesFile
    "Return the filename that contains the ImageMaker choices"
    ^'choices.txt' asFilename
```

We've seen references to MyImageMaker above, so we now need to create it as a subclass of ImageMaker. In MyImageMaker we override a few methods to keep dialogs from coming up, and to specify file paths. Override getZoneDirectory to remove the Dialogs and to set the directory to self myBaseDirectory. **Override** makeImageFile **to remove the Dialogs and to set the** imagePrefix **to self** myImageName. **Override** refreshView **to be an empty method, and** warnUser **to return** true.

```
MyImagerMaker>>myBaseDirectory
    "The directory where the utils subdirectory resides"
    ^'c:\visual' copy
```

```
MyImagerMaker>>myImageName
    ^'myApp' copy
```

In VisualWorks 2.5, one additional step needs to be taken. The first time your new application image is loaded, VisualWorks does some operations to optimize memory use and increase performance, then saves the image again. So, if you are creating an image as part of an automatic process, your scripts should create the new application image, *and then start up the new application image*. The code above will automatically save the optimized application image, then exit.

Common to VisualWorks 2.0 and 2.5

The following methods are common to both VisualWorks 2.0 and 2.5.

```
ImageCreator>>myRemoveSelfAsDependent
    "Remove ourself as a dependent of ObjectMemory.
    We don't want this code to run every time the application is started."
    (ObjectMemory dependents includes: self class)
        ifTrue: [ObjectMemory removeDependent: self class]
```

In myOpenApplication **we assume we can send** open **to the application class. If you need another message sent, you could define a new method** myStartMessage, **which returned a symbol. You would then start the application by** self myApplication perform: self myStartMessage.

```
ImageCreator>>myOpenApplication
    "Open the application. We need to make sure that the user is not prompted for
    the window position. When you accept this method, it will ask you to declare your
    application class. Make it Undeclared. "
    |prompt |
    prompt := ScheduledWindow promptForOpen.
    ScheduledWindow promptForOpen: false.
    self myApplication open.
    ScheduledWindow promptForOpen: prompt
```

```
ImageCreator>>myFileInApplication
    "File in the application code."
    self myInstallFile fileIn.
```

```
ImageCreator>>myInstallEmergencyHandler
    "Install the application Emergency Handler."
    Exception emergencyHandler:
        [:ex :context | self handleException: ex context: context]
```

```
ImageCreator>>myInstallFile
    "Return the filename that files in the application code"
    ^'install.st' asFilename
```

```
ImageCreator>>myApplication
    "Return the class that starts up the application"
    ^MyApplication
```

In the method that sets up the new emergency handler you will want to put something more sensible than the code shown here, but what you put will depend on how your application handles errors.

```
ImageCreator>> handleException: ex context: aContext
    "Do some error handling then quit"
    Dialog warn: 'Error: ' , ex errorString , ' in ' , aContext printString , ' Quitting application'.
    ObjectMemory quit
```

We now have a mechanism for creating new images automatically, with little or no human intervention.

Saving the mklm image

After filing in either the Stripper or ImageMaker followed by the ImageCreator, we need to save the image under a name, such as mklm. This is the image that will create our deployment image, using all the code we wrote above. The obvious way to save mklm is to use the File menu to either save the image or exit VisualWorks and save. However, this will create a change file, which will grow every time mklm files in the application code. By adding two methods to the class side of ImageCreator we can save the image without a change file:

```
ImageCreator class>>saveImage
    "Save the image that will be used to create the production image."
    "self saveImage"
    ObjectMemory globalGarbageCollect.
    ObjectMemory
        snapshotAs: self myImageName
        thenQuit: true
        withLoadPolicy: 1
```

```
ImageCreator class>>myImageName
    "Return the name of the image that will be used to create the deployment image"
    ^'mklm' copy
```

Rather than saving the image from the file menu, you can now evaluate ImageCreator saveImage, which will save the image with no change file, then quit. An alternative mechanism is to save the image with the name snapshot. VisualWorks treats this name specially and does not create a change file. After creating the image, you would then rename snapshot.im to mklm.im.

Runtime Packager

In Smalltalk, method parameters are not typed, and polymorphism allows many classes to define the same method name. It is therefore very difficult to statically tell if classes are referenced and methods are invoked. The consequence is that the stripping process can be rather hit and miss as you try to figure out what you can strip from the image.

Runtime Packager, from Advanced Boolean Concepts, provides additional capabilities that make it easier to determine what you can strip and what your application needs. It allows you to specify which classes and methods you want included, which ones you want removed, and which you are not sure about. It will then use both static and dynamic analysis to check your application to determine which classes and methods are safe to remove.

Runtime Packager will statically check all the message sends, starting at the message send that starts your application and following the message send tree until there are no further references. It also allows you to run the application in a special test mode in which it records all the classes and methods that were previously marked for deletion, but which are referenced in the running application. It automatically returns them to the image and continues running the tests. Once all the static and dynamic analysis is done, it creates a stripped image.

At the time of writing, Runtime Packager was available for $495 for a single user, and $1,200 for a site license. For more information, contact:

Advanced Boolean Concepts, Ltd.
3704 Cameron Mills Road
Alexandria, VA 22305, USA
Phone: (703) 548-5073
Fax: (703) 548-6053
Email: advbool@advbool.com
Web page: http://www.advbool.com/advbool/

Chapter

34

ENVY

When organizations start developing in Smalltalk, they often use the fileIn and fileOut mechanism to manage changes to classes and methods. After a while, especially if the number of people working on an application increases, most organizations look for a way to better manage source code and configurations. The dominant player in this field for Smalltalk is Object Technology International, Inc. (OTI), with their *ENVY®/Developer* product. The part of ENVY/Developer that manages source code and configurations is called *ENVY®/Manager*, and this is what most developers are referring to when they talk about *ENVY*. This chapter provides an overview of ENVY/Manager and gives, perhaps, a few pointers to those already using it.

ENVY/Manager helps you manage code development. In brief, it provides a source code repository that stores and tracks all changes to methods and classes. It allows developers to modify and test their code in isolation from each other, possibly even working on parallel versions of the same code. Once developers are satisfied that their code works, they can release it for general use. Other developers now have the choice of loading the new code into their images or continuing with the older version until they are ready to integrate. Between the extremes of isolation and integrating all the code released by a developer, ENVY/Manager also provides a way for developers to view or load individual classes or methods that another developer is working on. At the project level, ENVY/Manager keeps track of product releases. By creating a configuration map that specifies the versions of the classes that comprise a release, you can easily recreate any release of your application. We'll look at each of these facets in the following sections.

Code Sharing

ENVY/Manager keeps the source code in a central repository called a *library*, so all developers have access to the same code (it actually keeps both source code and byte-compiled code for faster access). ENVY/Manager is conceptually a client-server application, where developers work in client images, which communicate with the library server. Thus, whenever anyone makes a change to a class or a method, all other developers have access to that change should they want to view it or load it into their image (subject to security, which we'll talk about shortly).

ENVY/Manager automatically keeps track of every revision to every class and method, rather than using the more common manual check-out, check-in mechanism used by source code managers such as RCS and SCCS. The manual check-out, check-in mechanism works well with large source files where work can be fairly well-compartmentalized and source files can be checked out for relatively long periods of time. However, the Smalltalk object-oriented paradigm means that changes are likely to affect many cooperating classes, and because methods are generally short, a developer is likely to make small changes to many methods. In this world, tracking all changes is a lot less intrusive than a manual check-out and check-in scheme.

Because all the versions of the code are stored, it becomes a very simple matter to go back to a previous version if necessary. Even if methods or classes are deleted from the local image, they still exist in the repository and can easily be found by looking for *available* methods or classes in the appropriate browser.

ENVY/Manager makes it very easy for developers to work on code in parallel. For example, one developer might be working on a class for the next release of the product, while another developer is making bug fixes to support a previous release and another is trying out some optimization techniques. All three developers can work on their changes without affecting each other, then when it comes time to integrate the changes, ENVY/Manager provides tools to show the differences between versions and to load alternative versions.

Applications and Subapplications

In ENVY/Manager, everything is done within the context of an *application*, which is simply a collection or grouping of classes. Thus, within applications you have many classes, all pertaining to the application. To further organize the classes, you can create subapplications within the application. For example, a common way to organize an application (let's call it EmployeeApp), is to have three subapplications, one for the domain model classes, one for the user interface classes, and one for the data access classes. So we might call the subapplications EmployeeDomainApp, EmployeeUIApp, and EmployeeDataAccessApp. Subapplications are also commonly used to break out platform-specific code, because when an application is loaded it can use logic to determine which subapplications to load. (In what follows, we'll use the term "application" to mean either an application or a subapplication, unless explicitly stated otherwise.)

When an application is created it contains exactly one class, which has the same name as the application. This class serves several purposes. It starts off being a class template, which developers can use to create new classes. It also provides an opportunity to write class side methods that will be invoked on pre-defined occasions (related to loading or unloading the application and starting and exiting the image). The most useful is the loaded method. Because source files are not filed in, class side initialize methods are not automatically invoked. Instead, you have to invoke them explicitly in the loaded method, which is executed when the application is loaded into the image. (Another, less known method is addToSystemMenu, which allows you to easily extend the ENVY/Manager menu.)

In ENVY/Manager, every class is *defined* in a single application. However, you can *extend* a class in another application, which gives you the opportunity to add application-specific behavior to that class (note, however, that you can't *modify* a base method in an extension). For example, suppose you are working on two products that share some, but not all, code. ProductOne needs a new method foo added to Object. You might create a new application called ProductOneSystemExtensions, then extend Object by adding foo to Object in this application.

Version Control

Applications and classes can exist in one of two basic states: as *versions,* which cannot be modified, or as *editions,* which can be modified. You can tell the state of an application, because versions display with a version name and editions display with a time stamp between parentheses.

ENVY/Manager allows developers to modify any method of any class (subject to access control). To modify any component, its container must be modifiable — that is, it must be an edition. So, while methods are always editions, to modify a method, the class has to be an edition too. Similarly, to modify a class, the containing application or subapplication must be an edition. Fortunately, ENVY/Manager makes this all very easy. The developer simply has to modify and accept a method and the enclosing class will automatically be made an edition (if it's not already one). If the application containing the class is not already an edition, ENVY/Manager will also ask the developer if he wants to create a *scratch edition* of the application when he accepts the method (we'll talk about the difference between an edition and a scratch edition later).

Visibility

All changes are recorded in the library — every change to every method. However, changes are not automatically propagated to other developers' images, so developers can work in isolation, unaffected by other people's work. However, if a developer chooses, he can view or load other people's changes. In a normal development environment a developer will load changes for two reasons: to integrate his code with that of others, and to load in a class or method to get an immediate fix from another developer. Let's look at the visibility of the different types of components, because the rules for viewing and loading them are different.

Methods

A developer can browse all editions of an individual method and load any edition into his image (remember that all methods exist as editions in the library, and every time you accept a method a new edition is recorded).

Classes

A developer can browse all editions and versions of a class and can load any version of the class. However, editions of a class can be loaded only by the person who created the edition.

Applications

A developer can browse all editions and versions of an application or subapplication. He can also load any edition or version. But which classes are loaded when he loads another edition or version of the application? Only those classes that have been *released* to the application. By definition, releasing a class makes it available to the application and denotes that is should be loaded when the application is loaded. A class must be versioned — made immutable — before it can be released to an application. Similarly, if an application consists of several subapplications, loading the application will load the released versions or editions of the subapplications.

Products and Subsystems

A developer will often want to load in the current baseline of the product under development, or of a subsystem. Loading in the current baseline gives the developer a chance to test his changes with all the released changes. Just as an application is a collection of classes that have meaning together, a *configuration map* (often known as a config map) is a collection of applications that have meaning together. By loading in a configuration map, the developer loads in all the application versions or editions that have been specified in the configuration map. The order of loading of applications is controlled by specifying the *prerequisites* of each application.

Configuration maps provide a one-step way to load a specified set of applications. The main reasons to manage configurations are: to load the latest development build, to load end-user builds, and to give the ability to recreate releases of the product should it be necessary to track down a problem in a previous release. Typically, an organization would have several different configuration maps: one for loading the latest development build, one for each major component or subsystem, and one for creating an end-user image.

Scratch editions

Scratch editions of an application are similar to editions, but have the quality of being automatically created and are therefore unintrusive. However, you cannot release classes into a scratch edition of an application, and scratch editions cannot be browsed or loaded by other developers. Thus, if you exit the image without saving it, you will not be able to load the scratch edition you were working on and will have to individually load all the appropriate editions or versions of the classes you modified. Most developers let ENVY/Manager create a scratch edition for them, then convert it to a "regular" edition at a convenient stopping point. Besides being a convenience, scratch editions are useful in their own right for adding debug code that will later be removed (such as self halt). Because you are only adding debug code and then removing it, you don't really want an edition of the application to be permanently recorded in the library (although all the method changes are recorded). Scratch editions display with the version name surrounded by double angle brackets.

Management of Applications and Classes

ENVY/Manager works on the premise that applications have *managers* and classes have *owners* (the concepts are the same; just the terminology differs). Each application has a manager who is responsible for understanding the application and the relationships between the classes in the application. Each class has an owner who is responsible for the integrity and consistency of the class. The idea is that a class is likely to be better encapsulated, with a more consistent public interface, if one person is responsible for it. Having one person responsible for the class provides both accountability and continuity of perspective.

Classes have to be versioned to make them available to other developers, and have to be versioned and released to make them available to their containing applications. Only the class owner can release a class to its containing application. Similarly, subapplications have to be released to make them available to their containing application. Only the subapplication manager can release a subapplication. Applications are always available to load, and hence are always released.

However, while only owners and managers can release components, any developer can make changes to classes and methods. If a developer realizes he needs to modify some code in a class he doesn't own, he simply creates a new edition of the class, makes the change, and keeps working. When he is done with his changes he will typically create a new version of the class. Because he can't release the new version of the class, he tells the owner of the class about the new version and the class owner browses it. The owner can release the new version of the class, or he can modify it or rewrite it to maintain the internal class consistency, then version it and release the new version.

Perhaps this sounds too permissive, with anyone allowed to view or change any code. ENVY/Manager allows you to control access to code by setting privileges. Associated with each application is an application group, which consists of the class owners (only members of the group can own classes in the application) and developers who have an interest in or a need to know about the workings of the classes. You can restrict access to the classes in the application to just owners of the classes (by having no other group members), to group members, or to the world. Among other things, access can be separately restricted for looking at public methods, looking at private methods, and creating editions of a class for modifying code.

An Example of Controlling Parallel Development

Because ENVY/Manager allows multiple developers to create editions of the same class and, to modify the same methods, let's see how the process of releasing this code would work. Suppose two developers are working on the same class, which neither owns. They both create editions of the class and scratch editions of the application. After making their changes, they each version the class, each giving it a different version ID. To make things easier for the class owner, they might name the version with their name and the date. That's as far as they can go because neither is the owner of the class. Now they tell the owner of the class the ID of the version they created.

The owner of the class can browse these new versions and can also browse differences between his version and either of the new versions, or between the two new versions. The owner can then choose how to integrate the new changes, whether by loading in entire methods, by cutting and pasting, or by rewriting. Once he has created a new edition and incorporated the changes, the owner then versions and releases the class, then asks the application manager to version the application.

Code Reviews

ENVY/Manager makes it possible to do on-line code reviews. The general process is that, once a developer is ready to have his code reviewed, he versions all the classes and applications, then informs the reviewers that the code is ready for review. The reviewers then load in the code and review it in their images. They might add comments, rewrite methods, or even restructure methods within classes. Once done with their review they inform the original developer, who looks at the changes and decides which changes to integrate. This process also makes it easier to stagger the reviews. Rather than have three developers simultaneously review the code and make changes, a better option is to have one person review the code, integrate any proposed changes, have the next developer review the results of the integration, integrate his proposed changes, then have the last developer review this integration.

In describing the mechanics of doing on-line code reviews, I am assuming that you are using the security provided by ENVY/Manager, and that developers cannot simply become other users. I am also assuming that anyone asked to review code is a member of that application group.

The code author versions and releases all his classes and the application managers version the containing applications. The application managers then create new editions of the applications and re-version them with a name, such as *For Review, 96/03/20*. There are now versions of the applications for the reviewer, and editions of the applications that can be used to continue development or can be re-versioned. Next, the application managers change the application manager of the "for review" version of each application. This is a key point; each edition or version of an application can have a different manager and different class owners (the default is to keep the same manager and owners as the previous version). Finally, the code author creates a new configuration map of the applications that will be reviewed, again naming it something like *For Review, 96/03/20*, and changes the manager of the configuration map to be the reviewer.

The author then tells the reviewer that the code is ready for review, and gives him the name of the configuration map. The reviewer loads the map and starts browsing all the code, making code changes where appropriate. Once the reviewer is done, he versions the classes he has changed, giving them names such as *Reviewed by Bill, 96/03/24*. At this point he can't release the classes because he is not the owner, so he simply makes himself the class owner and releases the class. (He can do this, because he has already been made the manager of the review version of the application. It seems a little confusing, but by becoming the owner of the class in this edition of the application he is *not* changing the ownership of the class in the mainline code.) The reviewer then versions the application with a similar name. Finally, he creates a new version of the configuration map with a similar name.

The author then looks at the new configuration map to see which applications have been changed. He does not load the configuration map; instead he goes to each application that has been modified and browses changes. Depending on how much work he has done in the meantime, he will either browse changes between the *For Review* and *Reviewed* versions of the application, or between the current and *Reviewed* versions. If the application has subapplications, he will have to also browse changes for each subapplication. As he looks at the changes, he can load in the alternative code if he chooses. Figure 34-1 illustrates the process of reviewing a single application.

For additional information on using ENVY/Manager to manage code reviews, see "Implementing Peer Code Reviews in Smalltalk," by S. Sridhar, in the July/August 1992 issue of *The Smalltalk Report*. Note,

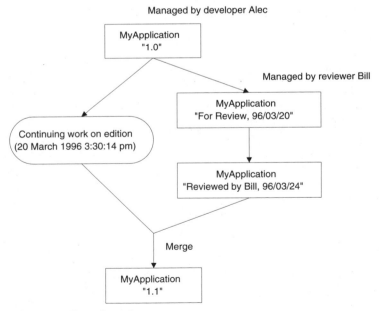

Figure 34-1. The code review process

however, that this article describes a process in which there is little security, and developers can simply become another user to accomplish the described tasks.

Additional Information

You can reach OTI at the following addresses:

Object Technology International, Inc.
2670 Queensview Drive
Ottawa, Canada K2B 8K1
Voice: (613) 820-1200
Fax: (613) 820-1202

Object Technology, Inc.
301 East Bethany Home Road
Suite A-100
Phoenix, AZ 85012, USA
Voice: (602) 222-9519
Fax: (602) 222-8503
e-mail: info@oti.com
Web page: http://www.oti.com

For a product review of ENVY/Manager version 1.43, see the review by Jan Steinman and Barbara Yates of Bytesmiths in the October, 1992 issue of *The Smalltalk Report*. The review, with some updated information, can also be found at the web address:

http://www.bytesmiths.com/pubs/9209Envy.html.

35

Public Domain Code and Information

To the best of my knowledge, the following information was correct at the time I wrote it. However, things change, so there are no guarantees that the information is still correct.

Magazines

The main magazine for Smalltalk developers is *The Smalltalk Report*. There is also a regular Smalltalk column in *The Journal Of Object-Oriented Programming*. Both magazines are published by SIGS publications, at the address below:

The Smalltalk Report
SIGS Publications
PO Box 5050
Brentwood, TN 37024-5050
Current price: $89 a year (9 issues)

The Journal Of Object-Oriented Programming
SIGS Publications
PO Box 5049
Brentwood, TN 37024-9737
Current price: $79 a year (9 issues)

SIGS subscriptions:
e-mail: subscriptions@sigs.com
Voice: 1-800-361-1279
Fax: 615-370-4845

SIGS information
Web: http://www.sigs.com
e-mail: info@sigs.com
Voice: 212-242-7447

Back Issues: 212-242-7447
Reprints: 717-560-2001

Products and Information

The Smalltalk Store

The Smalltalk Store provides one-stop shopping for a variety of Smalltalk products, usually at a price slightly lower than the vendor price.

The Smalltalk Store
565 Esplanade, Suite 402
Redondo Beach, CA 90277
Voice: 1-800-431-2226
310-543-1530
Fax: 310-540-6908
e-mail: stsales@smalltalk.com
Compuserve: 71361,1636
Web page: http://www.smalltalk.com

Public domain code

The main archives for public domain Smalltalk code are at the University of Manchester in England, and at the University of Illinois (UIUC). UIUC mirrors the Manchester archives and also has its own archives. You can get code from UIUC using the World Wide Web or by anonymous ftp. ParcPlace also has some source code available from the World Wide Web.

Usenet

On the Internet, the newsgroup comp.lang.smalltalk usually contains a lot of good material on Smalltalk programming. The *Smalltalk Frequently Asked Questions* (FAQ) is periodically posted to comp.lang.smalltalk and news.answers. Ralph Johnson's compilation of classic bugs is periodically posted to comp.lang.smalltalk.

The World Wide Web

Here are some Smalltalk-related Web pages. Some of them lead to other interesting Smalltalk Web pages, so if you start here you can end up at a lot of other sites with Smalltalk information.

UIUC Smalltalk Archive
  http://st-www.cs.uiuc.edu
Smalltalk FAQ
  http://xcf.berkeley.edu/pub/misc/smalltalk/FAQ
Smalltalk FAQ (plain text):
  http://xcf.berkeley.edu/pub/misc/smalltalk/FAQ/FAQ.txt
Another Smalltalk FAQ:
  http://www.cis.ohio-state.edu/hypertext/faq/usenet/smalltalk-faq
    /faq.html
Patterns Home Page
  http://st-www.cs.uiuc.edu/users/patterns/patterns.html
Portland Patterns Repository
  http://c2.com/ppr/titles.html
Jeff McAffer's home page
  http://www.oti.com/jeffspg/smaltalk.htm
The Smalltalk Developer's Site
  http://www.rwi.com/smalltalk/smalltalk.html
Yahoo Smalltalk page
  http://www.yahoo.com/Computers_and_Internet/Programming_
    Languages/Smalltalk/
ParcPlace-Digitalk
  http://www.parcplace.com/
VisualAge
  http://www.software.ibm.com/software/ad/vastub.html

Anonymous FTP

If you don't have a Web client, you can get to the Smalltalk archives at st.cs.uiuc.edu using anonymous ftp. If your ftp program can't find this address, the IP address is currently 128.174.241.10.

If you've never used anonymous ftp before, here are some basic instructions. Start by ftp'ing to the site (ftp st.cs.uiuc.edu). When asked for your login, enter anonymous and give your e-mail address as the password. You can use cd to change directory, and ls to list the directory. To get a file, use get (e.g., get speed.st). To get multiple files you can use mget (eg, mget s*.st).

Once you are on st.cs.uiuc.edu, you can cd to /pub. In that directory you will find a document called Index, which is worth getting, then reading. In /pub/Smalltalk you will find other directories. The directory MANCHESTER is a mirror of the archives at the University of Manchester, and contains a file called CATALOGUE, which describes all the files available in the Manchester archives. Other directories under /pub/Smalltalk contain files for the various flavors and releases of Smalltalk. In Smalltalk/st-docs you will find Ralph Johnson's compilation of classic Smalltalk bugs, as well as job listings for Smalltalk jobs.

Source Files

This book comes with an accompanying diskette, containing code and examples. Neither the author nor the publisher warranties the code or examples in any way. There is no warranty that they are correct, or that they will fulfill their stated purpose. In particular, you include any additions or changes to system classes at your own risk.

On the diskette are three different types of code. First, the .ex files in the examples directory contain example code that can be highlighted and evaluated. The files contain code matching the examples in the text. However, these files should *not* be filed in. Instead, you can look at them using a File List or a File Editor, and evaluate the code directly in these tools. Or, if you prefer, you can cut and paste the code from these tools into a Workspace and evaluate it there.

Second, the files in the classes directory contain classes that can be filed in. These classes illustrate points that are made in the text. Normally there is an examples protocol on the class side that contains methods to execute.

Third, the files in the sysadds and sysmods directory contain additions and modifications to system classes. Note that there is always a risk in making changes to system classes, so incorporate these changes at your own risk.

The source code and examples are licensed to only one person per copy of this book. That person is free to use the code and examples in his or her own development environment or applications as he or she sees fit. However, the licensed person may not distribute the code or examples to other people.

Source Files Mentioned in Chapters

This section shows which source files are referenced in which chapters.

16	Processes	psq.st, process.st
18	Cleaning up at termination	cleanup.st
19	The dependency mechanism	depend.st
20	Error handling	errormsg.st
21	Debugging	debug.st, role.st
22	Common errors	literal.st
25	Hooks into the system	copydemo.st, framewrk.st, hooks.st
26	Changing widgets at run time	focus.st, listdemo.st, widgets.st
29	Meta-Programming	metademo.st
30	Testing	testing.st
31	Customizing your environment	launch20.st, launch25.st
33	Managing source code	custom.st, imcr20.st, imcr25.st, install.st, install2.st, local.st

New Classes and Subclasses

These files can be found in the directory classes. Each file contains a class or classes, for which the code is shown and discussed in the book. The files can be directly filed into the image.

cleanup.st	Class to close files, terminate processes, etc., at termination
copydemo.st	Example of copying, both with and without using postCopy
custom.st	Class to customize your development environment
debug.st	Three classes: (1) a class that logs to a file or to the Transcript; (2) a class that intercepts messages being sent to an object; (3) an example for using the inspector to change values
depend.st	Examples illustrating the dependency mechanism
errormsg.st	Example showing the use of error message classes and subclasses
focus.st	Example of determining which widget has requested the focus
framewrk.st	Extensions to the Extended Framework
hooks.st	Examples of using various system hooks
imcr20.st	Classes to automatically create deployment image for VisualWorks 2.0
imcr25.st	Classes to automatically create deployment image for VisualWorks 2.0
launch20.st	Subclass of VisualLauncher for VisualWorks 2.0
launch25.st	Subclass of VisualLauncher for VisualWorks 2.5
listdemo.st	Example of setting up code to intercept double-clicks and keyboard input
literal.st	An example of modifying literal strings
metademo.st	Example showing methods and variables in a class and its metaclass
process.st	Subclass of Process that includes a name variable
psq.st	Priority Shared Queue
role.st	An example showing an object assuming different roles
testing.st	Test Manager and Test case classes and subclasses
widgets.st	Examples of modifying widgets and menus at run time

Files for Installing Applications

These files can be found in the directory manage. Each file illustrates some aspect of managing application or development environment code, and filing code into the image.

install.st   Installs modifications to system classes, files in application code, and
                  customizes the environment

install2.st   Shows how to discover the directory from which the file-in is being done

local.st   Local development environment changes

System Class Additions

These files can be found in the directory sysadds. Each file adds methods to a system class. Use at your own risk.

behavior.st   Additions to Behavior to return all instances of a class and its
                  subclasses, and to change instances into empty strings

blockcl.st   Additions to BlockClosure to fork processes with names

c-browse.st   Additions to class side of Browser for looking at all methods in a
                  specified protocol

c-para.st   Addition to class side of ParagraphEditor to return the keyboard

char.st   Addition to Character to return character as a string

chararr.st   Additions to CharacterArray to trim white space, to capitalize the
                  first letter, and to return an array of substrings

class.st   Additions to Class to copy a class and to create accessors when
                  accepting a class definition

inspect.st   Additions to Inspector for inspecting owners of and reference paths
                  to an object

keyproc.st   Addition to KeyboardProcessor to help track which widget has
                  requested the focus.

object.st   Additions to Object, which add functionality for halting, displaying
                  objects, printing to the Transcript, and marking methods

stream.st   Addition to Stream to read a line and strip comments.

sequence.st   Additions to SequenceableCollection to append an object, and to find
                  the first occurrence of an object starting at a specified position

System Class Modifications

These files can be found in the directory sysmods. Each file modifies existing methods in a system class. Use at your own risk.

behavior.st   Modification to Behavior to provide a different method template.

inspect.st   Modifications to the Inspector menu to allow you to browse owners of
                  and reference paths to the object being inspected

keyproc.st   Modification to KeyboardProcessor to track which widget has
                  requested the focus. You must add a new instance variable by hand.

standard.st   Modification to StandardSystemController to allow the VisualWorks
                  launcher to be invoked from the Window menu.

B

Source Code for Chapter 24

This appendix shows the code for the examples in Chapter 24, in full. To save space I've done some minor things, such as to show only the class names and the instance variable names in the class definition.

Superclasses

```
ApplicationModel subclass: #MyInput
    instanceVariableNames: 'person '

MyInput class>>open: aModel
    ^self openOn: (self new initialize: aModel)

ApplicationModel subclass: #MyView
    instanceVariableNames: 'person '

MyView class>>open: aModel
    ^self openOn: (self new initialize: aModel)

Model subclass: #MyPerson
    instanceVariableNames: 'name age '
```

Example One

```
MyInput subclass: #MyInput1
    instanceVariableNames: 'name age '

MyInput1>>initialize: aPerson
    person := aPerson.
    name := String new asValue.
    name onChangeSend: #nameChanged to: self.
    age := 0 asValue.
    age onChangeSend: #ageChanged to: self
```

```
MyInput1>>age
    ^age

MyInput1>>name
    ^name

MyInput1>>ageChanged
    person age: self age value

MyInput1>>nameChanged
    person name: self name value

MyView subclass: #MyView1
    instanceVariableNames: 'name age '

MyView1>>initialize: aPerson
    person := aPerson.
    person addDependent: self.
    name := String new asValue.
    age := 0 asValue.

MyView1>>age
    ^age

MyView1>>name
    ^name

MyView1>>update: aSymbol with: aValue from: anObject
    aSymbol == #name ifTrue: [self name value: aValue].
    aSymbol == #age ifTrue: [self age value: aValue]

MyPerson subclass: #MyPerson1
    instanceVariableNames: ' '

MyPerson1>>age: aValue
    age := aValue.
    self changed: #age with: age

MyPerson1>>name: aValue
    name := aValue.
    self changed: #name with: name
```

Example Two

```
MyInput subclass: #MyInput2
    instanceVariableNames: 'name age '

MyInput2>>initialize: aPerson
    person := aPerson.
    name := String new asValue.
    name onChangeSend: #nameChanged to: self.
    age := 0 asValue.
    age onChangeSend: #ageChanged to: self.
```

```
MyInput2>>age
    ^age

MyInput2>>name
    ^name

MyInput2>>ageChanged
    person age value: self age value

MyInput2>>nameChanged
    person name value: self name value

MyView subclass: #MyView2
    instanceVariableNames: 'name age '

MyView2>>initialize: aPerson
    person := aPerson.
    person name onChangeSend: #nameChanged to: self.
    person age onChangeSend: #ageChanged to: self.
    name := String new asValue.
    age := 0 asValue.

MyView2>>age
    ^age

MyView2>>name
    ^name

MyView2>>ageChanged
    self age value: person age value.

MyView2>>nameChanged
    self name value: person name value.

MyPerson subclass: #MyPerson2
    instanceVariableNames: ' '

MyPerson2>>age
    ^age isNil
        ifTrue: [age := 0 asValue]
        ifFalse: [age]

MyPerson2>>name
    ^name isNil
        ifTrue: [name := String new asValue]
        ifFalse: [name]
```

Example Three

```
MyInput subclass: #MyInput3
    instanceVariableNames: ''

MyInput3>>initialize: aPerson
    person := aPerson.
```

```
MyInput3>>age
    ^(AspectAdaptor subject: person sendsUpdates: true)
        forAspect: #age.

MyInput3>>name
    ^(AspectAdaptor subject: person sendsUpdates: true)
        forAspect: #name.

MyView subclass: #MyView3
    instanceVariableNames: ''

MyView3>>initialize: aPerson
    person := aPerson

MyView3>>age
    ^(AspectAdaptor subject: person sendsUpdates: true)
        forAspect: #age.

MyView3>>name
    ^(AspectAdaptor subject: person sendsUpdates: true)
        forAspect: #name.

MyPerson subclass: #MyPerson3
    instanceVariableNames: ' '

MyPerson3>>age
    ^age

MyPerson3>>age: aValue
    age := aValue.
    self changed: #age

MyPerson3>>name
    ^name

MyPerson3>>name: aValue
    name := aValue.
    self changed: #name
```

Example Four

```
MyInput subclass: #MyInput4
    instanceVariableNames: ''

MyInput4>>initialize: aPerson
    person := aPerson asValue

MyInput4>>age
    |adaptor |
    adaptor := AspectAdaptor subjectChannel: person sendsUpdates: true.
    adaptor
        accessWith: #yearsOld
        assignWith: # yearsOld:
        aspect: #age.
    ^adaptor
```

```
MyInput4>>name
    |adaptor |
    adaptor := AspectAdaptor subjectChannel: person sendsUpdates: true.
    adaptor
        accessWith: # called
        assignWith: # called:
        aspect: #name.
    ^adaptor

MyView subclass: #MyView4
    instanceVariableNames: ''

MyView4>>initialize: aPerson
    person := aPerson asValue

MyView4>>age
    |adaptor |
    adaptor := AspectAdaptor subjectChannel: person sendsUpdates: true.
    adaptor
        accessWith: # yearsOld
        assignWith: # yearsOld:
        aspect: #age.
    ^adaptor

MyView4>>name
    |adaptor |
    adaptor := AspectAdaptor subjectChannel: person sendsUpdates: true.
    adaptor
        accessWith: # called
        assignWith: # called:
        aspect: #name.
    ^adaptor

MyPerson subclass: #MyPerson4
    instanceVariableNames: ' '

MyPerson4>> yearsOld
    ^age

MyPerson4>> yearsOld: aValue
    age := aValue.
    self changed: #age

MyPerson4>>called
    ^name

MyPerson4>> called: aValue
    name := aValue.
    self changed: #name
```

Example Five

```
MyInput subclass: #MyInput5
    instanceVariableNames: 'trigger '
```

MyInput5>>initialize: aPerson
    person := aPerson.
    trigger := false asValue

MyInput5>>accept
    trigger value: true

MyInput5>>age
    |adaptor |
    adaptor := AspectAdaptor subject: person sendsUpdates: true.
    adaptor forAspect: #age.
    ^BufferedValueHolder subject: adaptor triggerChannel: trigger.

MyInput5>>name
    |adaptor |
    adaptor := AspectAdaptor subject: person sendsUpdates: true.
    adaptor forAspect: #name.
    ^BufferedValueHolder subject: adaptor triggerChannel: trigger.

MyView subclass: #MyView5
    instanceVariableNames: ''

MyView5>>initialize: aPerson
    person := aPerson

MyView5>>age
    ^(AspectAdaptor subject: person sendsUpdates: true)
        forAspect: #age.

MyView5>>name
    ^(AspectAdaptor subject: person sendsUpdates: true)
        forAspect: #name.

Model subclass: #MyPerson5
    instanceVariableNames: ''

MyPerson5>>age
    ^age

MyPerson5>>age: aValue
    age := aValue.
    self changed: #age

MyPerson5>>name
    ^name

MyPerson5>>name: aValue
    name := aValue.
    self changed: #name

Example Six

```
MyInput subclass: #MyInput6
    instanceVariableNames: ''

MyInput6>>initialize: aPerson
    person := aPerson asValue.

MyInput6>>person
    ^person

MyView subclass: #MyView6
    instanceVariableNames: ''

MyView6>>initialize: aPerson
    person := aPerson asValue.

MyView6>>person
    ^person

Model subclass: #MyPerson6
    instanceVariableNames: ' '

MyPerson6>>age
    ^age

MyPerson6>>age: aValue
    age := aValue.
    self changed: #age

MyPerson6>>name
    ^name

MyPerson6>>name: aValue
    name := aValue.
    self changed: #name
```

Example Seven

```
MyInput subclass: #MyInput7
    instanceVariableNames: 'trigger '

MyInput7>>initialize: aPerson
    person := aPerson asValue.
    trigger := false asValue.

MyInput7>>person
    ^person
```

```
MyInput7>>trigger
    ^trigger
```

```
MyInput7>>accept
    trigger value: true.
```

```
MyView subclass: #MyView7
    instanceVariableNames: ''
```

```
MyView7>>initialize: aPerson
    person := aPerson asValue.
```

```
MyView7>>person
    ^person
```

```
MyPerson subclass: #MyPerson7
    instanceVariableNames: ''
```

```
MyPerson7>>age
    ^age
```

```
MyPerson7>>age: aValue
    age := aValue.
    Transcript cr; show: 'Age changed'.
    self changed: #age
```

```
MyPerson7>>name
    ^name
```

```
MyPerson7>>name: aValue
    name := aValue.
    Transcript cr; show: 'Name changed'.
    self changed: #name
```

Example Eight

```
MyInput subclass: #MyInput8
    instanceVariableNames: ''
```

```
MyInput8>>initialize: aPerson
    person := aPerson.
```

```
MyInput8>>age
    ^(PluggableAdaptor on: person)
        getBlock: [:model | model age]
        putBlock: [:model :aValue | model age: aValue * 3]
        updateBlock: [:model :aspect :parameter | aspect == #age]
```

```
MyInput8>>name
    ^(PluggableAdaptor on: person)
        getBlock: [:model | model name]
        putBlock: [:model :aValue | model name: aValue asLowercase]
        updateBlock: [:model :aspect :parameter | aspect == #name]
```

```
MyView subclass: #MyView8
    instanceVariableNames: ''

MyView8>>initialize: aPerson
    person := aPerson.

MyView8>>age
    ^(PluggableAdaptor on: person)
        getBlock: [:model | model age * 10]
        putBlock: [:model :aValue | ]
        updateBlock: [:model :aspect :parameter | aspect == #age]

MyView8>>name
    ^(PluggableAdaptor on: person)
        getBlock: [:model | model name asUppercase]
        putBlock: [:model :aValue | ]
        updateBlock: [:model :aspect :parameter | aspect == #name ]

Model subclass: #MyPerson8
    instanceVariableNames: ' '

MyPerson8>>age
    ^age isNil
        ifTrue: [age := 0]
        ifFalse: [age]

MyPerson8>>age: aNumber
    age := aNumber.
    self changed: #age

MyPerson8>>name
    ^name isNil
        ifTrue: [name := String new]
        ifFalse: [name]

MyPerson8>>name: aString
    name := aString.
    self changed: #name
```

Index